# THE
# DISARMING
# OF CANADA

# THE
# DISARMING
# OF CANADA

## JOHN HASEK

KEY PORTER·BOOKS

**Canadian Cataloguing in Publication Data**

Hasek, John, 1938-
　　The disarming of Canada

Includes index.
ISBN 1-55013-045-5

1. Canada - Armed Forces.　2. Canada - Defenses.
I. Title.

UA600.H38 1987　　　355'.033071　　　C87-094283-2

Key Porter Books Limited
70 The Esplanade
Toronto, Ontario
Canada M5E 1R2

Design: Marie Bartholomew
Cover photo: Gregg Eligh
Typesetting: Imprint Typesetting
Printing and Binding: T.H. Best Printing Company Limited
Printed and bound in Canada

87 88 89 90　6 5 4 3 2 1

To the soldiers of the Republic of South Vietnam, to my classmate in Fort Bragg, the late Captain J.J. Carroll USMC as well as to all the American and other soldiers who fought in Vietnam, my brother officers and men of the Ghana Army 1965-67 and to the Canadian soldier, past, present and future.

Dead or living, drunk or dry,
  Soldier I wish you well.
              —A.E. Houseman

# Acknowledgements

My thanks to the following: Glenna for raising the family during my long obsession; my mother for our freedom and my late father for going to Klettendorf camp during the war and for following us after; Eva who gave me back my Czech heritage and memories of what oppression is, and for nursing me through the writing of this book and for editing the original version; and my editor Rick Archbold for forcing me back to Clausewitz for authority.

# Contents

# Prologue

*Knowledge dispels fear.*                    Ringway Parachute School Motto

January 1984

There is only a dim red glow in the functional cabin of the C-130 Hercules transport aircraft. The main lights have been switched off so that the sixty paratroopers in the back can get their night vision. It is three o'clock in the afternoon, but men of the 3rd Commando of the Canadian Airborne Regiment are preparing to do a night jump. In the Canadian North it is the time of the long night.

Three of the C-130s carry the troops and the fourth their toboggans, packed with all that the soldiers need to survive and fight in the arctic winter. They took off from Trenton, Ontario, more than a thousand miles to the south. The heat has been turned down in the back of the aircraft to prevent sweating in the men's heavy arctic clothing. Inside the planes' cavernous bellies, it is chilly as the troopers huddle together in their parkas and white camouflage suits. Sweat now can be extremely dangerous. Once the soldier is on the ground and the adrenalin rush of his thousand-foot descent into the unknown has worn off, he cools off very quickly, his wet clothing turning into a refrigerator.

The men now rousing themselves in the semi-darkness, are the elite of the Canadian Armed Forces. Most of them have been sleeping during the three-hour flight, despite the spartan seating and crammed conditions. Experienced soldiers sleep when they can, not knowing when they will be able to rest next. It also helps that controlled fear makes men drowsy.

Merely to be able to survive in the cold of the arctic winter is an achievement. To parachute into the frozen night and after arriving be prepared to fight takes skill, self-confidence and professionalism unsurpassed by any troops in the world.

"Get ready!" a jumpmaster yells, and the men repeat it in chorus, "Get ready!" Holding the clips that will attach their parachute static lines to the plane at the ready, they push themselves forward on the folding benches which line the outside bulkhead and run down the centre of the plane.

"Stand up, hook up!" the port and starboard jumpmasters shout, and the troops struggle to their feet. They fold and fasten the benches to the bulkhead and jam themselves into two single files, now called "sticks," facing the rear of the aircraft. Then they clip the static lines to the thick steel wire, called the anchor-line cable, that runs over their heads. This will pull open their parachutes once they have cleared the aircraft.

"Check your static line!" Each trooper tugs on the line of the man ahead of him before tracing it to where it disappears into the back-mounted parachute pack. Only then does he check his own line.

"Check your equipment!" First the main parachute on the back; then rifle and snowshoes over one shoulder; now the bulging rucksack, rigged in front and hanging on the thighs below the reserve parachute — all are quickly scanned and felt by each man and his buddy behind him. The last two men in each line turn around so that the last man on the stick can have his back checked.

"Sound off for equipment check!" The last man in each stick hits the man ahead of him and yells "OK," and this is carried on until the first man of the starboard and port stick point to the jumpmasters as they shout their OKs.

Suddenly, the plane slows down with a jolt and the jumpmasters, with the aid of the airforce loadmaster, slide up the two rear doors.

The engine noise increases to a roar as the frigid arctic air rushes into the cabin. Small, pin-bright, red lights near the doors come on to signal that there is one minute left before the first man exits. Through his headset the loadmaster has learned from the plane's navigator that the estimated wind speed on the ground is six knots. Now he mimes this information to the paratroopers by blowing over his opened palm and then holding up six fingers. Six knots — just perfect for a good roll on reaching the ground. The men jam tightly together as the jumpmasters clip their own static lines to the anchor-line cable to become stick leaders, and poise in the port and starboard doors.

As soon as the red light is replaced by a green light, jumpmasters and jumpers shout "GO" in unison and start to follow the stick leaders out of the door. One by one the two sticks shuffle towards the tail of the aircraft and jump out of the port and starboard doors, each one instantly disappearing into the darkness.

Actually, *jumping* is a misnomer. Each soldier is laden with rifle, ammunition, snowshoes and rucksack; in addition, some have radio sets as well as parts of the platoon heavy weapons. With the added weight of the two parachutes, helmet, arctic sleeping bag, rations and all the other items necessary to survive the northern cold, a man can hardly walk, let alone jump. The trick is merely to fall out of the aircraft without getting entangled in one's own or somebody else's equipment.

Instead of the crisp one-two tango step taught at the parachute school, the troopers stagger down to the end of the aeroplane, each man pushing the man ahead of him towards the black, cold doorway. As the first man on each side steps out, he is immediately whipped off by the icy rush of the propeller blast. In rapid succession he is followed by another and another. There is a minute of noise and confusion in the aircraft when to the roar of the prop-blast is added the howl of steel on steel as the static-line clips slide down and clash together at the end of the anchor-line cable. Then there is an eerie emptiness in the plane's belly. Only the loadmaster is left, to pull in the streaming static lines and deployment bags which trail past the tail of the Hercules. That done, he pulls down the doors, and the engines' roar also fades.

Outside in the arctic night the men have no sensation of falling. The force of air pushed by the propellers, compounded by the 120 m.p.h. airspeed, creates a wind that smooths out the pull of gravity. Then the parachute unpeels off the back, brakes his forward and downward movement, and suddenly he is hanging, suspended in time and space.

For a moment, which seems like eternity, there is peace and solitude. Above him is the perfect translucent shape of his opened parachute canopy and the deep darkness of the sky, broken only by stars and the shimmering Northern Lights. The snow-covered ground gleams brightly below. He is suddenly aware of other forms hanging under their parachutes all over the sky.

Within less than a minute each man automatically does his drills preparatory to landing: check canopy; check all around that there is no immediate danger of collision with another jumper; undo reserve parachute belly band; check drift over the ground. Now for the first time there is an awareness of movement, but it is gentle and rather detached from the man's immediate concerns. Next check for possible obstacles in the approximate landing area. Now, quickly release snowshoes, rifle and pack on a lowering line fixed to the parachute harness. There is a sharp tug as they fall to dangle twenty feet below the paratrooper. They will land separately from the man and not hurt him as he rolls.

The ground now starts to rush upwards, but only for an instant. As the paratrooper sinks below the horizon all details vanish and the ground turns black, while the sky, which was black before, now has all the light. In preparation for impact, his feet and knees are tightly together, legs slightly bent, muscles tensed. His arms are up above his head, hands on the riser straps leading to the canopy suspension lines. He tucks in his head and elbows, and as another quick rush of adrenalin surges through his body, he waits for the ground to hit him.

The exact moment and manner of impact are always a surprise, for the jumper does not know the degree of his lateral movement and cannot judge the speed of his fall. The moment his feet touch the snow, he automatically rolls over the ground in the direction of his drift, thereby lessening the shock. When the snow is deep, he sometimes only sinks into it.

As he lies on the ground, he releases one set of suspension lines in order to collapse his chute and then bangs the quick release box to shed his harness. Each soldier now straps on his snowshoes, shoulders his pack and picks up his weapon. Then he goes to the rendezvous point where he and his comrades sort themselves out into their tactical groups. Those who make up the Commando headquarters and four of the five platoons are regular infantry. These are the Canadian equivalent of the famous Gurkhas; they do not look nearly as exotic, but they can soldier just as well as the men from Nepal.

Most are from the Atlantic provinces, some from the poor parts of Toronto, Hamilton, Montreal and other urban areas. All are career soldiers. The non-commissioned officers have done several tours of peacekeeping already; many of the younger troopers have at least one tour of Cyprus under their belts. Others have come to the Airborne Regiment after serving for three years with the Canadian Brigade in Europe.

Many are from areas where opportunities are so limited and the jobs available so tough, that the army is a good alternative. There are Newfoundlanders from the outports, who grew up fishing from small dories in the open Atlantic without ever learning to swim. There are boys from the backwoods of Northern Ontario and Quebec, young men from Indian reservations, sons of the poorer Prairie communities, jobless miners from Cape Breton. The army is where they can all change their luck. It is a microcosm, but a microcosm for the most part of the marginal, the undereducated, the dispossessed, forgotten Canadian.

The men find their toboggans, step into the harnesses and begin to pull the boatlike sleds. The wind has dropped off and the soft squeal of the runners over the virgin snow seems magnified under the silent dome of the arctic sky. The order of march is: one platoon,

Commando headquarters, two, three, four and five platoons.

The fifth platoon, which has dropped so suddenly into the empty Arctic, comprises a very different slice of the Canadian mosaic. The twenty-four men and their officer are not regular force paratroopers, but rather militiamen from the Queen's Own Rifles of Canada. They are part-time soldiers, who are the barely flickering pilot flame of the Swiss system in Canada's armed forces.

All are from Toronto and its surrounding area and they make an odd assortment. Two are policemen. One is a lawyer, happy to take orders from his sergeant, who dropped out of grade eleven at Toronto's Central Tech five years ago and has not held a steady civilian job since. Four others are still in high school; two in community colleges. The platoon commander is a history student at the University of Toronto, who is taking eight years to get his honours degree rather than the normal four. Some of the rest are unemployed. Unlike all other countries, Canada does not require employers to give time off to those who serve in our military reserves.

But there is little difference in expertise between the regulars and the reservists who snowshoe off into the cold night. On one exercise when the regulars are short of people, the Queen's Own lieutenant takes over as the operations officer of the commando and a militia sergeant commands a section of regulars.

Just like their regular counterparts, the young men from Toronto are most certainly not attempting to solve the problems of the world. What they are doing is trying to help themselves through school, community college or university by part-time soldiering. They could probably make more money, and also find easier acceptance from their peers and the community at large, by slinging Big Macs. But they prefer the adventure of being airborne infantrymen to the safety and warmth of a fast food restaurant.

The number two rifleman, in the second section of the airborne platoon of the Queen's Own Rifles, is a little older than the others and has lost most of his hair. He is the lawyer, thirty-seven years old and working for a prestigious firm. A product of the sixties, he arrived at the conclusion — a little late and on his own — that the country needed other defences than the plaintive chants of folksingers and the mouthing of peaceful intentions.

The young lawyer decided to join the Queen's Own Rifles only after he had been admitted to the bar, but he is not an officer. The calendar of an officer in the regiment is time consuming and what little time the fledgling lawyer could give, he wanted to spend soldiering. He also did not have the leisure time for the course of study that would have qualified him as a militia officer, a course which requires more reading and writing every year. He therefore joined as a rifleman.

He keeps himself in such top physical condition that he can beat every man in the company in every run and endurance march. He has great leadership qualities and his presence pushes the other men to excellence. He would be a much greater asset as an officer, but he simply cannot take the time to get commissioned. Even more sadly, he is seen by most of his contemporaries as an oddball. To them, the idea of defending their country is as remote as the teachings of Carl von Clausewitz.

After a five-mile march, the men put up their tents, blow up air mattresses, and except for those unlucky enough to get the first shift of sentry or radio watch duty, thankfully crawl into their sleeping bags. Despite the intense arctic cold, they are warm enough and immediately fall asleep.

When Canadians hear of these men, which is rarely, they are justly proud. Our soldiers are as good as any in the world. But the total number of fighting troops in the Canadian Airborne Regiment is less than four hundred, the total for the whole regular infantry is less than six thousand. The number of militiamen trained to these standards is tinier still; in addition to some forty in the Queen's Own, there are three smaller groups — one in Quebec, one in Alberta and one in British Columbia.

These men are good soldiers, but their tiny numbers could not dislodge even a small diversionary probe of Canada's North. The number of properly trained combat arms officers and men in the

Canadian army is so small that today in order to train more than an extra twelve battalion-sized units, we would have to withdraw some of our forces from Europe. On the 5th of May 1945 the Canadian Army had more than one hundred battalion-sized combat arms units in the field in North West Europe.

# PART ONE

# THE CONTINUUM OF CONFLICT

# CHAPTER ONE

# Arms and the Man

*We therefore conclude that war does not belong in the realm of arts and sciences; rather it is a part of man's social existence. War is a clash between major interests, which is resolved by bloodshed — that is the only way in which it differs from other conflicts. Rather than comparing it to art we could more accurately compare it to commerce, which is also a conflict of human interests and activities, and it is still closer to politics, which in turn may be considered as a kind of commerce on a larger scale. Politics, moreover, is the womb in which war develops — where its outlines already exist in their hidden rudimentary form, like the characteristics of living creatures in their embryos.*

Carl von Clausewitz

Although Canada is not at war in the traditional sense and the chances of a conventional war being fought on our soil are small, there is a continuing indirect attack on the Western democratic nations. Canada, instead of being the country which made such a vital contribution to defending the democratic way of life in wars past, has become a weak link in the Western alliance.

This book is about the disarming of Canada in the postwar period and the serious threat that this poses, not only to our own and to Western security, but also to Canada's existence as a sovereign nation. I have no doubt that, if called, Canadians would fight again, but next time the call may come too late or not be heard at all: "For if the trumpet calls with an uncertain sound, who will prepare for battle?"

This book is about the steps I believe are necessary to provide Canada with an adequate defence against the kinds of conflict we can expect in the nuclear age. It is also about the changes which we must make to turn our country once more into a strong, unafraid partner in the defence of democracy.

In order to make my case, I believe it is important and necessary to understand something of military strategy and of the history of conflict — subjects currently and dangerously unfashionable in the English-speaking world. My earliest childhood memories are of war and fear. As a child in Czechoslovakia, I knew the fear of the Nazi death camps and experienced the danger of Allied bombs. As a man and as a soldier, I have learned that it is the children, the young and the soldiers who are war's greatest victims.

Man's greatest gift is the ability for superior communication. Our ability to communicate enables us to co-operate and thus to adapt better to our environment and even to change it. By working towards a common goal, our ancestors could get more food and better shelter. But when it came to the division of the benefits of this co-operation, there was competition and conflict.

Human conflict can be resolved by an authority acceptable to both sides; however, no mortal power can mediate forever. When authority fails, the conflict is resolved by the disputant who applies the greater force. Force can be manifested in many ways: intellectual, moral, economic, political and physical. Can anyone doubt the power of love or of laughter? But violence, the brute application of force, can override all other categories. The simplest definition of war is the use of violence by one society against another.

Strategy is the planning for victory against an intelligent human opponent, who is planning strategies for your defeat. Strategic planning is necessary for success and survival in any enterprise where there is competition from other humans. In military strategy there is the added factor of violence. With the addition of violence, we enter into a continuum of conflict on which war and peace are relative terms which can only apply when all sides are agreed on the rules. What may be accepted as an act of war at one time, under one set of rules, may merely become an act of terrorism or a police action at another.

The ultimate force with which a state defends itself against violence is its army. Traditionally, in war, victory goes to the army that is bigger, better armed, better led and better organized, but the will to win can make up for deficiencies in size, leadership and equipment.

Such use of force is costly to maintain, more costly to employ. The less of it needed the better. The more concentrated that it can be, the more economical its use. Superior concentration and economy can give an advantage to smaller countries with stronger wills. The current Afghan resistance to Soviet might and the recent victory of the North Vietnamese are but two examples of the truth behind these strategic platitudes. The willingness to use violence and escalate its destructiveness may suffice in winning, for as the great Chinese strategist Sun Tzu said five hundred years before the birth of Christ: "Supreme excellence consists in breaking the enemy's resistance without fighting."

In conflict, as in poker, there must always be a willingness to up the ante. Steadfastness of resolve and the signalling of this will is the single most important principle of war, as it is in politics and business. In times of relative social and political stability, this escalation operates within well-defined parameters, accepted by all belligerents. Carl von Clausewitz, the Prussian soldier, who 150 years ago wrote what is generally accepted as the most important treatise of all time on the theory and practice of war, called this a "limited, constricted form of war."

European wars in the century leading up to the French Revolution were thus "limited," and though bloody and nasty enough for the participants, were relatively low on the conflict continuum. The major European nations were ruled by royal oligarchies, members of which were interrelated and called each other cousin. As a result, there was tacit agreement on the limits to which either side would go to alter the balance of power. The more refined that such a system gets, the less is the violence needed to be able to judge the outcome. Apparently in ancient China, during one such period of social stagnation, opposing generals would merely tactically deploy their armies and then after inspecting each other's deployment, agree on who would have won, declare him the winner and retire from the field with their armies unharmed and the political situation re-aligned.

During periods of social revolution or great technological change, limited forms of war are sometimes replaced by conditions closer to an ultimate abstraction called "absolute war" by Clause-witz. Then neither side can predict what the final outcome of the new correlation of forces will be, and therefore neither is willing to admit defeat. And so the fighting will escalate beyond the point where the gains resulting from conquest can in any way make up for the losses caused by the violence.

In a pendulum's swing that began in the late eighteenth century, warfare became increasingly damaging and frequently less re-strained. But, with the end of the Second World War and the invention of nuclear weapons, a new limit seemed to have been placed on total war. This, however, does not lessen the utility of the nuclear threat as a psychological weapon, nor does it rule out accidental usage. The nuclear umbrella combined with an ignorance of the nature of conflict has made some forms of aggression easier. As early as 1954, the highly respected British strategist, Captain B.H. Liddell Hart wrote that: "To the extent that [the H-bomb] reduces the likelihood of all-out war, it increases the possibilities of "limited war" pursued by indirect and widespread local aggres-sion."

The industrial and social revolutions of the late eighteenth and early nineteenth century released untapped human energy and initiative. One of the direct results of this was that new human and industrial power could be channelled into armies as well as new weapons and transport. For the first time in modern Europe, not only the physical, but also the mental capabilities of the individual soldier started to be used. Some of the newly enlisted citizens could read and soldiered with some personal conviction, not just for the sake of measly pay and rotten rations.

The well-ordered nature of war was upset, when, after repeated losses, the citizen army of the French Republic began to beat the smaller, well-trained armies of the monarchies. At the same time that the French were having their social revolution, the industrial revolution was beginning in England and soon spread to the continent. Developments in machinery, manufacturing, agriculture and transportation permitted an unprecedented increase in population and made many more men available for the new armies.

Sufficient food could now be produced by fewer farm workers for much greater numbers of people. Modern methods of transport and communication could move the food and distribute it to larger population centres. New methods of mass production could be used to arm the bigger armies and the railways could move them at great speeds.

Eventually all the Continental powers, instead of having small forces of mercenary or professional soldiers, made service in the military part of an expanded notion of citizenship. Prussia, where the welfare and education of the common man was most advanced, also had the best army of the period. It was said that it was not a state with an army, but an army with a state. Russia and Turkey, which had huge armies, but whose inhabitants were largely illiterate serfs, had problems in matching the proficiency, flexibility and strength of the European citizen armies. As the ancient Greeks had demonstrated to the Persians, free men made better soldiers than slaves.

During the nineteenth century, neither Britain nor the United States needed the great numbers of soldiers required by the European nations. For home defence the British relied on a strong navy and a decentralized, inefficient local militia, while their regular army was more an Empire police force, used in penny packets against unruly natives. The control of the seas gave British force great flexibility, but it did not have the mass or the administrative support for the sustained, all-out warfare of which the Continental armies were capable. Britain could not even suppress the revolt of the semi-developed colonies in North America.

After gaining its independence and ending the counter-revolutionary threat in 1812, the USA was never seriously threatened. Like its mother country, it also kept only a tiny, professional army, isolated from mainstream society. Its main use was to pacify the West and assert American authority among the much smaller powers emerging in the Western Hemisphere.

British victories were not won by huge numbers. During the Napoleonic Wars, it was a small British army and Spanish guerrillas who tied up a much greater French force on the Iberian Peninsula. Later, the celebrated victory at Waterloo was only a coup de grâce. Wellington had 67,000 soldiers, but only 24,000 of these were British. The rest were Hanoverians, other assorted Germans and Flammands. Napoleon had only 74,000, for despite the miracle of his political comeback, in 1815 the French Emperor lacked military strength. He had lost the great majority of his army to geography and the weather during his previous reign; of the half million men with him in Russia only 20,000 came back.

On the Continent the new warfare required an ever greater number of professional officers. The planning and co-ordination necessary to turn the industrialized nation into a nation at arms could no longer be done by a commander and his personal aides. Large staffs became necessary to orchestrate the movement and concentrate the huge new armies, to bring to bear and use increasingly sophisticated weapons, as well as to understand and plan the logistics of procurement for the resupply of men and machinery.

In the past, officers had simply been appointed, or even raised their own regiments, and had picked up their knowledge mainly by experience. Promotion depended as much on patronage and seniority as on success in battle. In most of the pre-revolutionary armies, appointments and promotions were purchased, a system which survived in the British Army into the second half of the nineteenth century.

In the new mass armies, an aristocratic lineage and "a good seat on a horse" were no longer sufficient for promotion. As warfare became more complicated, professional training of one kind or another for all officers became a requirement. In the past, a general's staff was composed of officers whom the general picked to translate his strategic or general (hence the rank), plans and orders into tactical specifics. Most of the other needs of an army were solved by haphazard methods at the regimental level. Pillage, forage and local procurement were sufficient to provide the smaller armies with all but their ordnance needs. Civilian entrepreneurs followed the armies and did whatever was profitable.

These methods could not be used on a large scale. Now there had to be officers who understood and could co-ordinate artillery, engineering, ordnance, logistics, transport, medical care and evacuation, veterinary needs, food procurement and preparation, and intelligence gathering as well as being versed in tactical operations.

At the lower level, these functions could be carried out by specialists with non-combat status or by semi-educated officers, commissioned from the ranks. In the higher formations, an intimate understanding of command, tactics and leadership were more important than detailed knowledge of the support trade, so combat officers had to be trained in what are considered the more mundane and less glamorous matters of the military art.

Academies for young men embarking on a military career and staff colleges for serving officers became a standard part of military establishments. On the continent this led to the development of the General Staff system. The brightest officers were now carefully picked early in their careers to become members of the General Staff, or as it was called in Germany, the Great General Staff.

A young officer first had to prove himself by commanding infantry, cavalry, artillery or combat engineer troops. After much study and examination, a handful — some years as few as half a dozen — would become members of the General Staff, and they would keep this coveted designation for the rest of their careers. In the German Army to this day a red stripe down the trouser leg and the letters GS after his rank, distinguish a General Staff officer from his colleagues.

In addition to their primary tasks of leading men in battle, the General Staff were taught the intricacies of the state at war. Their professional development was carefully planned, and increasingly senior staff assignments were interposed between tours of commanding ever larger units and formations. Thereby, the officer broadened and updated his practical skills while broadening and improving his abilities as a staff officer. In addition to attending as students, the General Staff officers returned to the academies and staff colleges as instructors and professors. Clausewitz himself followed this pattern of professional development.

When General Staff officers became the senior commanders and staff officers in the system, they knew the art of war from the practical as well as the theoretical side. The general staff system also ensured that at every level of the field armies there were some officers who understood the big picture and could advise their seniors if the plans at the lower level were not in fact conforming to the overall aim.

One of the principles of the General Staff was that its members analyzed plans at every level and questioned them if found faulty. Only when such plans became direct orders to action did this questioning cease. Such in-house analysis of strategy and policies was just as rigorous in peace as in war. It helped to keep bureaucratic expediency and empire building in check by questioning not only proposed changes, but also the status quo.

During the nineteenth century, the plans of the General Staffs of Prussia, Austro-Hungary, France, and to a lesser extent, Russia, were used for the running of the nation in wartime. In times between wars, the staffs honed timetables, schedules and secret arrangements which could mobilize the entire country from a nation at peace to one where the military aims and goals took precedence over all else.

When war threatened, the great majority of young Europeans became instant soldiers, having earlier been trained during their conscription period. The factories switched to making ammunition and weapons, and the railways deployed men and material for war, with their normal duties far down the list of priorities. At such times, the civil government became a rubber stamp for the General Staff, and the commander-in-chief had power that was subordinate only to the monarch, president, or whomever was the head of state. The national press was converted into a massive propaganda tool.

In the nineteenth century, Britain and the United States, with no serious threat against them and no mass armies, did not need to develop a proper system of a General Staff for strategic planning and mobilization of the nation. Although military academies and later, staff colleges, were developed, strategy was never seriously taught. The technical aspects of the soldier's trade became the main parts of the teaching curricula. West Point, the US Military Academy, especially emphasized engineering and science. Canada's Royal Military College copied a great deal from West Point, and to this day, instead of channelling the best students into the humanities, train them as engineers.

In England there also remained a traditional suspicion and dislike of martial authority, which was probably a residue from the days of Oliver Cromwell and his Majors General. In America, many of whose citizens had come to the New World to escape military service or war itself, the Congress enacted a law against the formation of a general staff.

There were early signs that the lack of a proper staff was a great weakness in time of war. A large portion of the 20,000 British fatalities in Crimea were victims of the atrocious medical and logistical services, rather than of enemy action. In 1870, Germany had fifteen army corps in action against France within two weeks; twelve years later, the British needed a month to put together a single army corps for their "quick action" campaign in Egypt. In America during the Civil War, the overwhelmingly powerful Union took four years to bring down the Confederacy at enormous cost in blood and wealth.

On the other hand, in Europe, although Clausewitz and the lesser military theorists all clearly spelled out the necessary subordination of a powerful professional officer corps to the ruling civil power, the dangers to the internal freedom of the state were always present. Under Frederick the Great, Prussia had developed the most powerful and efficient General Staff in all Europe. Although some of the side benefits of needing lots of healthy, thinking soldiers, were the most advanced systems of education, medical care and general welfare in Europe, the overall results were evil. The officer class became all-powerful, arrogant and the symbol of the increasing militarization of Europe.

As the Continental General Staffs assumed ever greater powers, it became almost inevitable that their constantly improving plans would eventually be used. In 1914 came the pay-off. A Serbian nationalist assassinated an Austrian Archduke in Sarajevo, Bosnia, and following this minor act of terror came threats and stiff diplomatic notes, then threats of mobilization, followed by actual mobilization, then further threats and finally declarations of war.

Paradoxically, given that the war was precipitated by the over-planning of the Continental General Staffs, the small British professional army was committed to the Western Front because of a lack of proper military planning. General Henry Wilson, who had great political connections but no General Staff to control and advise him, became extremely close to the French military commanders and at the outbreak of hostilities committed an expeditionary force to stand shoulder to shoulder with his friends. Strategically, the British Army would have been better off and more useful doing something else, such as attacking properly in the Dardanelles. However, once the initial troops were on the Continent, the British Empire was on its way to losing much of its wealth, power and a generation of young men.

The militarization of Europe in the nineteenth century not only helped to precipitate the First World War, but also contributed to its ferocity and length. The first principle of war is selection and maintenance of the aim: picking your objective and sticking to it. The second principle, learned by every soldier and football coach, is "offensive action." This applies even when you are not in any way an aggressor. For even though Clausewitz argued that "the defensive is the more effective form of war," he also realized that "even the weakest party must possess some way of making the enemy conscious of his presence, some means of threatening him."

Unless you at least threaten to attack, you must lose. Your enemy can concentrate all his resources and planning for the offensive, without having to worry about protecting himself. The time and method of his attack are entirely under his control. Adhering to this principle, the opposing armies of Germany, France, Austria and Russia were soon deep in each other's territories. When the revolving door effect stopped, Europe was committed to a long war of attrition.

Shaken and revolted by the magnitude of the carnage of the Great War, the remaining European democracies started to evolve new methods of behaviour to prevent such societal suicide from happening again. They changed the emphasis of their strategic plans from offensive action to defensive. Pacifism, isolationism and neutrality were among the ways by which various nations hoped to avoid war in the future. Laws and treaties were enacted to prevent war, or limit its effect. The League of Nations was founded to bring moral and economic pressure to bear in the international forum. Utopian, and in my opinion dangerous, dreams of some form of world federalism, with centralized military force were also part of the scheme.

The concentration on defence left potential enemies with the initiative, enabling them to safely concentrate their resources on offensive planning. The warnings of soldiers and others familiar with the nature of war were ignored. The fact that brute force can cut across and negate moral power, the power of law and the power of reason, was forgotten.

The totalitarian socialist philosophies, with expansion and domination as central motifs of their dogma, adopted the General Staff system organization of the nineteenth century to their own purposes. Unlike the monarch whom they replaced, for the totalitarian dictators, militarization of the state was not only reserved for times of declared war, but also became a tool of the permanent struggle to world communism for the Soviets and of the Nazis' dream of *lebensraum*.

The double tragedy of the Continental General Staffs was that while they helped to precipitate the First World War, they failed to prevent the Second. In Russia the officer corps had no chance of taking a hand in the internal affairs of the state, because Stalin's purges of the thirties had exterminated nearly all the experienced, senior officers who had been left from the Tsarist army, as well as many of the brighter, young officers who had started soldiering during the revolution. At the same time, the German officer corps quickly became subordinate to the Nazi dictator. Many saw in Hitler their opportunity for military honour and glory, and although collectively they despised and feared him, they did nothing to prevent him from consolidating his power. The German Great General Staff masked its ambition and its misgivings behind blind obedience to the civil power, no matter how evil. Only when he was losing the war was there an attempt by a segment of the General Staff to remove him.

As Stalin was exterminating millions of Ukrainians and Hitler starting his concentration camps, the League of Nations was proving to be even less effective than the contemporary United Nations has proven to be. Mussolini thumbed his nose at its moral pressure, and its economic sanctions were ineffective. When Mussolini butchered the defenceless Ethiopians unopposed, this should have been sufficient warning to the democracies, but it was not. Many conservatives lauded fascism because it was seen as a way of restoring law and order in post-war Europe, while the left-wing idealists suppressed news of the Soviet genocide because of communism's supposed championship of the working man.

With the French cowering behind the Maginot Line, the British smug behind the English Channel and America removed from the European scene by a renewed isolationism, the world was once again left vulnerable to a pitiless war. And this time, the rise of totalitarianism and the rapidity of technological advances made for the closest thing to absolute war yet seen.

Despite the warnings of his generals, Hitler opened up the second front by attacking the USSR. This allied the democracies with a system devoted to their destruction. Britain and the USA backed the

Soviet Union not only with material, but also with propaganda, which put the seal of approval on a system that had murdered millions of its own citizens and made slaves of the rest. Joseph Stalin, as bloody a dictator as Hitler, became benevolent old "Uncle Joe."

The democracies had turned themselves into Sparta-like dictatorships for the duration of the war in order to mobilize all their powers for its conduct. With enormous effort and the help of the USSR, in May 1945 they finally defeated Hitler's fascism. But they paid heavily for their alliance of convenience with the Soviet Union. All the countries freed from their fascist yokes by the Red Army became subject to a more durable form of tyranny.

With the end of the war in the Pacific, the democracies demobilized as fast as they could. The prewar weaknesses resurfaced and were made even more dangerous by the advent of the nuclear age. Their huge citizen armies put on civilian clothes and started raising children and buying cars, refrigerators and houses. The giant industries quickly reverted from turning out tanks, ammunition and Liberty ships to making goods for the new families. But as we now know, the defeat of fascism and Japanese imperialism did not end the conflict between democracy and totalitarianism. With the majority of military strategists again removed from the high councils of the USA and Britain, the West was ill prepared to meet the new dangers.

The USSR demobilized only partly; it kept up a huge army and failed to civilianize its industry. The Yalta agreement had established the line where the victorious armies of the West and the East were supposed to meet. Now Stalin consolidated his power and kept control of the countries that he was supposed to liberate.

In 1946, Western military planners knew that although the Soviets had not demobilized and had maintained weapon production at the wartime level, their capability did not match any possible hostile intentions. War damage to Soviet industry was estimated to be 25 percent of the prewar capital stock. Strategists estimated that the Red Army could overrun any one of the following: Continental Europe; Turkey, Iran and Afghanistan; or Korea, Manchuria and

North China. But even the most pessimistic did not believe that the Soviets could wage a major war before 1950.

Several factors changed the perceived balance of power dramatically, causing those military and political leaders with access to accurate information about Soviet intentions and capability to become increasingly worried. Their major fear was that Soviet appreciation of the new Western weakness would permit political and low-level insurgency activities in the peripheral areas to become bolder. This was evident not only from Czechoslovakia, which fell to communism in 1948, but also from Greece, Turkey and Iran, all of which beat off vigorous attempts by the Communists to seize control.

Even Western Europe was seriously threatened and Averell Harriman, head of a group making a study on the European Recovery Program, warned that Communist demonstrations in France and Italy were more than a tactical manoeuvre. There were strikes and anti-government demonstrations all over Europe, and Stalin was confident enough to openly re-establish Cominform, the agency for stoking the fires of subversion and revolution worldwide. Meanwhile, China had also fallen to the Communists.

Paradoxically, the subversive campaign was beginning to run out of steam just as it was getting under way, for although the United States was now weaker militarily, this weakness was becoming apparent coincidentally with the strengthening of Europe by economic means. The aid provided by the Marshall Plan promised to ruin the long-term chances of the subversive war and the support for the Communist parties in the non-Communist world. The Soviets were aware of this danger to their plans and did not allow any of the nations within their sphere of influence to accept the aid.

Finally, Western weakness was caused by the perennial problem of the isolation of the military within American society. Because the Americans retained the draft, the isolation was not as great as it had been between the wars and not as absolute as it was in Canada; nevertheless, it increased as the war receded into history.

The American military had never developed a peacetime army

that was properly integrated into mainstream society. The regular, long-serving soldiers who comprised the majority of the standing army were isolated in camps and forts, far away from main population centres. The officers, educated at their own academies and staff colleges, with heavy emphasis on engineering, were not in touch with civilian academe or with the opinion makers in society.

The US military chiefs, although they bridled at the weakening of conventional defences caused by the massive demobilization, were lulled into its acceptance by the American monopoly of nuclear weapons. Assessment of the will to use them was beyond their political sensitivity and outside the parameters of their responsibility. They were not trained to think politically or strategically in light of new global realities.

Lacking a General Staff and unable to form correct psychological and political assessments, they assumed, in the absence of clear directives from the civil power, that the atomic weapons would be used in a future conflict. Given the Soviet superiority in manpower and tactical airpower, the Joint Chiefs of Staff Strategic Plan of 1947, called BROILER, presumed that an adequate stockpile of atomic bombs would be available at the outset of a major conflict and more would be produced during hostilities. This presumption was never confirmed by the President, nor by the State Department, nor by the National Security Council. The NSC came into existence in 1947 to fill some of the gap caused by the lack of a strategic General Staff. The extra layers of bureaucracy formed by the State Department and the NSC only muddied the waters between the President, who is the Commander-in-Chief of the Armed Forces, and his closest military advisers.

In retrospect, it can be seen that the American generals' assumption was incorrect. Although President Harry S. Truman had authorized the bombing of Hiroshima and Nagasaki to save the lives of some million GIs, even then there should have been doubt that an American president would do the same for the less direct threat to American lives which a Communist takeover of Europe represented. But the US Air Force chiefs had neither the training, the inclination, nor the authority, to think in terms of policy at this level.

Truman was not only playing poker with the Russians, he was also bluffing the American public and his own service chiefs. This is beautifully demonstrated by his behaviour during the 1948 Berlin blockade. Immediately following the successful February coup in Czechoslovakia, the USSR attempted to take over West Berlin on the cheap by blocking off the long narrow corridor which was the only link with the free part of the city deep in East German territory. They had tactical air and ground superiority, and they knew that no conventional military threat could be used in reply to their action. So the Soviets estimated that if West Berliners did not submit immediately, hunger and cold would force the city to capitulate before the following spring.

In response, the Allies mounted Operation Vittles, a massive airlift of enough food and fuel to maintain the two million West Berliners. Simultaneously, the Americans played their ace in the hole; they deployed ninety B-29 Superfortress bombers from the United States to England. The Superfortress was the bomber type that had been used to drop the atomic bombs on Hiroshima and Nagasaki in 1945. The common belief at the time was that Truman was simply using the threat of the nuclear club to make the Soviets back off, but he was far too good a poker player to massively up the ante so suddenly. Besides, his hand was not that strong. In fact, the deployment merely signalled the intention of an intention.

Although the Americans in 1948 had a few atomic bombs and two dozen B-29s capable of delivering them, the means to strike a decisive nuclear blow simply did not exist. US military planners had calculated that it would take some 200 bombs to destroy the Soviet war machine and break Soviet resistance. Even the existing bombs needed highly skilled teams to assemble them for use, and these experts had long been dispersed to civilian life. In 1948, only two bombs could be assembled per day.

Of course there were no atomic bombs sent and the ninety B-29s flown to Europe were in any case only capable of carrying conventional bombs. The Strategic Air Command generals did not understand the more subtle uses of military power. They considered the deployment of the B-29s to be "a strictly political move and not a show of force." The record does not indicate what *they* meant by a "show of force," nor how the Air Force generals knew the line delineating it from a political move, since that same question has puzzled strategists since the time of Clausewitz.

As a result, the operational commanders were left totally in the dark as to the "reason why." The leader of the first B-29 squadron arriving in Germany suspected that his beautiful bombers and their elite crews were there to haul coal to the beleaguered Berliners. He was very relieved when his aircraft were merely ordered to fly normal training missions.

The Soviets must have known that the aircraft sent over to Europe were not equipped with the nuclear bomb. At this time they had penetrated the British secret service and probably had key moles and agents of influence in the American State Department giving them an accurate finger on the pulse of US foreign policy. They almost certainly knew more than the American taxpayers and Western journalists. Most probably they were better informed than the US tactical military commanders, and possibly had a better feel for Truman's intention than even his own senior military advisers.

The Berlin blockade demonstrated that although the Soviets were prepared to use military power, they did not want war. If they could not win with the sudden bluff, they were prepared to wait out the blockade until the Berliners were forced into their camp. To the surprise of all, Operation Vittles was successful; air transport proved capable of keeping Berlin alive indefinitely. This, together with the very low signal of a threat behind a threat sent by Truman in the form of the B-29s, was sufficient. With the coming of spring, Stalin called off the blockade and West Berlin remained free.

Despite what the President and the Kremlin both knew, the American public thought that the threat of nuclear weapons had prevented both defeat and the escalation of conflict, which in a sense is exactly what did happen. And as often happens in a democracy, where ultimately the people do make the decisions, the perception became reality.

Having seen how well the nuclear stick (apparently) worked, Congress rejected a Universal Military Training Plan, favoured by Truman, which would have seen the enlistment of every able-bodied young American man for a short period of compulsory service. This would have cost an estimated $4 billion. Instead, Congress approved a $22-million increase in the Air Force budget to build the seventy air groups (roughly equivalent to an army brigade) that the airmen wanted. This was the beginning of the West's modern strategic predicament: we have substituted weapons we intend never to use for soldiers we may be forced to use. This too is the central theme of the disarming of Canada: fear of the atom bomb has been substituted for genuine military power.

In 1950, a year after the end of the Berlin crisis, the Communists called the nuclear bluff in Korea, by using a small, backward nation as the sacrificial lamb. As a result, America realized that a credible, flexible, conventional response had to be built back into the system. But this was done only reluctantly and, instead of a universal military service, an unjust draft system was used to keep up the numbers of men in the army.

While the Soviets started on the long road to catch up to the American nuclear lead, the US Strategic Air Command became the most powerful force on earth and a symbol of the Cold War. Politically, in the short run, it all made sense; young American men were overjoyed that they did not all have to train as foot soldiers, for service in the infantry is never popular. Now, when democracy could be defended by a few glamorous aircrews with Armageddon under their wings, it made even less sense to learn how to live in holes in the ground, carry heavy loads on foot, and learn how to kill or be killed in the most unpleasant of circumstances.

Sheltering behind the American nuclear shield, the Europeans were quite happy rebuilding their shattered economies with little defence spending. Their young men who had survived the war could spend the time and energy saved from long military conscription in making Europe wealthy again. Despite the Korean example, some Europeans chose to believe that even though the Americans would not use the bomb to rescue friendly Asiatics, they would use it to come to the aid of their white European cousins. Others, namely the British and the French, rapidly built their own deterrent.

Dwight D. Eisenhower, the president who followed Truman, had been a professional soldier and the Supreme Commander of the Allied Forces in Europe during the Second World War. He understood the dangers of the cosy arrangement between manufacturers and the military by which weapon systems are pushed without an overall strategic plan. When he left office in 1960, he dubbed the lobbies of the individual service interests allied with parts of the weapons industry the "military-industrial complex." Although he understood the problem, he did nothing during his two terms to end it by the only method which might have worked — the establishment of a proper general staff system and the integration of the military into society. Only a knowledgeable, unified General Staff with a mandate for strategic planning could have identified for the president those weapon systems which were necessary for security of the nation and those which were being pushed by an alliance of vested interests. It would also have made the cosy arrangements between the interests of the individual services and weapons manufacturers much more difficult.

As the years passed, the people in the American defence establishment with the most serious and weighty military responsibility were not those who had actually fought the nasty, bloody little wars in the Third World, but those who were the priests of the Apocalypse: the crews of the bombers carrying the hydrogen bombs; the nuclear submariners; the missile warriors sitting in their underground bunkers ready to destroy civilization with a push of their fingers while studying for their masters degrees in accounting; and, above all,the bureaucrats. These troops replaced the citizen soldiers as the main keepers of Western security.

The fact that the primary use of nuclear weapons is psychological is still not fully realized by the majority of Western military strategists. What had been dubbed the Cold War, should more accurately be called the Psychological War. The war which the generation of postwar officers trained for was the shadow on the wall of the cave. The real war was the constant conflict on the peripheries of the two power blocks, diminishing in intensity as it got closer to the heartlands of the great powers and to the main theatre, the psychological front in Europe. Therefore, the more violent the conflict, the less its importance in the crucial struggle for the minds of the people of the democratic nations.

In retrospect it can be seen that the threat of nuclear weapons has placed new limits on war's form. Not only have the chances of nuclear war between the superpowers decreased over the years, but the constraints of the nuclear era have also prevented a conventional war in the homelands of the two power blocks. But the balance is fragile, for the constraints are largely technological and can be destabilized by one of many emerging trends. Not least of these is the development or ownership of nuclear weapons by any of a number of so-called crazy states. The standoff does not and cannot prevent the continuing indirect attack by the Soviet Union and other totalitarian communist states against Western democracy. Like it or not, Canada is a combatant in this global conflict, however ineffective her forces may be.

# CHAPTER TWO

# The Indirect Attack

*. . . by reducing the act of violence, war, to a means of policy, Clausewitz gives as its end not victory but the return to peace.*

Raymond Aron

The battle for men's minds has always been more important than the battle for physical territory, yet this fact is consistently overlooked by the West. The reasons for this blindness are complex, but the adoption of the ideas of Carl von Clausewitz by the Communists and the repression of these same ideas in the West is one of the causes of this phenomenon.

Western intellectuals have commonly held the ideas of Clausewitz responsible for the disastrous Great War. Clausewitz's great work, *On War*, was the bible of the European General Staffs, and the unchecked power and efficiency of these staffs were certainly two of the factors which precipitated the conflict. The mobilization of entire nations ensured the thoroughness and duration of the slaughter, but the blame for this cannot be laid on Clausewitz. All that he did was describe and systemize what the social and industrial revolutions and Napoleon had already started. From these observable phenomena, he derived the framework for a philosophy of conflict.

As Raymond Aron, who was himself one of the few great military philosophers of the twentieth century, says of his nineteenth century predecessor in the seminal *Clausewitz; Philosopher of war*:

He does not wish to be a philosopher of war in the sense that Kant, author of the treatise on perpetual peace, is considered a philosopher of war. He neither condemns nor approves of war, he takes it as a given primary fact.

In fact, because Clausewitz demonstrated that "the only source of war is politics — the intercourse of politics and peoples," his theories, instead of encouraging war, when properly understood, can be used to tame it. As he himself put it:

. . . policy converts the overwhelmingly destructive element of war into a mere instrument. It changes the battle-sword that a man needs both hands and his entire strength to wield, and with which he strikes once and no more, into a light, handy rapier — sometimes just a foil for the exchange of thrusts, feints and parries.

In his writings Clausewitz made a clear distinction between the military and the civil power, and subordinated the former to the latter. He also recognized a division between war and peace, but he realized that it was not always a clear one and subject to change.

In Chapter 26 of Book VI, "The People in Arms," he distilled the experience of Napoleon's army in the Iberian Peninsula into a theory about popular uprisings. This chapter of his book analyzes the guerrilla warfare which the Spanish population conducted against the French invaders and shows how it was a further step towards total war and was itself the result of the removal of conventional barriers during the period.

A popular uprising should, in general, be considered as an outgrowth of the way in which the conventional barriers have been swept away in our lifetime by the elemental violence of war. It is in fact, a broadening and intensification of the fermentation process known as war. The system of requisitioning, and the enormous growth of armies resulting from it and from universal conscription, the employment of militia — all of these run in the same direction when viewed from the standpoint of the older, narrower military system, and that also leads to the calling out of the home guard and arming the people.

The innovations first mentioned were the natural, inevitable consequences of the breaking down of barriers. They added so immensely to the strength of the side that first employed them that the opponent was carried along and had to follow suit. This will also hold true of the people's war. Any nation that uses it intelligently, will as a rule, gain some superiority over those who disdain its use. If this is so, the question only remains whether mankind at large will gain by this further expansion of the element of war; a question to which the answer should be the same as to the question of war itself. We shall leave both to philosophers. But it can be argued that the resources expended in an insurrection might be put to better use in other kinds of warfare. No lengthy investigation is needed, however, to uncover the fact that these resources are, for the most part, not otherwise available and cannot be disposed of at will. Indeed, a significant part of them, the psychological element, is called into being only by this type of usage.

When citizens are turned into committed, unpaid soldiers, the army and the state become one and the all powerful "psychological element is called into being." By this Clausewitz meant that when all citizens have a direct part in the conflict, it unifies the will to resist and win. When Clausewitz said that these resources are not otherwise available and cannot be disposed at will, he meant that the people armed do not have the training, the organization, the discipline or the logistics to fight anywhere except at home in a desperate cause which unites them. There is no way of projecting this power outside the locality of the armed citizen. His experience of guerrilla warfare in Spain made him describe this tactic as essentially a defensive one. It needed a revolutionary ideology with a world-wide application to turn "the people's war" into an offensive weapon.

The people who have not yet been conquered by the enemy will be the most eager to arm against him; they will set an example that will gradually be followed by their neighbours. The flames will spread like a brushfire, until they reach the area on which the enemy is based, threatening his lines of communication and his very existence.

The French used this defensive tactic in a limited and rather unsuccessful way in the war of 1870, by arming some civilians and organizing them around the infamous *francs tireurs*; but no General Staff used it for offensive war until the "total war" of 1914-1918. Then the Germans realized that communism, by appealing to a greater loyalty than nationalism, could be used to attack Russia from within, and arranged for the exiled Lenin and his fellow Bolsheviks to return to Russia.

The Germans did this out of desperation when they realized that the war was going to be a lengthy one. They had long feared a war on two fronts, against the French in the West and the Russians in the East. Of the two, they regarded the Russians as the greater threat. That was why, in 1914, they launched a rapid attack, designed to quickly knock France from the conflict. Then they would be able to concentrate maximum force on the more slowly mobilizing Russians.

The Russia of 1914 was not the backward, archaic tyranny of popular belief. The modern myth of pre-revolutionary backwardness and poverty is mostly the result of Soviet disinformation exploiting Western racial prejudice. Modern historical research indicates that nineteenth-century Russia had experienced a blossoming of human energy similar to that which had spread across Western Europe a century before.

For eighteen of the last twenty-five years before the war, Russia led the world in economic growth. In 1908, universal primary education was introduced, and by 1914 literacy was nearly 50 percent. By 1916, 89 percent of the cultivated land and 94 percent of the livestock were owned by the peasantry. The population doubled between 1860 and 1914.

By 1917, helped by the changes brought on by the war, the increasing trickle of Russian liberalization had become the flood of a successful revolution. In this situation German strategists saw a chance of beating Russia. They were prepared to help the chaos by sending back the most virulent revolutionaries. Lenin, who with some of his Bolsheviks, was living in exile in Switzerland, believed in world communism and in any means that would give him and his followers the power to work for this goal.

So the Germans arranged for Lenin and his small group of plotters to travel to Moscow in a sealed train. Their function was to corrupt Russia from within and then pull the shattered state out of the war. The Bolsheviks seized control in November of 1917 and made peace with the Germans as arranged. But by then the United States had finally entered the conflict and the Central Powers were doomed anyway. However, while the guns fell silent in the West, the germ of totalitarianism, which had destroyed the emerging democracy in Russia, kept spreading. As surely as the war ended the old empires and sealed the fate of European colonialism, it gave rise to communism and fascism.

In combining Marx and Clausewitz, Lenin had converted communism from an unrealizable Utopian dream into a cancer of the evolving Western democratic system. Marxist-Clausewitzian-Leninism not only destroyed national boundaries, but by declaring the permanency of the class war, it also destroyed the boundary between war and peace. The aim of universal peace through universal communism became supreme and all means were justified in its achievement.

Until then, peace for nations which were part of the emerging democratic system was a legal term which covered a situation existing when war was not declared. Violence by one state against another was a contravention of peace, although this distinction was seldom followed precisely. Absolute peace was, like total war, an abstraction only to be found in the afterlife. It served to establish some trust in the international system. In destroying the boundary between war and peace, communism also changed the meaning of the words themselves. For the Communists, absolute peace will be realized only with the achievement of world communism. Therefore the conflict leading up to this is described as the "permanent struggle for peace."

Since 1917 the Marxist-Leninist campaign for peace has meant unceasing conflict against the bourgeoisie. As George Orwell explained in *1984*, Peace is War. In keeping with this principle, neither the Soviet Union nor any other Communist government has ever declared war on anybody — they have merely intensified the struggle. Invasions of other states have fulfilled requests for fraternal assistance against counterrevolution.

The permanent struggle of the Soviets against the bourgeoisie is waged by an ongoing peace offensive. This takes a dual form: military preparedness combined with a constant subversive attack aimed at the unilateral disarmament of the West. The translation of the Politburo's general strategy into tactical campaigns is planned in the Kremlin by what is now known as the International Department and is funnelled to the West by local Communist parties and by front organizations. The better known of these include the World Peace Council, the Christian Peace Conference, the International Organization of Journalists, the International Union of Students, the World Federation of Democratic Youth, the Women's International Democratic Federation, Women's International League for Peace and Freedom, the International Union of Students, the World Federation of Trade Unions, the International Association of Democratic Lawyers and the World Federation of Scientific Workers.

To spread the party message at the local level are organizations which openly list their affiliation with one of the Front organizations. For example, the Canadian Peace Congress and the Toronto Association for Peace are affiliated with the World Peace Council, while the Congress of Canadian Women lists its affiliation with the Women's International Democratic Federation. There are also various ethnic organizations which support Soviet policies while vigorously promoting anti-Americanism. Then there are pro-Marxist, anti-Soviet organizations which help to spread the message. These, as well as some of the so-called Euro-Communist parties at times villify the Soviet Union, but never relinquish their attack on the bourgeoisie.

There are organizations started on official Soviet and freelance Western initiative such as the Physicians for Social Responsibility or ones with only a few Communist members in the original organization, but with some members having easy access to the Soviet Union. This access as well as popularity with mainline media would be jeopardized if an anti-Soviet line was included in its policies.

While the machinery for the peace campaign periodically changes in structure and name, its strategy and general method remain constant. The committed elements within the democratic country work clandestinely as well as openly to destroy the fabric of the existing society. Some recruits to the cause join the local Communist party or some other far left organization. Others are instructed to stay away from open association but work for the cause from other venues. The points of attack as well as their intensity vary according to time and place. Although the intellectual and political preparation goes on the whole time, it can be switched to support for local terrorism, or even to actual armed uprising, when the overall situation is suitable.

How the political mechanism is attacked depends on the political structure of the target country as well as on the local situation. In the English-speaking nations, all levels of government are subject to pressure, and success at any level is exploited. Thus if there appears to be a strong anti-Communist central government — and this could even be one which is socialist — the local levels will become the focus of attention. (Britain during the Margaret Thatcher era has seen a proliferation of so called "loony left" local councils.) If a large bureaucracy is built up around semi-independent "non-governmental organizations," these become, because of their non-elected status, ideal targets for infiltration.

Today, the largest and most effective front organization for the dissemination and coordination of world-wide Soviet peace strategies is the World Peace Council. The WPC, having been thrown out of Paris and Vienna, currently operates from Helsinki. It is funded by the Soviet government and staffed largely by non-Soviet Communists and Communist sympathizers. However, the USSR maintains direct control by a leavening of Soviets in key positions as well as by its control of the purse-strings.

Lenin's study of Clausewitz taught him that a simple Marxist revolution usually would not suffice to destroy capitalism in a sovereign nation. Clausewitz had written:

For an uprising by itself to produce such a crisis presupposes an occupied area [i.e. occupied by the enemy, which for Lenin meant the existing order] is of a size that, in Europe, does not exist outside Russia, or a disproportion between the invading army and the size of the country that would never occur in practice. To be realistic, one must therefore think of a general insurrection within the framework of a war conducted by the regular army, and coordinated in one all-encompassing plan.

Therefore, military force became a vital part of the permanent struggle, and the result of Lenin's ideas can be seen today. The Soviets have given military preparedness such priority that now their conventional and nuclear muscle makes them a military superpower. While the USA still matches the USSR in nuclear weapons and exceeds it in naval power, the Soviet armed forces are by far the largest in the world. There are 17 million Soviet citizens who have military training and an obligation to serve on a part-time basis or if called. Of these, 12 million are in the regular, reserve, KGB and internal security forces. A further 5 million are instructors in over 330,000 units formed in schools, colleges and workers' centres all over the USSR. There young Soviets aged fifteen and over get instruction in weapons training, shooting, parachuting and flight training. Compared to this, the United States has a total of 4.5 million regulars and reserves, which includes the Civil Air Patrol and also the little-known, and mostly dormant, State Militias. The latter are volunteer groups organized as skeleton military units in some sixteen states.

Even Communist China with a population four times as numerous as the USSR has only 13 million organized and armed regulars and reserves, with another 6 million militia which has some basic training, but is generally unarmed. Unlike China, the USSR also has the means to project this human power, the ability to move and employ its military force beyond its borders. In fact, the Soviet logistical capability to move and support many troops anywhere in the world has been steadily built up since the end of the Second World War.

As long as the West retains some power and cohesion, the Soviet Communists will be loath to use their military forces in a direct attack. As Clausewitz pointed out, the waiting game from a defensive position is the best strategy in war:

> . . . defence is easier than attack, assuming that both sides have equal means. Just what is it that makes preservation and protection so much easier? It is the fact that time which is allowed to pass unused accumulates to the credit of the defender. He reaps where he did not sow. Any omission of attack — whether from bad judgement, fear or indolence — accrues to the defender's benefit.

This does not negate the need for offensive action:

> Pure defense, however, would be completely contrary to the idea of war, since it would mean that only one side was waging it. Therefore, defense in war can only be relative and the characteristic feature of waiting should be applied only to the basic concept, not to all of its components.

Lenin, by wedding Marx's "class war" to the Clausewitzian description of "the people in arms," took a strategy for the defence of a sovereign nation and turned it into an attack on a world scale. Clausewitz stipulated that in a general uprising:

> Militia and armed bands of civilians cannot and should not be employed against the main force — or indeed against any sizeable enemy force. They are not supposed to pulverize the core but to nibble at the shell and around the edges.

With the entire world at stake and the democratic nations as the main theatre of the psychological war, the constant violence we observe in the Third World becomes easier to understand. This not only "will deny [the West] these areas altogether," it will also help immeasurably in the psycho-political war in the heartland of the democracies. As Clausewitz wrote:

Once this influence of the political objective is admitted, as it must be, there is no stopping it; consequently we must also be willing to wage such minimal wars, which consist in merely threatening the enemy, with negotiations held in reserve.

This theory of war helps to explain modern Soviet actions and to predict their strategies. More importantly, in it also lie the seeds of democratic victory. A strong defence, coupled with psychological attack, cannot fail to "reap where [we] did not sow." The ever increasing problems of communism, whether they lead to a final failure of the system, or, as is far less likely, to successful reform, means that the waiting game is indeed a winning strategy for democracy against totalitarianism.

The psychological manipulation of behaviour has a long history in the Soviet Union. I. P. Pavlov's experiments with the conditioning of animal behaviour rank him with Freud as one of the fathers of modern psychology. Since Pavlov, the Soviets have been steadily progressing in research and development of the more practical uses of psychology. In the West the psychology of manipulation has been used mainly in the arena of commerce; meanwhile, the Soviets have been perfecting its use for psychological war.

Various parts of the modern campaign have been noted — the Cold War is an inadequate attempt to describe it — but there has been no appreciation of the enormous unified attack being mounted by all the Communist powers and of the gravity of the threat that the sum of the parts presents. Although it has been the major and the only successful part of the permanent struggle, this has escaped the notice of the majority of the military technocrats who are responsible for the defence of the democracies. Unfortunately, psychological warfare has only been a peripheral part of the study of conflict in the West.

The destruction of veridical communications is the heart of the psychological war. It is communications which hold a society together and which give democracy such overwhelming strength, and it is trust as much as technological progress which has been responsible for the communication explosion in the West.

The key to the power of communications in a democracy is trust — trust that the medium is not being manipulated purely by those in power in order to control society. The greater the trust and the greater the common base of knowledge underlying the trust, the speedier and more comprehensive the communication. In order for such trust to be maintained, there must be methods of verification and comparison and these can only exist in a free society.

This trust in communications is ultimately based on belief in a supreme authority, as opposed to a secular, human power. To verify information we ask, "On what authority do you have that?" When we swear that the evidence that we give is the truth, the authentication that we use is a symbol of authority in culture, such as the Bible or the Koran. As there is no similar cultural touchstone of authority in communications under communism, instead of largely being a method of exchanging information, communication becomes a method of control and propaganda.

In keeping with Lenin's original aim of overthrowing the governments of non-Communist countries, communications become the prime weapon to infiltrate and corrupt democratic society. No opportunity is missed to weaken and divide the old order, for as Lenin wrote:

> A more powerful enemy can be conquered only by exerting the utmost effort and by necessarily, most carefully, solicitously, cautiously, and skillfully taking advantage of every 'rift', even the smallest, among the enemies, of every antagonism of interest among the bourgeoisie of various countries, between various groups or types of bourgeoisie within different countries, by taking advantage of every, even the smallest, opportunity of gaining a mass ally, even though this ally be only temporary, vacillating, unstable, unreliable and conditional. Those who have not understood this have not understood a particle of Marxism, or of scientific contemporary socialism in general.

Misunderstanding of the psychological front in the modern world is a major weakness of the Western alliance. This is a great tragedy, for the indirect attack is cheap, safe and potentially the best strategy for the West. Decentralization of decision making in the post-industrial democracies, which to date has been seen as a weakness, coupled with the massive lead in communications, potentially give the West an unbeatable advantage with little danger of escalating violence.

Until this is understood by Western decision makers, fear and ignorance will remain our greatest enemies. The less united and more demoralized that the West becomes, the greater the psychological utility of Soviet nuclear and conventional military power will be. While fear and lack of cohesion alone perhaps cannot lead to the defeat of democracy by totalitarianism, the weakening of the West increases enormously the danger of another uncontrolled war in the industrialized world. For, as the Communist block rapidly falls further behind the West in everything save military might, time is running out and the waiting game becomes one of diminishing returns for the Soviets.

To "take advantage of every rift," every real or perceived injustice is exploited. Then the disaffected subgroups are weaved into a collective web of hostility to the majority and, while this gives each minority an illusion of extra strength, it ultimately works against the group's primary purpose. Its energy is diverted into destroying the entire status quo instead of trying to reform the part which affects it.

The ensuing polarization helps to undermine democratic society as a whole, because even those members of the majority who would have been sympathetic to a particular grievance, now become hostile. Institutions, which are the building blocks on which a society is built, are all attacked. The family, religious organizations, unions, educational institutions, political parties, as well as all levels of government and civil service bureaucracies of all kinds become targets for corruption. The trust and authority holding the existing order together begin to dissolve with the spread of hatred, fear and envy.

The authorities that are the most difficult to infiltrate and corrupt, such as the armed forces and police, are isolated and alienated. In the Russia of 1917, the failure to do this properly was a major lesson for the Communists. Since then, in places like Czechoslovakia, East Germany, Hungary and Poland, we can see the results of this tactic. Attempts at alienation and isolation of the army and the police are also a major part of the indirect attack against our own societies. The American experience in Vietnam shows how this can work against an army. Both the on-going British problems in Ulster and the current anti-police drive in the United Kingdom are examples of the indirect attack at work.

In addition to controlling their own information process, a major part of the Communist indirect attack is the attempt to manipulate the communication process in the West. The more obvious way that this is done is by propaganda, where the use of two contradictory themes is a time-honoured tactic. Thus the USSR is presented as arming only to defend itself, while spreading fear of its implacable, resolute might. At the same time we are told that it is the USA which poses the greatest danger to world peace, and the West which must make the concessions; it is the American scorpion in the bottle which must have its poison removed.

The Western strategy of nuclear deterrence has greatly helped in this Soviet strategy of fear. In placing a reliance on the deterrent value of the nuclear weapon, the Western powers have required fewer and fewer of their citizens to become soldiers. The security and defence of the democracies has been left increasingly to professionals, technocrats and the bureaucracy. This has not only left the average citizen ignorant of all aspects of conflict, but also left him with the feeling of personal uninvolvement in the security of his own society. Uninvolvement turns into helplessness, despair and fear. Ultimately it can lead to submission.

The conventional, that is non-nuclear, military balance is also used to spread fear. The fact that the Warsaw Pact has bigger armies, more tanks, more divisions, more soldiers and greater reserves than NATO is never hidden. In fact, misleading propaganda about how the individual Soviet bloc soldier is better trained, tougher and meaner than his Western counterparts is actively pushed. The grave weaknesses of the whole Communist military establishment, such as the lack of initiative of the officer corps, inferior technology, unreliable armies in the satellite countries and lack of flexibility, are of course never mentioned from the other side of the Iron Curtain and seldom mentioned in the West. Western defence bureaucrats and arms manufacturers unwittingly play into this hand. To keep their share of the budget, they also constantly harp on Soviet strengths and Western weaknesses.

The attempted Soviet manipulation of communications in the West is the other half of the disinformation campaign. Here the media and the education system are the most important targets.

Some of the methods of manipulation of Western media have been described in print as well as in Kit Vincent's excellent documentary film, "The Deception Network," shown recently by CTV. The manipulation of the learning process is slower in action and more difficult to uncover; it includes the politicization of education and the suppression of source material. A specific Canadian example of this process will be found in chapter eleven.

One of the most suggestive pieces of circumstantial evidence for this form of psychological warfare is the attempted suppression in the West of Clausewitz's section on revolutionary war, the part of his work that would be most useful in mounting a Western defence against the indirect attack.

According to Raymond Aron, until 1955, there was no readily available translation of Clausewitz's *On War*. Book VI, "the implications of which only revolutionaries have grasped," was not even included in the extracts published in the USA. In 1968, a popular English edition of *On War* was finally published by Penguin Books. But not only was Book VI entirely omitted, in the course of laying out a philosophy for "peace studies" for the reader, the editor offered the following additional help:

> The disavowal of aggressive war as an instrument of policy by the Soviet Union can perhaps be partly attributed to a change of climate in world public opinion: almost everyone is for peace.

However, there is evidence that the disavowal represents a genuine orientation of the Soviet leadership, reflection of the profound aversion to war of their population and of an intense standing commitment to build a great civilization on Communist principles.

Further on, despite all evidence to the contrary, and overlooking the largest army in the world which that year invaded Czechoslovakia, the editor wrote:

> . . . whatever the reason, whether the absence of martial inclinations in the Russian people, or the peculiar position of the Soviet Union in the international system, or the ideological underpinnings of Soviet foreign policy, or the pre-occupation of the Soviet leaders with peaceful economic development, the Clausewitzian philosophy was never firmly established in the USSR.

Whereas:

> . . . the Clausewitzian philosophy of war now enjoys the greatest prestige in the military circles of the United States and among their advisory entourage . . . [and that] . . . Probably a major factor in the restraint exercised by the United States [is] the fact that the Soviet Union had acquired its own retaliatory weapon, in consequence of which retaliation for infringements on the "Free World" became a risky matter.

For good measure, the editor* then labelled leading Western strategists as "Neo-Clausewitzian." He reserved special scorn for Raymond Aron:

---

* In the 1980s, Anatol Rapoport, the editor who wrote these interesting interpretations of Clausewitz became the first professor and founding chairman of peace studies at the University of Toronto, as well as president of Scientists for Peace and advisor to the Toronto Board of Education Committee on "Thinking and Acting in the Nuclear Age."

Among the numerous tracts of the Neo-Clausewitzians the most ambitious, to my knowledge, is "Peace and War" by Raymond Aron. Aron presents himself as a Westerner concerned with the precious heritage of Western civilization . . . an essential component of the defence of the "Free World" is resistance to subversion.

Another, little understood part of the disinformation campaign, which is used internally as well as externally, is the use of mass deception. This is a ploy which preceded the Communist rule in Russia. An early example of conjuring with perceptions on a mass scale is the story of Potemkin's village. This concerned an elaborate scheme by the eighteenth-century Russian Prince Potemkin to convince his Empress lover, Catherine the Great, and her advisers, that the funds which she had given him as governor of the newly conquered province of Crimea had been well spent. When Catherine came to inspect her new colony, the route on which she travelled was lined with false-front houses; newly planted gardens; smiling well-fed household servants, dressed-up as serfs, waving from the side of the road; and other illusions to give an air of prosperity to what were in fact dirt poor villages. At the end of each day's journey, while Catherine and her lover partied at a local inn, the next part of the illusion was prepared under cover of night.

Although the story is mainly apocryphal, it has become an integral part of the Soviet psyche. Potemkin's successors and their pupils have not been idle. A similar ploy convinced the playwright George Bernard Shaw, a visiting former President of France, Raymond Poincaré, as well as a world willing to believe, that there were happy well-fed peasants in the Ukraine, while Stalin's 1932-33 man-made famine killed off between seven and ten million people.

The effectiveness of the indirect attack and of the updated methods of mass deception now in use were brought home to me when I served a tour with the International Commission for Control and Supervision of the Ceasefire in Vietnam (ICCS).

The long conflict in Indo-China had begun another act and we were new characters on the stage. On January 27, 1973, the Americans and the South Vietnamese had signed a ceasefire agreement with the North Vietnamese and the Viet Cong in Paris. The ICCS was part of the complicated machinery which was put in place so that neither side took undue advantage of the situation to better its military position.

On reflecting on my experience in Vietnam, I realized that the whole period of American involvement was one of successful mass deception of the Western world. We, the Canadian members of the ICCS, had not only been preconditioned, but our perceptions were continually being scrambled from the moment we set foot in Southeast Asia.

Just before dawn on January 29, 1973, a Canadian military Boeing 707 landed at the Thon Son Nhut airbase in Saigon. Minutes before, the airfield had been under rocket attack and a fat, shaken, young American airman who was helping the passengers to disembark, muttered that during his year in Vietnam this was his first time under hostile fire.

The tired Canadians getting off the aircraft were not too interested in his grumbling. Looking like misplaced, overgrown Boy Scouts in their light green shirts and dark green pants, they were part of the first operational commitment of the Canadian Armed Forces following the unification of the Royal Canadian Navy, the Canadian Army and the Royal Canadian Air Force. The hurriedly assembled contingent was composed of officers from every branch, who were there to judge and report on ground operations. Many had once been sailors, airmen or army non-combatants. They had no knowledge of even basic small unit tactics and infantry weapons, let alone how to recognize what was happening in the strange, multilayered battleground of Vietnam. The official post-unification policy was that they were all interchangeable.

They and their External Affairs colleagues of the contingent were equally politically naive. The brief indoctrination in Montreal prior to leaving did not lessen their naivete. Intelligence briefings were squeezed in between the drawing of tropical uniforms and lectures on the new strains of VD raging through Southeast Asia.

Vietnam was divided into seven regions, for the purpose of the ceasefire agreement. On the briefing map, which had no more intelligence information on it than a *Time* magazine map of the day, the areas under Communist control were shown as pink leopard spots. As I was to be the Senior Staff Officer for Operations in Region IV, I took a particular interest in that part of the Coastal Plain and Central Highlands which the region comprised. With the exception of our headquarters, which was located in the town of Phan Thiet, the whole region appeared to be pink.

A week after arrival in Saigon, we deployed to Phan Thiet, a fishing town on the South China Sea, about ninety miles east of Saigon. Its 80,000 inhabitants were crammed into an area that in North America would house a village. The small, unsubstantial houses and narrow, twisting streets ran back from a long, curving beach of sparkling pale yellow sand. The town was overlooked by a 150-foot bluff rising from the southern end of the beach.

Towards the end of their rule of Indo-China, the French had built a small airfield on the bluff's flat top. The surviving colonial administration buildings, yellow stucco with gracefully curved red tiled roofs, stood in dignified contrast to the utilitarian pierced-steel-planking mats of the single runway.

After the departure of the French, the South Vietnamese airforce became the owners of the airfield. When the American forces became heavily involved in the fighting against the Communists, the US Army took over the airstrip's management for a time. At one point a regiment of the 7th Air Cavalry Division, those helicopter-mounted descendants of Custer's famous horsemen, themselves immortalized and ridiculed in the film *Apocalypse Now*, was supposedly housed there.

During our stay in 1973, there were no aircraft based on Phan Thiet airfield. The only air traffic was an occasional visit by an Air America light plane or helicopter. Formerly this small airline had done most of its business flying clandestine missions for the Central Intelligence Agency. Now it had the contract to provide air transport for the ICCS.

The headquarters of Region IV of the ICCS occupied one of the American-built prefab shacks on the other side of the runway from the more substantial French buildings. The whole airfield was enclosed in barbed wire, gun positions and ancient, unreliably marked minefields laid by generations of nervous occupants. Half a mile away, in the town itself, the Canadians of Region IV lived with their Indonesian, Hungarian and Polish colleagues.

No one had thought that the ceasefire would end the conflict. We had been led to believe that we were there merely to record and protest the inevitable Communist takeover. All of us had come to Vietnam thinking that the non-Communist government was doomed and that the United States had lost this distant war. Our first impressions only reinforced our perceptions, as they were designed to do.

We had been flown from Saigon to the Phan Thiet airfield by Huey helicopters and then were driven to our quarters in town. As we left the airfield defences, mortar rounds exploded some distance from the road. The American soldier driving the staff car was not as shaken by this as had been the airman at Thon Son Nhut, but he also remarked that this was an unusual occurrence.

During the first weeks in Phan Thiet, there were other incidents — a rocket attack caused damage and injuries in the suburbs; a mortar bomb dropped into the crowded market near our living quarters killed and wounded some women and children. Every day for the first week after our arrival, there was action on the plain outside town, for which we had a grandstand view from the airfield on the bluff. Some days we could see South Vietnamese armoured personnel carriers in the dusty fields, or one of their A-39 jets bombing, or a helicopter strafing with rockets and machine guns.

The South Vietnamese told us that they were merely replying to nuisance raids from small groups of Communist infiltrators, as in fact, in the heavy-handed fashion inherited from the Americans, they were. But in my mind I knew that all this was merely preparation for the final takeover, which would happen once the last American forces had gone. I was not alone in my apprehension. The Canadian government ordered several ships from the tiny Pacific portion of the fleet to steam around in the South China Sea so that somehow, some of us could be rescued when the situation got desperate.

In the coming weeks, I gradually found that my impressions had been wrong and that the Communist superiority in South Vietnam was a mirage. Certainly, some areas resembled a country at war, as we had expected. This was particularly so in Region I, bordering on North Vietnam. There, dug-in South Vietnamese divisions faced regular divisions of North Vietnamese regulars. The fortified defensive positions were reminiscent of the trench lines of the First World War. Most of the rest of the country had little damage. The war would periodically break out with the suddenness of a summer hurricane and then depart, and once the dead and wounded were removed, it would not leave much more permanent damage than a storm.

There were indeed regions with large areas under Communist control, but these were only a fraction of what we had expected. Most of the areas coloured pink on our original maps turned out to be jungle, some of which certainly held Communist units, but most of which should not have been coloured pink, but green for neutral.

The South Vietnamese control was so complete in my region, that it was almost entirely defended by Regional and Popular for-ces — the latter only part-time soldiers. Unlike regulars, regional troops could not be sent to serve outside their native province. This meant that they were never too far from home and could still help their families with the harvest. The Popular forces were even more localized. They were just villagers armed with rifles, who guarded their village at night and farmed in the daytime.

Finding out who was in control was not easy. The only way to judge which side had caused a violation of the ceasefire, was to know who was the attacker. To do that, first we had to get to the scene of the outbreak of fighting with the aid of the Joint Military Commis-sion (JMC), which was formed from the opposing armies.

The South Vietnamese Army (ARVN) representatives of the

JMC smilingly told us that they owned every occupied hamlet and every arable piece of land in the region and, providing that we gave them a bit of notice, they would get us a safe passage to any part of the region. The Communist representatives insisted that they were the owners of the whole region and indeed of every square inch of Vietnam.

We tried to clear this up. What about Phan Thiet itself?, we asked the Communists, pointing out that they were virtual prisoners in their compound on the airfield, with ARVN soldiers guarding them. The only answer was a polite smile and the offer of more tea. We blamed this apparent misunderstanding on the culture and faulty interpreting.

Without agreement as to safe passage from both sides, we could not convince the Poles and Hungarians to venture outside Phan Thiet. The only way to find out what really was going on was to see for ourselves. Gradually, as we started to trust the South Vietnamese, we extended our areas of operation. In the end, we discovered that most of our area of South Vietnam was free of Communist control.

During this period, between January and June of 1973, the military situation kept improving for the South Vietnamese Army, but the psychological war of perceptions continued steadily to be lost. This turned out to be far more conclusive than the tactical battles, or who in fact controlled the most ground. American and international opinion sealed the fate of the South Vietnamese, just as it had forced the USA out of the war.

As we had expected, there was no real ceasefire, but the war was not very intense. There were few pitched battles; the key to the conflict lay in small actions and scattered acts of terror. For example, on May 20, 1973, we received a routine complaint from the South Vietnamese representative on the local Joint Military Commission. Would the ICCS investigate a ceasefire violation in the hamlet of Long Hiep, where the previous evening a grenade explosion had killed three villagers and wounded a dozen others.

The investigation of ceasefire incidents had seemed simple

enough when we read the protocols of the ceasefire agreement on the aeroplane taking us to Vietnam. If fighting broke out, the attacked party would complain to the closest ICCS team through the Joint Military Commission. A four-nation observer team would go to the area and rule which side had violated the ceasefire. The reality was quite different.

As the ceasefire violations were almost invariably caused by the Communist forces, the Polish and Hungarian ICCS delegations would come up with all sorts of reasons to delay an investigation. By the time the observers arrived, the incident was usually over and culpability difficult to prove.

This time it was a repetition of the same old stalling tactics. The Region IV ICCS held a meeting of the Regional Executive Committee to decide if we should investigate. While the Canadians and Indonesians were eager to move, the Poles and Hungarians stalled as much as they could and were even more reluctant to go than usual. A short while before, on Easter Sunday, a bomb had exploded in a Roman Catholic churchyard in the region, killing some twenty children and wounding nearly one hundred others as they attended an Easter pageant. Captain Alex Miller, the local Canadian team leader, had for once managed to convince his Communist colleagues to accompany him and an Indonesian officer to the site.

The villagers had no doubt about who planted the bomb and why; it was the familiar pattern of destroying the traditional local hierarchy. They also had no difficulty in making the connection between the terror and the Communist portion of the ICCS investigating team. In their anger they threw stones and jeered at the jeeps with the Polish and Hungarian officers.

With this incident still fresh in the minds of our Warsaw Pact colleagues, in the end, on this occasion, the Indonesian officer and I went to Long Hiep on our own. By the time we got there, the incident was already cold. But the South Vietnamese were keeping a prisoner to show me. He had been caught hiding outside the village and the ARVN captain who had called me was most anxious that I talk to him.

The prisoner turned out to be a frightened fourteen-year-old boy from the hamlet. While we were questioning him, I began to realize again how little I knew of the war in Vietnam. Here is a reconstruction of the interview as I recorded it in my field notebook:

Ngai's mother, Nguong, was pregnant and had four children already when her conscript soldier husband had been killed fighting the North Vietnamese Army during the Spring offensive of 1968. Since then she had been supplementing her tiny pension by farming. It was a hard life and she resented the authorities which had taken away her man. Her resentment was so success-fully fuelled by Communist propaganda that she eventually came to feel that the real cause of her grief was the government and the army, rather than the invaders from North Vietnam. Nguong became a Communist sympathizer.

She did not have much time to mollycoddle a dreamy, lazy fourteen-year-old boy and Ngai had also become resentful. He had left school after only one year, when he could barely read and write, because he had to help to feed the family. His day started early when he had to take the family water buffalo to the river to water it. He had to do this while his three sisters and little brother were still in bed.

Once in a while in the early mornings at the river he met members of the local Communist band, called an Arrow Action Team Viet Cong. It was outside the occupied hamlets that they collected what they called their taxes. In order to ensure a peaceful life and prevent too many acts of terrorism, the villagers gave enough rice and foodstuffs to the guerrillas to keep them alive.

The guerrillas agreed with Ngai that his mother treated him unfairly. They also told him that the only thing that he had to look forward to was service in the Government Army when he turned eighteen and to being killed just like his father. He would be much better off and help to end the whole unjust system, if he ran away with them and became a fighter for the cause of freedom.

Before dawn on the 25th of December, 1972, Ngai left the

buffalo at home and went to the river alone. He went off with the guerrillas to the jungle leaving his angry mother to reorganize her life. Ngai's older sister, Nhum, took over the water buffalo duties.

Life with the guerrillas was considerably more difficult for Ngai than it had been at home. He had never-ending chores, and he was always cleaning somebody's weapons. Periodically he had to help rebuild the camp in another part of the jungle.

In between the work they had lectures, which always seemed to be about the same thing. How the villagers were being exploited by the richer and more powerful people, about the injustice and the misery, about the dreadful war which had killed his and so many other fathers and which had to be stopped. He also learned how to handle a rifle and to pull the pin from a hand grenade.

One evening in May the commandant of the guerrilla group gave Ngai two hand grenades and told him that he had to go and throw one at the soldiers in his village and the other at the hamlet chief. This was necessary, for the hamlet chief and the young soldiers were lackeys of the government which was keeping the other people in the hamlet so poor.

Ngai got to the little dusty main street at dusk, just as people were returning from the paddies and the coconut groves. He hid between two houses and waited. Suddenly a group of shadowy figures started coming towards his hiding place. He got very frightened and forgot that he had to throw his grenades in the village chief's house and the police station. Instead, he pulled the pin and threw one of the grenades towards the approaching people and ran. Four seconds later came the bang and then the screams. He ran on into the darkness with the shouts of anger and screams of pain of many people following him.

When he was out of breath he crawled into a bush about a quarter of a mile from the village. When he stopped shaking, he got very tired and fell fast asleep.

Ngai was awakened by the voices of old friends from the

village. They were going out to the fields to start the morning's work. As they passed his bush he heard them talking about the people killed and wounded the night before. Now he really got frightened; perhaps he had killed his mother, one of his sisters or his five-year-old brother. He ran to the village chief's house and threw himself on the ground, crying.

When we returned, the Poles and the Hungarians discounted our report, which was based on the grenade fragments, the mute evidence of the dead as well as verbal reports from the boy himself and the wounded farmers. They said that this was probably a case of a curious child experimenting with explosives. They wanted this incident, the explosion in the churchyard, and all the other acts of terror, large or small, to seem unconnected with the world of nuclear overkill and the grand strategic plans of the superpowers.

Baron de Jomini, the Swiss-born Napoleonic soldier, whose *The Art of War* is second only to Clausewitz's *On War* in its insight into conflict, wrote:

> As a soldier, preferring loyal and chivalrous warfare to organized assassination, . . . I acknowledge that my prejudices are in favour of the good old times when the French and English Guards courteously invited each other to fire first, — as at Fontenoy, — preferring them to the frightful epoch when priests, women and children . . . plotted the murder of individual soldiers.

And I shared his sentiments, but like him, I knew that I had to learn far more about this form of warfare, in which children were used as a cheap, discardable weapon.

How did it happen that the US forces, having won every tactical battle, had gone home in disgrace? That the South Vietnamese, whose army was strong and confident, whose cause was obviously just, were vilified and cut off from support? That the defeated, demoralized, Communist forces were being touted as the glorious victors? I gradually realized that the same old principles of illusion, evident in the story of Potemkin's village had been transformed, updated and used as an effective measure in the psychological conflict. Clausewitz's insight was more pertinent than ever: "Psychological forces exert a decisive influence on the elements involved in war."

A series of seemingly unconnected happenings suddenly had meaning when put in the context of the war of perceptions and helped to explain why my expectations of what I would find in Vietnam were totally at odds to the actual situation. The perception had been fuelled by the media and by the lack of any credible alternate views.

At the time of the ceasefire negotiations in Paris, there were co-ordinated actions all over the West to show the resolve and strength of the insurgency forces in South Vietnam. Canada was not excluded from this show of solidarity; a few days before leaving for Vietnam in January of 1973, I saw a large pro-North Vietnam and Viet Cong demonstration in Montreal. This was only one small part of the international Potemkin village.

As a result of this skilled campaign, the sympathy of the Western public was gained for North Vietnam, although it was the South that was under attack by the Communist North. Even though the public perceived the Communists as much stronger militarily after the withdrawal of the last Americans, they still saw them as the glamorous underdogs.

This also seemed to be the official Canadian view, fuelled by a distrust of American intelligence. Our own authorities were as ignorant of the true situation in Vietnam as was the public at large, despite having access to far more information.

When, sixty days after the ceasefire, the last of the American forces went home, this event had little military significance. The South Vietnamese were confident enough in their control that they lifted the nighttime curfew, which had been in effect in the country for some fifteen years. The little clubs and restaurants in Phan Thiet stayed open till the wee hours, each with a gramophone blaring music into the street. The lights stayed on as the people celebrated the retreat of fear from the night.

It was against this background that I made a memorable visit to a "teamsite" in ICCS Region III, which was next to mine. Each region's ceasefire observers were located at numerous such team-sites. The great majority of these were in South Vietnamese territory. One of few sites in Communist territory, and the only one with an airfield, was in the neighbouring ICCS region. It was called Duc Tho II and was located at an airstrip that had been built and used by American forces before being captured by the North Vietnamese. Colonel Keith MacGregor, the regional commander, had organized a liaison flight there to establish communications by air. He had a spare seat on the flight and allowed me to go along.

The chubby, jovial Air America pilot put the single-engined Pilatus Porter into a maximum climb straight off the runway as we departed from Pleiku. The scrap heap of wrecked Huey helicopters, Skyraiders, Caribou, Boxcars and Dakotas at the end of the runway demonstrated how easy it is for an infiltrator to shoot down an aeroplane if it lingers at low altitude as it is landing or taking off.

Although the wrecks were all from before the ceasefire, the Communists still shot at everything that flew over their heads. Unless the flight was co-ordinated perfectly beforehand, the ICCS plane was liable to be shot at despite the distinctive stripes on its tail. Nine ICCS deaths in Region I were a grim reminder of this.

We circled over Pleiku until we reached 10,000 feet, well above the range of automatic weapons and even safe from the nasty, shoulder-held, heat-seeking Soviet missiles which were very common in Vietnam at the time. Some of the country below us was heavily pockmarked with artillery and bomb craters. It was worse than anything that I had seen in any of the other regions up to then and almost resembled the devastation that most people watching television in the sixties imagined Vietnam was.

When we were over the runway of Duc Tho II preparing to land, the pilot stood the Porter on its nose and performed a remarkable imitation of a wartime Stuka dive bomber. He was reducing the risk of some of the unseen people with guns below us shooting us down on our mission of peace.

It could be seen from the air that Duc Tho II had been a large military airfield, with some hardstand dispersal areas and the foundations of what had probably been an original settlement, which had been enlarged by the airfield administrative buildings. At ground level, the long, coarse grass hid the foundations of the structures which had once been there. One nearly demolished building and a couple of burnt-out American tanks were all that remained of past battles. The skeleton of the old building was being used as a terminal. In addition, the Communists had put up a wooden control tower. The contraption looked like a flimsy, low, hunting blind.

We were greeted by the local ICCS team members and North Vietnamese, dressed in the pith helmets and the rankless sand-coloured uniforms of the Provisional Revolutionary Government, for officially by the terms of the ceasefire agreement, the North Vietnamese had gone home at the same time as the Americans. To celebrate the occasion of the first ICCS flight to Communist territory in South Vietnam, the Communists had put a table, chairs and a rattan screen inside the roofless building. Here they served us tea. Before sitting down to the table, we were invited to wash up. The toilet facilities consisted of another table, this one outside, with a row of tin washbasins on it. To relieve oneself, there were only the bushes and the long grass.

The only other object of note on this, the main airport of the Provisional Revolutionary Government of South Vietnam, was a blackboard. Chalked on it were the regulations for visitors to the field. Although one of the prohibited actions was the taking of photographs, the guards happily posed by the board while I photographed it. This is what it said:

## - THE RULE -

In order to keep safety and order on the airfield, the local liberation Army's high Command establishes the rules as followed:

I. Those who want to come in the Dacto, must have warrants of the L.H.G.

II. Before coming in DACTO II airfield to study or on business, the guests must hand over the warrants to the guard and follow the direction of the authorized men on the airfield.

III. Gurantee operation in every time, avoid any accident for men, cars etc.

IV. Men and cars must go on the roads already fixed. When studying, repairing the taking off or landing line, there is a red or green mark from the leading tower, every body must go away from the taking off or landing line.

BAN: Ban on bringing along the explosive causing explosion on the airport. Ban on going wantonly on the runway. Ban on coming near the airplane if no business. Ban on smoking, firing, cars coming near the airplanes. ! Ban on TAKING film and picture.

Those who don't implement these rules, must be kept and brought to the L.H.G. to be taken into examination.

May, 5, 1973

The L.H.Command

After tea and the photograph-taking, we climbed back into our aircraft and went back to Pleiku, leaving the two Canadian captains from the teamsite, who had previously come in over land, waving rather forlornly from their Soviet jeep.

Later I started to realize that the whole show had been put on for the benefit of our little Porter's eight passengers and pilot. The dating of the rule, a few days before our visit, should have told me this immediately, also the fact that it was only written in English. For there were no other "guests" or cars expected, and when the Rule decreed a "ban on smoking, firing, cars coming near the airplanes," it meant our Porter — there would be no other air traffic into Duc Tho II after we left.

The fact that I could take photographs of the sign, when it clearly banned the taking of any, showed only that the Communist soldiers themselves did not know what it said. Normally they were very swift to enforce any rules that they could.

It was later still that I realized why there were so few ceasefire teamsites in Communist territory. It was not only because there was less genuine Communist territory than we had suspected, but also by 1973 the North Vietnamese situation was so desperate that there were not even enough resources for many Potemkin facades.

The number of facades was not important, what mattered was how they were perceived in the West. No modern Potemkin illusion is possible without using the mass media. Therefore the more important part of the strategy was the manipulation of the media which carried the illusion. That is why the press, radio and the film industry have always been prime targets of the Soviet disinformation campaign.

The key to why the Vietnam Potemkin perceptual illusion succeeded on such a staggering scale is the nature of Western television. Vietnam was the first television war and the Communists managed to make Western TV carry the message of South Vietnamese defeat when the South was actually winning. They did this without the majority of the members of the industry being aware of how they were being used.

The instant transmission of a moving picture makes television an immensely powerful method of communication. However, this visual communication is more by means of emotions than by the transmission of verifiable facts. A false picture is just as emotionally powerful as a true one. The pictures television provides are as often as not illusions. This is especially so when the picture is of war.

The image of the boy who used to live next door getting his legs blown off in living colour makes the average housewife in Buffalo very receptive to the message accompanying the visual shock on her screen. Whichever thought gets attached to the picture will not soon be changed or forgotten.

War is one of the most complex of man's endeavours, and may be the most difficult to understand and report in any medium. Television is eminently unsuitable for providing clear, unemotional news of war. Unlike print reporters, TV cameramen, soundmen and correspondents have to record actual action. This is very dangerous, because they have to expose themselves to war at very close range. It is also very confusing, because they get easily disoriented in the fearful "fog of war." This is what happened in Vietnam.

The cameraman is the most forgotten and probably the most important person in the process. In order to get the best picture, he almost becomes an extension of his instrument. All he can do is give an artistic or emotional meaning to the image that he captures; there is no way that he can put it into an intellectual context. Although powerful, the picture he takes is still essentially neutral. It is like the crack of the bullet being fired without the thump that tells you its direction and distance.

The reporter who stands in front of the camera starts to shape the message that is attached to the image. But without military training, without access to the plans, to the thinking and to the intelligence available to the combat commander he can only convey what Clausewitz called the "friction" of the war. To put a broader meaning to his verbal caption to the moving image, he must rely on other sources. The person who is able to put a forceful tag onto the picture gets his message across.

In Vietnam, the Communists put across a limited number of simple slogans without any regard to their truth and little to their suitability. Eventually, enough of these messages got attached to the images coming home from Southeast Asia to swing the psychological mindset in the West in favour of the Communists, and the media war went to them almost by default. These simple slogans and clichés became attached to, and reinforced by, the emotionally powerful images that the technically brilliant but politically and militarily naive Western TV crews kept producing. To what extent this was originally just a happy coincidence of ideology meeting its medium and to what extent it was planned by the strategists in Hanoi and Moscow will probably never be known, but the more it worked, the more it was exploited.

The pictures have faded a little now and a whole new generation has grown up who cannot remember their original impact, but in the majority of people in the West they still elicit a Pavlovian response. Few can forget these images of Vietnam: the little naked girl running away from a napalm attack, her whole being personifying terror; the South Vietnamese police chief in a Saigon street summarily shooting with his revolver a captured Viet Cong guerrilla, both executioner and victim in casual civilian attire; Viet Cong soldiers in control of the ground floor of the American embassy and the US military policeman in the garden throwing a handgun up to the diplomat cut off on the second floor.

The messages that these images reinforced are also a little tarnished now, after the suicidal escape of the boat people, after the Vietnamese invasion of Cambodia, after the dark rumblings about the use of chemical and bacteriological agents by the North Vietnamese. But the catch phrase and slogans of the era are still bright and believable to many Western minds: at least the Viet Cong had a cause that they believed in; they would sweep away the corruption; they were primarily nationalist patriots, their communism was only an incidental tactic and really rather nice; "amerika," the most powerful nation on earth, was fighting the noble Viet Cong to keep the venal South Vietnamese in power, and losing; "Hey, hey, LBJ, how many kids did you kill today?" and the US Army represented all that was wrong with "amerika," capitalism, the West and U.S. imperialism; intellectual, sensitive and caring Americans were united against the war; they supported the draft dodgers and deserters who were streaming into Canada, made fun of those who served and vilified those who fought; the act of desertion was courageous, whereas courage in the line of duty was bestial and stupid; the US military was composed of power-mad, genocidal officers and heroin-addicted, conscript dropouts; etc, etc.

Despite loss of life, matériel, morale and prestige, the US forces won all the tactical battles in Vietnam, but the American military failed to attach timely captions to the ceaseless, raw pictures that kept coming out of Vietnam. Their combat leaders at the troop level were not supposed to talk to the press, nor were they trained to do so. Instead, each action would be explained later by an immaculately starched officer in one or another version of the briefings that soon came to be known as the "Saigon Follies" or "Dog and Pony Shows." The briefing explanations invariably came too late. All the body counts, all the lights at the end of all the tunnels, came to be treated by the media as lies and half truths because, by the time they were released, the violent image had already been captured and a simple slogan had been attached to it.

By January 1973, the U.S. Military had long lost all credibility with the Western media and opinion makers. The perception that the war had been lost militarily was so common that the promised material support to the Army of The Republic of South Vietnam (ARVN) was almost totally cut off by the US Congress. Just as important, the South Vietnamese nation had lost all moral support in the free world.

When the lack of ammunition, spare parts and weaponry was added to the total lack of moral support for South Vietnam, its eventual collapse became inevitable. The only surprise — further evidence of the low state of the North Vietnamese Army — was that it took two years instead of two months. In those two years, with US airpower no longer interdicting the supply route through Cambodia, the Ho Chi Minh Trail became a blacktop highway, with a bumper-to-bumper traffic of trucks containing Soviet-supplied arms and equipment. But even more vital than material refurbishing was time, which allowed the maturing of two cohorts of North Vietnamese boys to fill out the depleted ranks of the invading army.

But none of this was known and understood at the time. The Americans failed to grasp that insurgency warfare, until its final stages when it may turn into more conventional conflict, does not concern itself with the traditional balance sheet of war. Troop strengths, casualties, gains and losses of territory are all of no account. Perceptions are.

General Giap, the Soviet-trained architect of the earlier Communist victory over the French, played his hand in a classic revolutionary manner, with the unwitting help of the Western media. In what is probably the best-remembered action of the whole war, the Tet offensive of 1968, he sacrificed the majority of the Viet Cong in order to strike at the minds of the American public. For a brief moment the Communists were in control of places which were thought to be among the safest and the photographers and TV cameramen were there to freeze the moment into history.

Security was rapidly restored by the anti-Communist forces and the attacking Viet Cong were killed or captured. The remainder of the war was fought by the North Vietnamese army. The indigenous South Vietnamese Viet Cong had been destroyed as a fighting force, but remained a powerful psychological one. Viet Cong units, or of the Army of the Provisional Government of South Vietnam, as they were officially known, were brought up to strength with North Vietnamese conscripts, but fought to the end under their Viet Cong designations. The flags and the fiction of being South Vietnamese remained.

At the time it was thought by Western analysts that the Tet offensive had been designed as a blow at the brain and communications system of the anti-Communist forces in Vietnam in order to trigger a popular uprising. When this failed to happen, the US high command boasted of the military failure of the campaign. However, North Vietnam's objective had never been military. Tet was one part of a brilliant two-pronged attack aimed at discrediting the South Vietnamese and knocking the US back out of the war.

The dramatic action in the cities of South Vietnam was timed to coincide with the end of President Johnson's first elected term of office and was only one part of a much larger strategic picture. Tet had been preceded by an increase in the scope and intensity of the anti-war demonstrations in the United States and in the lands of the other leading democracies. There was dramatic footage of Viet Cong flags in Washington, of Old Glory being burnt in England and in France, images that coincided with the sudden violent Communist presence in the centres of South Vietnam.

The dual attack succeeded brilliantly. In March President Johnson announced not only that he would not seek re-election, but that America would seek "an honorable peace" in Vietnam. From now on every American soldier in Vietnam would know that he was fighting a war in which his commander-in-chief had already given up. Giap had achieved his aim; the bloody battles during the 1968 democratic convention in Chicago became merely a mopping-up action, which had the effect of further turning America against itself.

That year the assassinations of Robert Kennedy and Martin Luther King disrupted the democratic leadership still more. These events, together with the race riots in the United States and the student revolution in Paris, allowed the Soviet Army tanks to drive into Prague in August with hardly a murmur from the West.

To what extent the eventual outcome of the Vietnam War could have been changed had the American public been properly informed as to the military situation is open to conjecture. What is certain is that if the US military had learned from experience that the psychological aspects of an insurgency war are at least as important as the tactical victories, the army itself would not have become so alienated from the rest of American society.

During Vietnam the Americans made a great attempt at public relations. They are, after all, the modern masters of technical communications. But they failed to make sufficient allowance for the power, the speed and the lack of integrity of the most influential of the information purveyors, television.

*The Irony of Vietnam, the System Worked* by Leslie Gelb and Richard Polk, is an authoritative book that outlines without emotion the military strategies of that conflict and their results. It is not widely known; it would be too much to hope that mere books would change popular perceptions, conditioned by years of television. The authors confirm by statistics what I had judged subjectively, namely that the much maligned process of Vietnamization had worked. The Vietnamese had adapted American weapons and tactics to their own culture and organization and gone on to win the majority of battles. In the late sixties the fighting formations of the US Army and Marines were phased out so that eventually, in addition to naval and air support, only logistical troops and advisers were left in South Vietnam.

Of course, the American Army only played a part in the public relations process. The emotions as well as convictions of the many people involved in delivering the message were important. The selection, editing, and transmission of any particular image were largely beyond the control of the military, but it was the military leadership which failed to give what I call the psychomedia aspect of the conflict the attention that it deserved.

The army kept the public-relations function separate, rather than making it a vital part of command down to the lowest level. Instead of training all combat officers to talk to the press immediately and with authority, time and credibility were allowed to lapse until the formal briefings. Unless a war is important enough to a democracy to warrant the imposition of censorship on the press, or isolated enough like the action in Grenada to make the exclusion of the media from the fighting possible, every combat leader must be capable of giving, and authorized to give, his version of every action in which he takes part. There is no great indoctrination necessary for this, or no great sophistication required of the ordinary soldier. The truth as seen by the local commander will invariably be coloured by his aims and objectives and the media will eventually become sophisticated enough to realize that it is neither the soldier's job nor his inclination to give a balanced view.

For the combat commander, the governing principles of communicating with the media must be speed and truth. The trust built up will more than compensate for all the times that these principles backfire. Perhaps in the future it will be concluded that it was the lack of appreciation of the importance of fighting the media war that was the single greatest factor in the loss of South Vietnam to communism. Whereas the North Vietnamese had no real hope of a tactical victory, it was the electronic update of Potemkin's methods that permitted the north from going down in defeat. And the Soviet psychostrategists had won a major victory at a small price.

The reader may well ask why I have gone to such lengths, in a book about Canadian defence, to describe a situation that happened in Vietnam almost fifteen years ago and in which Canadians were nothing more than powerless observers. The answer is in what this teaches us about the nature of our enemy and its means of defeating us, even on our own soil.

South Vietnam lost its freedom because it lost the psychological war, not the one between men fighting in the field. The same war is still being fought much closer to home. There are no Communist guerrillas now operating in Canada, although I would argue that their moral equivalent has long been gnawing at our innards. But whatever the case, we must be prepared to combat both insurgency within and a subtle psychological war for our hearts and minds waged from without.

The indirect psychological attack may seem a remote and improbable form of warfare to most Canadians. But if we are ill prepared to wage it, then we risk losing our democratic way of life. This is true whether we plan our future defence as part of the Western alliance, as I believe we must, or opt, as some are now arguing, for official neutrality. In order to make such crucial decisions, we must first understand the current state of the Western alliance.

# CHAPTER THREE

# The Achilles Heel of the Western Alliance

*No matter how clearly we see the citizen and the soldier in the same man, how strongly we conceive of war as the business of the entire nation, opposed diametrically to the pattern set by the condottieri [mercenaries] of former times, the business of war will always remain individual and distinct. Consequently for as long as they practice this activity, soldiers will think of themselves as members of a kind of guild, in whose regulations, laws, and customs the spirit is given pride of place.*

Carl von Clausewitz

In order to discuss the implications of Canada's current defence situation, we must know the strategic problems of the democratic alliance. And since the USA is the most powerful member of the alliance, as well as its leader, it is essential to understand its military strengths and weaknesses.

There are two basic military problems which the English-speaking nations of the alliance have failed to address since the end of the Second World War. The first is the lack of a true general staff system and so of any sophisticated ability to develop timely and appropriate military strategies. The second, for which the first may partly be blamed, is the weakness of conventional forces and their alienation from mainstream society, which has led to their isolation from the political decision-making process.

These twin fault lines have been converging to cause a military crisis in the United States. As a result, the Western alliance grows weaker, even as it attempts to negotiate reductions in nuclear arms. However, there are signs that the crisis is forcing changes which could rectify the problems and make the world more secure instead of leading it into greater danger.

As I argued in Chapter 1, the historic reason why the English-speaking nations failed to militarize as thoroughly as did the Continental powers was because they were fortunate enough to be geographically removed from the main cockpit of war.

For these and other reasons, traditionally the USA has kept the military from the strategic decision-making process, believing that all it had to do when the threat became serious, was to bring its economic might to bear. At the close of the nineteenth century, the eminent Victorian soldier-statesman Field Marshall Wolseley, wrote in his introduction to the biography of the American Civil War General, Stonewall Jackson:

> The pleasing notion that, whenever war comes, money can obtain for the nation all that it requires is still, it would seem, an article of at least lip-faith with the politicians of the English speaking race throughout the world.
>
> Gold will certainly buy a nation powder, pills, and provisions; but no amount of wealth, even when supported by a patriotic willingness to enlist, can buy discipline, training, and a skilful leading. Without these there can be no such thing as an efficient army, and success in the field against serious opposition is merely the idle dream of those who know not war.

Today, the military is still isolated and there is no systematic method of military strategic planning. Also, despite expending a great deal of gold, because there is no obligation to serve, the armed forces of the USA are comparatively weak in numbers. There are just over four and a half million Americans in the regular, reserve and civilian paramilitary forces, which is around a quarter of the total Soviet citizens who have military training and an obligation to serve. The US Army has insufficient depth and mass for sustained warfare and would therefore be heavily overcommitted in a world war, or even one which had two or more conventional fronts. As a result, its war-fighting capability is questionable.

The framework for obtaining manpower for the military is basically very good. When desperate times call for the mobilization of large numbers of reserves, the state National Guards can be called out on a full-time basis and become a fully integrated part of the federal army. At other times, the Guard is broken up into individual state components, ensuring a grass-roots connection with the local society. Although it has training and mobilization tasks in the overall system, and is funded by the Federal Government, there remains a certain amount of control and a vital identification and cohesion with the individual state.

While the localization of the National Guard ensures that the reserves remain well integrated in the society at large, the regular army has traditionally had problems in retaining cohesion with the civilian population. Although at the moment there is a good deal of boosterism for the armed forces, this can quickly dissipate, as happened during the Vietnam War in the face of a skilled psychological campaign.

The root of the problem is a regular officer corps that has traditionally been isolated from the political leadership. West Point, while being geographically close, could not be further away from Harvard, in terms of ethos at least, than if it were on the moon. The pool of academics and opinion makers which influences and is often part of the government, has no institutional contact with the closed, fortlike Pentagon.

Having an officer corps removed from the decision-making process may superficially seem to be an advantage in reducing the threat to the civil power; however, it can lead to misunderstanding and frustration which is dangerous to the security of the nation. Furthermore, when in times of danger, the army expands, the regular officer corps becomes isolated from its own reserves, as well as from the uniformed rank and file of the active forces.

The results of this problem could be seen after the end of the Second World War. The demobilized soldiers ensured that the power of officers to discipline and punish soldiers was severely curtailed. The famous Doolittle Commission, which did this, is widely blamed for the abysmal performance of the US Army in the early days of the Korean War.

When this weakness was actively exploited during the Vietnam era, the final result was that the US Army became isolated not only from the people who elected the government, but finally even from the government that sent it to fight.

As the army began to disintegrate, in many instances the enlisted men no longer took orders from the officers. Discipline broke down to the extent that junior officers and senior non-commissioned officers were sometimes murdered by their men. These assassinations became widely advertised and were even given a popular name. The mere thought of "fragging" effectively sabotaged discipline and the automatic obedience to orders without which an army breaks down.

The success of the indirect attack and the inability of the American military to deal with it can be judged from the fact that this breakdown was occurring in an army which was winning, and doing so while suffering fewer and fewer casualties. The greatest disciplinary problems occurred in the non-fighting units and in rear areas. Drug use became epidemic and racial differences were exploited.

There were equally serious problems in Stateside units and with the US troops in Europe. There, drug-related offences and race riots became so endemic, that the US Army was in some ways in worse shape than it had been in Southeast Asia. In September of 1973, three months after returning from Vietnam, I went to the south of West Germany as part of the umpire staff for the fall exercises. To my amazement, I was cautioned not to walk unaccompanied when crossing a small copse, which lay between the mess hall and my quarters in the staging camp for the exercise. The routine mugging of lone soldiers by drug-addicted deserters had forced the authorities to put up a sign, ordering military personnel to walk in pairs.

In the wake of the Vietnam debacle, the political will for

maintaining the unfair draft system disappeared, and the US Army returned to an all-volunteer force for the first time since before the Second World War. At the same time, the Reserve Officer Training Corps was disbanded at many of the most prestigious universities. This removed an important source of bright junior leaders and heightened the intellectual isolation of the officer corps.

The end of the draft also killed the major motive for young men to join the reserves. In the past, service in the Guard or the reserves was a patriotic alternative to the draft. With the demise of the draft, the cost of manpower increased dramatically, and the army lost its mass.

The intellectual isolation and further loss of roots in society at large, increased a deeper, more dangerous gap in American security; the people's psychological preparedness for defence was weakened. The United States was less prepared for the strongest defence of all, Clausewitz's "The People Armed."

An important consequence of the isolation of military thinking is that civilian leaders and opinion makers do not understand the basic principles of conflict, while the military officers do not fully realize the finer nuances of political necessity. Selection and maintenance of the aim is the first and overriding principle of war, but in a democracy there is no single paramount aim. Any detailed long-term ends are neither possible, nor desirable. While principles such as liberty, equality and the various freedoms remain constant, the exact interpretation of their meaning as well as the degree to which society grants them vary. Therefore, no single end can ever fully justify the means. The democratic process itself becomes the end, whereas to a soldier the objective is paramount.

Due to the ambiguity of aims in a democracy, a close relationship between the military and civilian society becomes especially important, as well as a General Staff to constantly interpret the aims and objectives of security and defence in the light of societal changes. The military must, of course, steer clear of active participation in politics. However, there is a narrow, but crucial difference between knowledge and involvement.

Instead of studying the application of their trade to the political realm, senior American and Canadian officers subjugate themselves to a layer of non-elected civilians who filter military professional judgement before it reaches the elected leaders. By the time it reaches political decision makers, the message has been watered down, distorted or lost. The presidential appointment of veterans to high executive office, as well as the increasing political clout of those who experienced Vietnam combat at first hand, makes for at least some understanding of strategy and conflict resolution in the American polity. The Canadian system is worse, in that the advisory filter consists of professional civil servants, instead of non-bureaucratic appointees.

Without a general staff system, as exists in most of the forces of our non-English-speaking allies, as well as in those of our adversaries, the strategic layer of military expertise is missing in the US armed forces. Strategy is left to lobbyists, civilian academics and private think tanks. As all of these are dependent on political patronage, not only do they tend to produce strategy which is palatable to the reigning political party, but their influence changes with each change of administration. The resulting strategic discontinuity is compounded by a traditional and psychological discontinuity at the unit level. For unlike other armies patterned on the British, the American Army has never developed a continuous regimental system. So the same problems tend to be repeated, as the gaps in institutional memory leave the army unprepared for conflict and heavy handed during its resolution.

Since the United States has no General Staff for defence strategic planning, it relies on a military bureaucracy driven largely by vested personnel interests and equipment budgets. The procurement of weapons systems and the self-protective tendencies of the career military personnel give the only tangible continuity to the system. Like the Canadian system on a large size, this leads to waste, duplication and pork-barrelling.

With no professional body to fit weapons procurement into the strategic picture — including the cutting of unnecessary weapons programs — the Pentagon ignores two important principles of war. Concentration of force and economy of effort are both violated in the waste of money, equipment and, above all, brains. The much-decried military-industrial complex merely fills the vacuum which is thereby created.

As the United States is so unequivocally the leader of the free world, these problems are especially vexing, for not only do the strategies of the leader drive the strategies of the smaller members, but they also have a profound impact on the opposition. The lack of strategic planning, and therefore of predictability, is one of the factors which inspires fear in the USSR. The Soviets are understandably afraid of war with America. They know that Uncle Sam fought a bloody civil war over principle, and when aroused, as in WWII, has gone beyond mere victory with that "... terrible sword ... with which he strikes home once and no more, . . . [instead of] a light, handy rapier."

The Soviet fear of the unpredictability of democratic wrath has been as much of a deterrent as has America's nuclear arsenal. But there is another more important reason for the success of the Western alliance in avoiding a world war without capitulation by the democracies. It is that the USA, by constantly being the innovators in nuclear and conventional technology, unwittingly maintained the offensive in the psychological war. However, with the achievement of parity in the early 80s, the USSR took away much of this advantage from the West. And coincidentally with the loss in Vietnam, Western strategies became based far more on the defensive, a development that presents great new dangers for the West.

After selection and maintenance of the aim, the second most important principle of conflict is offensive action. This simply means that if you don't at least threaten to attack, eventually you will lose, for your enemy can pick his own time, place and means, as well as concentrating all his resources on the attack. He does not have to disperse his forces, or leave any in reserve to counter your possible offensive action.

This does not, however, contradict the fact that defence is still the most favourable position. For as Clausewitz put it:

The ultimate aim of defensive war, as we have seen, can never be an absolute negation. Even the weakest party must possess some way of making the enemy conscious of its presence, some means of threatening him.

In the late 1980s, the United States thus finds itself a superpower without the civilian/military structure or the conventional strength to convincingly project its power in its role as leader of the Western alliance. Until the structural reforms are made, any gains on the psychological front, such as the great renewal of self-confidence under President Ronald Reagan, could prove to be short-lived indeed.

Despite the appointment of a few knowledgeable ex-combat officers, backed up by a few excellent ex-officer senators and academics, there is still no sophisticated American military strategic planning and no communication of the real situation to the public. The Reagan administration's recent disarray over the so-called Irangate scandal resulted from desperate clandestine efforts by a handful of officers to make up for this lack. This is a great pity because the American officer corps of today is the most highly educated ever, and individual officers and ex-officers are extremely capable of strategic thinking and planning.

Since there is a wealth of competing strategy for the political executive to pick from, even when appropriate strategies are selected, they usually are adopted far too slowly and have had their effectiveness blunted by political compromise. A current example of this is the converging crises of manpower and funding in US defences, a problem which has reached an even more critical point in Canada.

In the decade since the draft ended, there has been widespread unease about the ability of the volunteer army to attract and retain sufficient good-quality soldiers. The changing political climate in the nation at large, as well as the poor employment prospects for young Americans in the early 1980s, have helped the army to recruit and keep sufficient numbers to maintain a good front. Morale and discipline have improved immeasurably since the sad days of the early 1970s and, as there has been no major emergency to test the system, plans have been tailored to fit the limited manpower available. Yet the basic criticisms of the volunteer army have remained unanswered and to these are now added new problems.

The last of the baby boom generation have now passed into their twenties and America's future cohorts reaching military age will be smaller. In addition, the predictions are that youth unemployment will not be as serious in the coming decade, thereby making the young less dependent on the army as an entrée into the workforce.

As well, the financial good times appear to have run out for the Pentagon: there may not be any further large increases in defence spending. The seriousness of these converging crises of manpower and money have not generally been recognized. This is because the true relationship of manpower and strategy has never been publicly examined by the military itself.

Charles Moskos, a leading American military sociologist, has long advocated a compromise solution to his country's manpower problem. His idea is based on using the existing system of financial aid for post-secondary education. It is an approach which is politically feasible and more desirable than either a return to a compulsory draft or staying with the status quo. To greatly simplify a sophisticated sociological blueprint, Moskos recommends that the only way a fit young American could get aid for post-secondary education would be by completing a term of full-time service or keeping an obligation for reserve service. At the moment many young Americans can get financial assistance without any commitment to service in the forces.

Although Moskos has been predicting the manpower crisis and advocating this solution for more than ten years, it is only now that his plans are gaining official acceptance and that parts have been acted upon. In the past three years, the strength of the reserves has risen by almost 50 percent, and there is increasing integration with the regular forces. But this is too little too late. The lag time between the idea and its execution has given opposing strategists a great chance to exploit the existing weakness.

Knowing the American weakness at the level of conventional forces has permitted the Soviets to press for nuclear disarmament to their great propaganda advantage. Although there was no chance that the Soviets were serious about their offer to ban all nuclear weapons, predictably the confused American response has made the USA appear less willing to do away with nuclear arms than its opponent.

The manpower problem in the USA is now coupled with a renewed isolationism. This is partly born of economics and partly from the reaction to the successful Soviet strategy of spreading fear and anti-Americanism in Europe. As a result, both the new right and the left in America seem to be meeting at the thought of bringing the troops home from Europe.

Nonetheless, if a partial US withdrawal is co-ordinated with intelligently negotiated concessions from the USSR and a continual strengthening and unifying of European defences, it could prove beneficial to the democratic alliance and to world peace. This is because it would make Europe more self-reliant. If it is hasty and carried out unilaterally, it could prove disastrous. Regardless, as Western Europe grows economically stronger compared to the USSR, its defence must increasingly be based on strong conventional reserves drawn from the European nations themselves.

A similar problem to the converging crises of money and manpower being experienced in the United States is also evident among the major allies. But the response of some, particularly the Germans, has been timely and smooth. Significantly, the changes were planned by their modern General Staff, one of the few well-developed and intellectually well integrated general staff systems in the Western alliance. With no fuss, the West Germans have built up their reserves over the past few years so that in conventional military terms there is now greater security on the NATO central front than at any time since the beginning of the alliance.

Elsewhere the outlook is also mixed. The British Army ended

National Service in the late 1950s and the regular army shrank faster than Great Britain shedded its oversea commitments. Lately, Britain has also had to place a much greater emphasis on its reserves. The British Army of the Rhine is now relying so much on its "Weekend Warriors" that it has been dubbed the "Channel Ferry Army."

The French have long been pioneers of a two-army model. They continue to have a large force of conscripts, which by law cannot serve outside Metropolitan France, and a small, mobile, highly trained force of professionals, capable of protecting French interests anywhere in the world.

A good, developing, conscriptionless British version of this two-army model could also be observed operating during the Falklands War of 1982. The highly trained and politically less exploitable regular Royal Marines, Parachute Regiment, Gurkhas and Guards went off to fight in the Malvinas while their place in the defence of Europe was taken up by reserves.

There is also a lesson in the value of different types of reserves to be learned from the British experience in Ulster. As was the case in Vietnam, the conflict in Northern Ireland has shown the value of local and reserve forces in internal security operations. This low-intensity form of warfare needs a lot of manpower, but the soldiers do not require a high level of training since they do not use heavy weapons and usually do not operate in units larger than sections of six to ten men and women.

The Ulster Defence Regiment soldiers can be operational after only thirty-five hours of training. As well, the logistical and administrative backup for this form of regional force is a fraction of that which is necessary for regular forces. It is interesting to note in this context that the average French conscript goes to a field unit with no training whatever and is trained in situ.

There was a further potential benefit of the use of locally raised reserves which the British army almost managed to exploit in Ulster. By recruiting from both religious groups, Britain greatly increased the chances of ending the conflict by means of a political compromise. Unfortunately, insufficient regular infantry troops were made available for the training and leadership cadre of the regiment when it was raised. Many of the key positions were filled by veterans of the discredited and disbanded police auxillary organization, the "B Specials," which had been a Protestant-dominated paramilitary police reaction force. Instead of being encouraged, the few Catholics who did join were made unwelcome and many quickly left. The remainder were easily terrorized by the IRA, who branded them traitors to the Catholic cause.

For the next decade the need for manpower is going to be one of the critical factors in the forces of the USA and its allies, including Canada. The trend towards greater reliance on reserve and local troops for home defence will grow. This will not only be less threatening to the Warsaw Pact than reliance on fewer, more mobile regulars, it will also increase the internal cohesion of the alliance members.

There will still be a need for highly trained and well-equipped regulars so that the democracies can project their power. But this ability will be mostly required for the high intensity end of the conflict continuum, with more and more examples of integrated deterrent forces such as NORAD and more systems such as the new NATO airborne warning aircraft. There is also a need for regular troops to act as members of multinational forces. However, the development of such co-operation to the level where international forces can cope with more than low-level peacekeeping, as in Cyprus, is still in the future.

Until America and its democratic allies redress the manpower imbalance, and until the other members of the Western alliance develop general staff systems on a par with that of West Germany, these twin weaknesses will continue to constitute the Achilles heel of Western defences. At the moment, of all the members of NATO, Canada is probably the most deficient in these crucial areas.

Will Canada be able to exert any influence on the future of the current disarmament negotiations? Where do our interests fit into the broad strategic picture of the West? How crucial to the alliance is Canada's full participation in it? I believe that the time has arrived for us to finally become a full partner in the defence of the West (something we cannot contemplate unless we are capable of defending our own territory from conventional attack). But there are two basic strategic options, both of which merit full and honest discussion.

# CHAPTER FOUR

# Canada: Neutrality or Alliances?

*We have laid it down as a necessity that good national reserves be prepared for the army, which will be less expensive in peace and will insure the defence of the country in war. This system was used by France in 1792, imitated by Austria in 1809, and by the whole of Germany in 1813.*

*. . . without being a utopian philanthropist, or a condottieri, a person may desire that wars of extermination may be banished from the code of nations, and the defences of nations by disciplined militia, with the aid of good political alliances, may be sufficient to insure their independence.*

Baron de Jomini, *The Art of War*

Canada's basic strategic interests are twofold. First we must be able to maintain our sovereignty. Second we must be able to project our power in the event that democracy (and by extension Canada) is threatened. Even if we were to choose the option of official neutrality, it would be no less necessary to be able to defend our borders from conventional attack or to protect our society from internal insurrection inspired from without.

Given the fact that we have fought for democracy in two world wars and share a continent with the West's premier power, it is difficult to imagine a neutral Canada. But in today's interdependent world even a neutral Canada would almost inevitably be drawn into a major world conflict.

Many Canadians currently seem to believe that it is possible to rely for protection on our allies, in particular on the United States. I hope that in the foregoing chapters I have demonstrated that it is just as true today as it was two hundred years ago when George

Washington said that "it is folly for one nation to look for disinterested favours from another." Whatever option we choose, we must have an army adequate to exercise it.

The question which this chapter addresses is whether the necessary reform of our armed forces should come within the context of a continuing commitment to NATO and NORAD or in the context of an officially neutral option, such as that of Finland, Austria, Sweden or Switzerland. When the regular armies and the reserves of these countries are added together, and considered in relation to their size, all of them have proportionally larger armed forces than any country in the NATO or Warsaw Pact alliance, including the Soviet Union. As an examination of three of these countries shows, neutrality is an arduous option, which in no way implies demilitarization.

The country now being held up as a model of neutrality by Canadian proponents of this option is Finland. What is not mentioned is that Finland was not Finlandized by choice. The Finns fought the USSR to a standstill twice during the Second World War to prevent being annexed along with Latvia, Lithuania and Estonia. Courage, luck, and an Afghan-like hatred of domination helped to save the Finns from the fate of their Baltic neighbours. Above all, the three annexed nations were smaller than Finland and lacked a topography which lends itself to protracted guerrilla action.

Finland is permitted internal democracy as long as it makes no criticism of the Soviets, no alliances with any other democratic nation, and no move to suppress communism at home. The cost of this enforced neutrality and limited democracy is enormous. Over 6.6 percent of GDP is spent on the defence budget compared to Canada's 2 percent, and 15 percent of Finland's population serves in the reserve or regular forces, as opposed to 0.4 percent of Canadians. From a population of less than 5 million, 700,000 are in the reserve forces. There is an obligatory forty days training a year for all reservists up to the age of fifty. Non-commissioned officers have to train seventy-five days per year. Reserve officers, who serve to age sixty, put in a full one hundred days each year.

The Finns had to sign a treaty of mutual protection with the Soviet Union, thus leaving the Soviets the option of coming "to their aid" should they fail to toe the line. The entire Finnish defence system is designed to make the Soviets pause before exercising their option of mutual protection. It was a similar option that was exercised by the Soviets in Czechoslovakia in the late 1960s and in Afghanistan a decade later.

Those who know what Finlandization really is hold Switzerland up as the example for Canada to follow. For it is as true today as it was in Machiavelli's day, when he wrote that: "The Swiss are armed to the teeth and are absolutely free."

Although the Swiss model is a useful one to look at, as with most models it cannot be transplanted whole to different circumstances. With an area of less than fifty thousand square kilometers, a quarter of which is covered by mountains and lakes, Switzerland could not be more different from Canada. It is two-thirds the size of New Brunswick, but has a population, at 6.3 million, ten times greater than that eastern Canadian province.

At one time the larger European countries used poor little Switzerland as a battleground, despite its high and forbidding terrain. In the early eighteenth century, a combined army of Russians and Austrians commanded by the old Russian general Suvorov, attempted to dislodge the French Army of Napoleon from Switzerland while the natives could only watch and learn more of the realities of war. They also learned because of economic necessity. As they had too many mouths to feed, the young and the adventurous went out to hire as mercenaries.

Succeeding generations of Swiss soldiers became Europe's most famous soldiers for hire. Today the Vatican's Swiss guard is the only visible remnant of the famous mercenary tradition, for the Swiss have since found better ways of using their talents to make money. But the invisible legacy helps to explain why Switzerland is such a unique and well-thought-out country, although for most tastes it suffers from a trifle too much regimentation.

It also helps to explain why Switzerland has long had the best defence system in Europe. The proof of the efficiency of its strategic plans has been its avoidance of the wars which have racked Europe during the past hundred years while countries with equally difficult topography have not been so fortunate.

During the nineteenth century, as the Swiss became wealthy and their defences more effective, they did not want to conquer others, but simply to retain their freedom and independence. Their philosophy became one of armed neutrality. For this they turned their country into a hedgehog; they fortified their passes and made every male citizen a soldier. They understood Clausewitz's message that the people armed is the ultimate defence against an aggressor.

During the twentieth century, the Swiss buttressed their neutrality on both the diplomatic and economic fronts. The Red Cross, which is the reversed image of the Swiss flag, became the symbol of medical neutrality, while the League of Nations and later some of the organizations of the United Nations set up their headquarters in Geneva. Meanwhile the Swiss quietly became bankers to the world's wealthy, perhaps the smartest neutrality-preserving tactic of all.

In addition to these passive measures and the fact of their geography, the Swiss stayed out of the two World Wars by means of thorough military planning and preparation. The people know this and are grateful to their non-fighting generals: streets and public monuments have been named after the military leaders who managed not to fight in the two World Wars.

The Swiss work hard at their defences. From a population of just over six million, over six hundred thousand trained, armed troops in combat formations can be prepared to defend the country on forty-eight hours notice. But uniformed troops are only the outward, easy-to-count part of the Swiss mobilization plan. In fact, the whole peaceful country of landscaped fields, tranquil cattle and jolly yodellers, becomes a bristling maze of fortifications, fields of fire and booby traps for attacking forces. Mountains open up to disgorge fighter aircraft and bridges can be blown up on signal. Industrial planning is co-ordinated with defence planning so that the Swiss can not only afford their defences, but even make money from export of items that are produced for the defence of the homeland.

There are problems, however. The success of the defensive strategies of preceding generations has inevitably placed less creative men in high positions. Now, instead of flair and daring (both essential characteristics of good fighting commanders) the modern Swiss generals have reached their positions only by hard work and administrative skill.

With all the effort that Switzerland puts into neutrality, it is firmly committed to the Western democratic system. Swiss strategic planners see only one possible threat — the Soviet Bloc — and they know that they could not exist without the Western alliance. For all its past merit, this fact makes their present neutrality seem somewhat hypocritical.

While the Swiss model seems to have run to its full development possibilities, there is another small, impoverished mountain nation — as Switzerland once was — whose sons go off as mercenaries today. Nepal is a small country nestled high up in the Himalayas with people as its main resource. The young Gurkhas have for generations gone to soldier in other nations' armies. On the surface they are merely effective, brave, mercenary soldiers. But there is more to them than their legendary courage. The reason for their effectiveness is that although they are mercenaries, unlike those Westerners who take up arms for pay in a foreign country, their motive is not primarily either money or ideology. They fight on foreign soil only partly because they want to improve their lot. They also want to help their own communities. This impulse makes them solid professional soldiers.

In the nineteenth century, soldiering away from home became an important adjunct of Gurkha society. Life was tough in the high mountain homeland which could not support all its inhabitants. Therefore, young men welcomed the opportunity to become soldiers in foreign lands. While in the army they were able to send money to support their families, as well as obtaining a much better education than was available at home. At the end of their service they returned to Nepal, and with their education, experience and their pensions were able to support themselves. As a result, they became important figures in their communities, where they had time to teach others and to take part in local politics.

The Gurkha brand of mercenary soldiering is as far removed from our situation as is the neutrality of the Swiss, but there are elements of both Switzerland and Nepal in the Canadian tradition and makeup. Our small professional military to a certain extent resembles the Nepalese model, whereas the Canadian militia has elements of the Swiss citizen soldier in it. The origins and historical development of both these Canadian models will be explored in Part 2.

What emerges from this examination of the neutrality option is that Canada is ill placed geographically and ill prepared historically to undertake such a role. We have for so long been part of the Western alliance and for so many years been wedded to American defence strategies, that neutrality would require an enormous psychological shift. This is true even if it were economically viable for us to become a neutral country. Even if it were desirable.

Less well understood is Canada's crucial position in the Western alliance, one which we are only partially and less and less adequately occupying. Soviet aims and goals have remained constant for seventy years. While the overall strategies for achieving these goals have also shown a remarkable consistency, the tactics, timing and emphasis of their attack change with changing circumstances. No opportunity for exploiting a weakness or widening a schism in the Western democracies is missed.

The exploitation of any success is a major principle at the strategic as well as at the tactical level. Thus it can be seen that the successful Communist hijacking of the Sandinista revolution in Nicaragua, which has been the signal for the intensification of the indirect attack in the Western hemisphere, also makes Canada a potential prime target.

Soviet strategists must inevitably see in Central America the possibility of a Western psychological defeat of much greater magnitude than Vietnam. It is not surprising, therefore, that the propaganda drive within the democracies has been intensifying of late. This time, because Canada is not only America's closest ally, but also America's geographic rear flank, our country is a natural target of the indirect attack. The intensity of the offensive, as well as its ultimate success, depends on how soft a target we prove to be.

We have already seen an intensification of the campaign to pull Canada out of NATO and NORAD. This is because our nation is the lynchpin in the alliance between the two most important centres of democracy, the USA and Western Europe. If this attempted splitting of the alliance is not countered, it could seriously destabilize the world balance of power by a sudden weakening of the West.

Canada may be crucial to the Western alliance, but how important is membership in the alliance to Canadian security? How does the Western alliance serve Canada's strategic interest, and would it serve us equally well if we contributed nothing but our good wishes?

Over the years, it has become almost a religious belief in Canada that NATO is somehow responsible for our security. The truth is that through our membership in NATO we are helping to promote the larger overall security system of the Western alliance, a system headed by the United States. But there are no plans for reciprocity; the NATO alliance is designed for reinforcing Western Europe. It is only our American neighbour who could or would help in the defence of Canada itself in order to maintain its own security.

There are no American or NATO strategic plans for the security of Canada per se. Each nation is responsible for its own defence. Only with its own basic security needs looked after can any nation contribute to overall alliance plans for collective security. Canada is the only member of the alliance which has virtually no plans for its own defence. We structure our armed forces entirely around our alliance contributions so that we cannot protect our own country without the aid of outside forces.

No matter what shape the democratic alliance takes in the future, and change it will, the defence of the USA and Canada will remain interdependent. If Canadian defence is not to become totally ineffective, or impossible to afford, we must decide what we can best do for ourselves and what must be integrated with the United States. As a general rule, the more intensive the level of conflict, the greater the integration. The NORAD agreement is an example of this form of integrated co-operation in air and space defence.

Recent Canadian reluctance to participate in the new Strategic Defense Initiative is an example of how a lack of understanding by Canadian politicians, coupled with an inability of the Americans to explain the strategies behind their policies, makes such co-operation difficult. And where cracks show in the alliance, our enemies will do everything in their power to exploit them.

This lack of integration at the strategic level is again evident in the latest Canadian defence initiative — the attempt to assert our sovereignty in the Arctic. But water is as indivisible as is space, and it would therefore make far more sense for a joint NATO command with US-Canadian crews manning submarines to maintain North American sovereignty over this strategically crucial region along our northern frontier. Instead we are now planning, at impossible cost, to buy and operate our own submarine force.

Being an intimate partner in defence with the USA is not easy at the best of times. As I have already demonstrated, American defence strategies are more difficult to predict than those of the USSR. More serious still, by and large they do not exist.

Canada is now and will likely remain a part of the Western alliance. Despite the superficial attractiveness of the neutrality option, it is not appropriate for our strategic situation. The unhappy truth is that Canada's military has so declined since the end of the Second World War that we would have trouble defending our borders from the modern equivalent of a Fenian attack let alone a serious military threat. When it comes to our part in the defence of Europe, we expend billions of dollars and still can't live up to our commitments. Canada's military apparatus is in a desperate state and getting worse. In order to arrive at solutions, we must understand how this happened and what solid foundations remain. That is the subject of the next part of this book.

# PART TWO

# THE DISARMING
# OF CANADA

# CHAPTER FIVE

# Canada's Military Roots (1669-1867)

*War is not to be regarded as an independent thing, but as a political instrument; and it is only by taking this point of view that we can avoid finding ourselves in opposition to all military history.*

Carl von Clausewitz

Despite the lack of a serious external threat to Canada since Confederation, the military has played a vital part in the formation of our modern country. But the importance of the regular and reserve forces in the making of the nation has been little appreciated, for in keeping with British and American practice, the Canadian Army has never had a general staff system and has therefore lacked an institutional head and memory. While we have kept archives and maintained tradition, we have no capability for absorbing the strategic lessons of the past and from them planning our defences for the future. This institutional fault has been exacerbated by Canada's colonial status, which did not end with the Confederation of 1867. At least in the case of the military, it is with us still.

Not only have we not had a General Staff, but our officer corps has always suffered from a belief that someone else was responsible for strategic planning. The professional officer has traditionally seen himself as the technician, or enforcer, of defence. His duty was, and is, to be an expert in the techniques and tactics of waging war, and when called upon, to do or die, but not to reason why. As a result, in addition to there being no cohesive plans for our defence today, we are increasingly unable to draw on our past to secure our future.

This contemporary situation is a tragedy, because in the rich mixture of our military history are the ingredients for a secure and united Canada. If instead of destroying our military traditions they were built on, we could have modern defence forces which were firmly anchored in the society at large. This would help to give our country the cohesion which it now so badly needs.

Before the 1968 Canadian Forces Reorganization Bill, the three Canadian services were in many respects indistinguishable from and interchangeable with their British counterparts. However, long before this and most apparently in the case of the Royal Canadian Air Force, the American influence was starting to replace the dominance of British traditions.

After Confederation the forces were a reflection of Canada. Like the country they defended, no distinct Canadian identity was apparent. While this bothered some Canadian politicians and Ottawa mandarins, through the late nineteenth and much of the twentieth century the forces were mostly content and proud to be British. But as with Canada itself, the major challenge in the military was the French minority. French Canada's language and traditions were neglected, especially in the Royal Canadian Navy and the Royal Canadian Air Force, when these services came into existence in the twentieth century.

It was mainly this fact, coupled with the lack of a Canadian strategic planning capability that caused the army conscription crises in each of the World Wars. Although of the three services, only the army was at all sensitive to the problem and to the potential strength which the French Canadians could bring to the military, it had not been able to do enough to keep the cultural fault line from developing into a major split under the major stress of the two wars.

The neglect of the French minority and the lack of a unified strategic thinking made integration and change necessary. But instead of building on existing institutions, the unification of the forces enacted by the governments of Lester B. Pearson and Pierre Elliott Trudeau destroyed many of the traditions which were a source of strength and pride. In order to understand the nature of the modern military crisis in Canada and the firm foundations that still survive, we must first understand its historical origins. These go back to the period that precedes the British conquest.

In New France, the colonial institutions and culture mixed with that of the indigenous Indians to form the basis of Canadian military tradition. Louis XIV saw that the territory of Canada was too huge and the dangers too unpredictable for him to be able to defend it adequately with regular French troops. In 1669 he therefore ordered the country to be divided into geographic areas, the inhabitants organized into companies and local seigneurs appointed to command them.

It took fourteen years and a new governor before the local companies were established, but they became an effective means of defending the French possessions in North America. Responsibility for defence became an integral part of first class citizenship. All male inhabitants between the ages of sixteen and sixty were liable to serve, and although this universality was seldom enforced, a man could work his farm and still fulfil his military obligations.

Discharged regular soldiers automatically joined the militia, bringing with them new techniques and helping to maintain the level of proficiency throughout. The militiamen became skilled in fighting under the rigorous local conditions, picking up many of the skills of the Indians. In addition to fighting, they were used extensively for transport duties as well as for public works. The system was also inexpensive since the militia were not paid.

In addition to the militia, and the few regulars from France, known as Troupes de Terre, the French also developed a full-time force purely for service in the colonies, known as Troupes de la Marine. Started from French regular troops and sometimes reinforced by recruits from France, the Troupes de la Marine were mostly raised from local men. They combined the discipline and predictability of regulars with many of the skills necessary for the ongoing guerrilla warfare, which was known in New France as *la petite guerre*.

The senior professional officers for all three parts of the army always came from France and this, coupled with tensions between the regulars and the locals, caused a fatal weakness in the system. The loss of Quebec can be partially attributed to an improper understanding of the division of responsibility between the professional soldier and his civilian leader and the deep cleavage between regular and local troops.

In 1759 when the British force under the command of Major General James Wolfe sailed up the St. Lawrence, the governor general of New France was Marquis de Vaudreuil, a native-born Canadian whose military experience had been limited to local troops and who had grown up in the atmosphere and tradition of *la petite guerre*. The military commander reporting to him was the Marquis de Montcalm, a French professional and perhaps the most competent officer on either side of the Seven Years' War between France and Britain. He was the only man to beat the British on four occasions: at Oswego, Fort William Henry, Fort Carillon and Montmorency.

Commanding the guard on the crest of the Heights of Abraham was Sieur de Vergor, like the governor a local. He had let a large number of his one hundred-man garrison go on leave to gather their crops and the thirty remaining men did not maintain a proper watch. When Montcalm discovered this military negligence, he attempted to have de Vergor replaced, but, as the latter was a friend of Vaudreuil, this did not happen. It was largely because of de Vergor's negligence that Wolfe's men were even able to get into a position to fight. Thus local politics had prevailed over military logic and Quebec was lost on the Plains of Abraham. It was a theme that would be repeated many times during Canada's military history.

Even before the seizure of Quebec, the North American colonies, because of their size, were just as difficult for the British to defend as they were for the French. There were never enough regular troops to protect the colonists against guerrilla attack, Indian or white. And, like the French, the British also fleshed out the regulars with locally raised militias. A division between alien regulars and homegrown militia, combined with the inability of the foreign professional officers to master local politics, was thus a feature of both cultures.

The full-time and part-time non-professional troops were not a replacement for regulars but a vital supplement. However, because of their usefulness in guerrilla warfare, because they were cheap, and because they were local boys, a North American myth grew up of their superiority against standing armies.

This was a problem for the French, the British and especially for the Americans, for whom regular soldiers were associated with the enemy while the "minutemen" were the heroes. When George Washington was attempting to raise a standing army during the Revolutionary War, he had great trouble in convincing his fellow Americans that " . . . men who have been free, and subject to no control, cannot be reduced to order in an instant . . . "

This misunderstanding of the need for professional control of the army, which had partly caused the loss of Quebec by the French, also contributed to the lack of control by the regulars of the militia in post-Confederation Canada as well as the inability of the officer corps to find its proper level in the social structure of the United States.

The British, after the loss of the thirteen colonies, managed to protect the remainder of their North American possessions efficiently and economically with the same graduated response capability (to use modern jargon for an old situation) they used elsewhere to keep the Empire in line.

The lowest level of conflict was guerrilla-type action, by Indians or small bands of irregulars. The defence against this was the responsibility of the local, part-time troops. At the intermediate level of conflict were the locally raised, full-time "fencibles." Their job was to maintain security against larger raids. These fencibles were local men and retired regulars, usually only engaged to serve in one colony. When it became necessary to defend by offensive action of more than a local type, as for instance in the War of 1812, the British imported professional European troops. The regular rank and file were often German Hessians commanded by senior British officers.

One of the reasons why the fencibles and the various militias, French and British, were effective was that their ranks were leavened with ex-regular soldiers. Many of the European regulars who served a tour of duty in the new land stayed on as settlers at the end of their term of service. In the North American colonies was a chance for free land and true independence in addition to their measly pension.

All in all, the system of local militias, bolstered by local fencibles, backed and commanded by British regulars, was a sound foundation on which to build a post-Confederation army. All that was needed was to substitute a corps of highly trained, mobile Canadian regulars, for the imported British ones and develop a professional officer corps for command, control and strategic planning.

Unfortunately, this solid base was undermined by Canada's continuing dependence on British models and British commanders. The inability of the British senior officers to appreciate the nuances of Canadian politics meant that they never fully controlled the militia.

To understand this part of the Canadian story we must first briefly examine the structure and developments of the Victorian Imperial Army.

After the defeat of Napoleon in 1815, Britain steered clear of wars on the Continent as much as possible. This permitted the regular army to become an instrument of the commercial and political interests that were shaping the colonial Empire. It did not have to defend the homeland and therefore developed in many ways in isolation from mainstream society. It was even remote from the militia and the part-time yeomanry who were responsible for local, or territorial, defence.

The militia and yeomanry regiments, later known collectively in Britain as the territorial army, were rather feudal institutions. Before the Industrial Revolution they were officered by the local landed gentry, who formed the troops from their own agricultural workers. Although there was some obligation on the part of gentry and peasant alike to be part of the reserve home defence forces, there was always an amateur air about them. Nonetheless, they were in many ways a pattern worthy of development, and it is their reflection that can be seen in the early Canadian militia.

Britain's regular army regiments had an independence far greater than was possible in the Continental armies, but this was the result of the geographic dispersion of the Empire and the slow communications of the era. If a decision had to be made, the local commander perforce made it.

This tradition of independent thinking, coupled with inadequate centralized planning and control, led to some dreadful errors, but in the end gave the British Army a unique strength. Subordinate commanders were frequently able to respond quickly and correctly to local developments as well as to exploit any advantage immediately. This in some ways made up for the lack of a British General Staff. The tradition has been carefully nurtured, and even now the British Army is second to none in its tactical and fighting skills. These are major assets in the decentralized, low-intensity war of today and could be seen at work in the Falklands campaign of 1982.

The Continental armies were forever trying to breed these qualities, which came naturally to the freebooting British, into their well-ordered armies. The Germans in an attempt to instil this independent spirit into their officers, gave the highest decoration for valour only for a gallant action carried out *against* orders. Obedient valour was only worth a second class decoration.

If the strength of the nineteenth-century British Army was its decentralized structure and flexible nature, its weakness was in its isolation. Not only were the regulars isolated — by distance, slow communication and totally different tasks — from the militia and yeomanry, but also from mainstream British society. This led to a strong sense of regimental identity and also to an ingrown officer corps that took no interest in matters of strategy. Unfortunately, it is the bad aspects of isolation that have come to dominate the character of the modern Canadian Forces.

The old regular army was recruited from those parts of British society which were in the most desperate of straits. Thus the regular British soldier was removed geographically when he went to some far outpost of the Empire, in addition to being a social outcast when he stayed at home. All the Continental armies of the time had more contact with their parent societies and all had some place in the social order. Only the conscript Russian Army's terms of service were equally final. When a Russian peasant was conscripted for service to the Tsar, his friends and relatives held a funeral service and a wake to mark the finality of his departure.

To make matters worse, the British Army developed outside the boundaries of normal civilian life. The closed, exclusive fraternity it became differed as much from other armies as it did from its parent society, for where the Continental armies were designed for the grand massed tests of strength between industrial nations, the British Army was designed for "wog bashing," a crude, soldier's term for service in the colonies.

Although it went by other names, the most poetic being Rudyard Kipling's the "white man's burden," wog bashing was the most descriptive; in addition to describing what the Imperial soldier actually did, it implied the belief in racial superiority which made the system work. Only by being convinced themselves of their absolute superiority could the members of this tiny army convince the natives of a large part of the world that they were the legal authority. The supremacy of European technology and weapons was a major factor in maintaining the myth.

The majority of the men who spent their lives administering the British Empire unquestioningly believed in the justice of what they were doing. They brought genuine advances to societies which were at an early stage of development or in some instances decayed and crumbling. When the mixture of reward and minor punishment occasionally went awry, force was mercilessly applied to restore British supremacy. The Indian Mutiny is the classic example of this. But mutual benefit as much as force must be seen as one of the prime reasons why the huge polyglot empire maintained cohesion for even as short a time as it did.

The force needed for action in the colonies usually required no higher a formation of troops than a brigade of some three thousand men. Such brigades were usually formed from three battalions temporarily "brigaded" together. The battalion usually consisted of four companies and numbered about one thousand all ranks. A battalion was the active portion of a regiment and the regiment was the heart and spirit of the British Army.

An infantry regiment had two battalions, one which served on home duty and provided the recruiting and training base for the battalion which was overseas. Sometimes a battalion would serve overseas for decades without rotating home.

A soldier's battalion was the only society that he knew or cared about. Once in it, he spent his entire life as a living part of an organization that was at once a home, a family, a history and a future to him. Many a son followed his father into the regiment. It fed him, clothed him and administered to all his physical and spiritual needs. On rare occasions it rewarded him, and frequently it punished him by the lash or sometimes summarily executed him.

At the height of the Empire, there were around one hundred infantry regiments of the line. There were also cavalry and artillery units, sappers and other supporting troops, but the heart of the army were the two hundred battalions of approximately one thousand all ranks each. In 1897, there were 212,000 men in the regular British Army. These troops maintained British rule and order over the largest Empire that the world had ever seen.

This small force had no mobilizable reserves for service in the colonies. It did not need them. In case of unforeseen trouble, there was another army in the service of Queen Victoria which was at least as large as the regular British Army and which had enormous reserves to draw on. This was the Indian Army. Thus the Victorian regiments were able to continue to live in a world apart.

There were many other ways in which the British Army differed from its contemporaries on the Continent. It was not a homogenized army; the regiments each recruited from a particular locality and trained their own recruits. As a result, the idiosyncracies of the system were so great as to make it almost incomprehensible to outsiders. This only increased the cohesion and the insularity. In fact the most important qualities of the nineteenth-century regiments were their individuality and their historical continuity, which gave their members a distinct identity firmly rooted in the past.

The names of the regiments reflected this rich diversity of tradition. Some were named after the county where they were raised and from which they recruited, such as the Royal Hampshires, the Worcestershires or the Gloucesters. Highland regiments such as the Gordons and the Camerons were named after the clans from which they were drawn. Still others were not called regiments at all. There were the Green Howards, the Rifle Brigade, the King's Own Scottish Borderers (known as the Kosbies), the Borderers from the English side of the same border and the Welsh Borderers. There were the Connaught Rangers, the King's Royal Rifle Corps and the Black Watch.

Some of the regiments established roots in the New World, where they combined with the earlier tradition of the seigneurial system to start the regimental system in the Canadian Militia. The Black Watch was an example of this. Many of the soldiers of the Imperial Black Watch regiment took their discharge in Canada and this, coupled with the large percentage of Scotsmen who made up the elite of Montreal in the mid-nineteenth century, helped in the choosing of a name for one of the most powerful militia regiments in the new country.

The members of a Victorian regiment had all the loyalty of a family. They did not fight for any grand concepts such as democracy, or even Queen and country. They fought for the regiment and for their comrades; for the men that they grew up with, lived with and expected to die with. There was the close bond of intimate knowledge, each man knowing what to expect from his comrade. He knew who might save his own skin when no one was looking, who could be trusted to remain at his post until death. He knew which officer might unnecessarily risk the lives of his men and who would sacrifice his own life for the youngest drummer boy. These soldiers were no braver and certainly no better than other men, but they had cohesion and mutual trust that can only come from intimate knowledge and lifetime bonding. This was the great strength in the social isolation of the regular British Army.

The closed, self-sufficient world of the regiment also affected the officers. They became even more insular and reactionary than was customary in other armies. They did not want change and as their birth gave them status, if not wealth, outside the army, they were not greatly concerned with promotion or service beyond the regiment. As a result, the regimental officer did not have to know any theories of war; it was enough to know the men. Not only was it unnecessary to be too knowledgeable, it was thought to be bad form and an unseemly sign of over-ambition. Talking about one's job off duty was also bad form and forbidden in the mess; one simply did not talk shop. The army was morally strong, but intellectually weak; tactically flexible, but strategically deficient.

This lack of thinking was partly due to the nature of soldiering in the outposts of the Empire. Most of the time, the action the army was required to carry out had only the most indirect connection with grand strategy or Britain's security. Most often it meant protecting or gaining a market for private interests or playing straight man for some deep diplomatic ploy. Even if a local commander's orders had some connection with an overall strategy, an officer twenty years out of England, in days when it took two weeks for dispatches to reach him from home, might be forgiven for not keeping up to date with the intricacies of Imperial politics.

Strengthening this anti-intellectual bias was the fact that promotion in the army had very little to do with merit and nothing whatsoever to do with theoretical knowledge. Until the reforms of the mid-nineteenth century, commissions and promotion were on the purchase system. To become an officer, a gentleman bought a commission in the regiment of his choice. Providing he could afford it and that he had the right background, this was all he had to do. Similarly, if he wanted to advance to the next higher rank, he had to buy it from the retiring officer who held the rank or from the colonel of the regiment.

The fact that the officers came from a high social class compensated to some extent for the lack of a formal general staff system, since it permitted contact with the most powerful in the land. Far more influence could be wielded at a weekend of shooting at one of the great country houses than by the writing of staff papers in Whitehall.

The abolition of the purchase system was fiercely resisted on the grounds that only gentlemen with a stake in the status quo could be trusted with the responsibility of leading troops. But even after it was gone, the mindset and the type of officer produced by it left its legacy. And this legacy became part of the inheritance of the Canadian Army. The officers' aristocratic background and lack of professional knowledge produced a curious pattern of thinking. He had no opinions, or rather no thoughts, on matters of strategy, but great authority in the limited but all-encompassing environment of the regiment. His duty and that of those subordinate to him, was but to do or die and God help the upstart who wanted to know the reasons why, or had the effrontery to think that he could have an input into the reasoning behind an order.

There was a reverse, positive side to this uniquely ingrown, insular officer corps. Individuality and independence permitted genius as well as stupidity to flourish where it might have been stifled in a more structured military. The frail General Wolfe would never have passed the physical required to get into any army today. Yet he was the adjutant of his regiment at the age of sixteen. At thirty-five, with a wealth of soldiering experience behind him, he captured the fortress of Quebec and ensured the British conquest of French North America. As he was being ferried to land prior to the battle, he is reputed to have mused that he would rather have written Gray's "Elegy Written in a Country Churchyard," than capture Quebec.

In sum, it can be seen that the Victorian British Army had both strengths and serious weaknesses to transmit to the forces of the fledgling Canadian nation. Around the time of Confederation, some attempt was made in Britain to integrate the regular army into society and join it more closely to the territorially grounded militia.

Although superficially this was done and many of the regular regiments were given local or county names, essentially nothing changed. The English Channel and the Royal Navy ensured that the regular force was not needed to keep out other armies and the militia was sufficient for local problems.

The old British regular army disappeared in the opening round of the First World War, just as the modern Canadian Army was about to be born. The British regulars made a stand that has entered the annals of military history as an unequalled example of superb training, discipline, courage and steadiness under fire. The tiny professional army, which was mostly experienced in small actions in distant places, fought the massive steam roller of the advancing German Army to a brief standstill at Mons. For two days in the hot late summer of 1914 one of the two corps of the British Expeditionary Force in France stopped the impetus of the German machine.

The Battle of Mons clearly showed both the strengths and the fatal weakness of the British system. Even the fact that the Second Corps made its stand when it did was an example of a subordinate commander disobeying orders to exploit a tactical situation and save his troops in the bargain.

The commander of the British Expeditionary Force, Sir John French, had quite rightly ordered a withdrawal with no holding of ground. But when the retreating Second Corps reached Mons, Lieutenant General Horace Smith-Dorrien, its commander, realized that his men could only maintain an orderly withdrawal if they had a short time to regroup and rest. He calculated that they could do this by pausing briefly, giving the advancing German armies a bloody nose and then continuing to withdraw before the enemy had time to annihilate the tiny British force. This was exactly what happened, although the choleric French never forgave Smith-Dorrien for disobeying orders.

The British infantrymen fired their Short Lee-Enfield rifles with such disciplined speed and co-ordinated accuracy, that the Germans were convinced they were advancing into machine-gun fire. In fact, in keeping with the innate conservatism which is one of the weaknesses of the regimental system, the British only had two machine-guns per battalion; one of the senior officers had vetoed the army having greater numbers because he "did not consider them a worthwhile replacement for trained men."

The action at Mons was successful because the tactical and technical skills of the British regulars were unmatched and probably unmatchable by the huge homogenized armies of their adversaries. But the British had no depth of reserves to draw on. As fine an instrument as the regulars may have been, they were only good for the opening round in a big war. The day and perhaps the war were saved, then as good soldiers, the "Old Contemptibles" withdrew into history.

A great many of the virtues of the British regimental system that triumphed at Mons were transplanted successfully to the Canadian Army and were enriched with homegrown variations. But some of the faults came with the virtues and these, too, grew larger in the new soil. One grave deficiency Canada inherited was the lack of a collective intellectual tradition in the British Army.

In Canada this problem was compounded because the Canadian officer corps had none of the compensating advantages of their British cousins. The British officer was recruited from a class with a tradition of intellectual achievement. Even though thinking was frowned upon, many of the British officers were brilliant in a dilettante manner. Canadian officers picked up the confident manner of their British models, but they were even further removed from the thinking an army needs to do its job.

The Canadian officers were colonials, a category not quite as low as a wog but certainly in no way capable of independent thought. As a result, it is deeply ingrained in the collective psyche of Canadian military leaders that there is someone out there doing the strategic thinking for them. The consequences of this are still being felt today.

# CHAPTER SIX

# Professional Generals, Political Colonels and the Great War (1867–1918)

*We must seriously consider our Canadian position which is most illegitimate. An army maintained in a country which does not permit us even to govern it. What an anomaly.*

Lord Disraeli, 1866

After Confederation, while the British continued giving the direction for Canadian defence, they wanted the new country to pick up the cost. But the canny Canadians, having become accustomed to bearing no responsibility and little of the cost of their own defence before 1867, in view of the ever decreasing external threat from the USA, thought that any expense, however small, was a waste of money.

In part because of this penny-pinching and in part because they were incapable of understanding and making use of the politics of the emerging nation, the British General Officers Commanding were hamstrung in their efforts to produce a model, integrated army without building in some of the faults entrenched in their own system. Even when they identified a crucial defence problem of the emerging nation, they failed to get their point across. Invariably they came second best to the "parliamentary colonels" of the Canadian militia, who although ignorant of war, managed to play it both ways, as soldiers and as politicians.

These militia politicians became a permanent feature of the Canadian defence scene due to the lack of a professional officer class with the proper standing in the emerging social structure of the new nation. They were, for the most part, community leaders, who because of their prominence in the civilian community also became leaders in the militia regiments. They in turn used their military ranks to gain greater prestige in the community and often a seat in Parliament. All of this was not necessarily bad, except that they had neither the self-discipline nor the professional knowledge of the regular officers whose place they usurped.

For example, the turn of the century French-speaking British General Officer Commanding, Major General Ivor Herbert, attempted to redress the balance between the English and the French in the emerging army. He was bitterly attacked and by the most notorious of all the "political colonels," Sam Hughes, later, and until 1917, Canada's Minister of Militia, a post corresponding to the modern position of Minister of Defence.

General Herbert saw the wisdom of retaining the loyalty of the French Canadians by permitting them to keep their own identity within a Canadian national structure. Hughes, however, even if it weren't for his own redneck prejudices, had his anti-French and anti-Catholic Orangeman constituents to keep happy. And so Herbert's progressive ideas were defeated in the political arena.

Ruining any chance the British Commanding Generals might have had was their haughty air of superiority to anything or anybody colonial. This was matched by the corresponding servility of the Canadians themselves. If it was to be the best, it had to be British. James Morris in *Pax Britannica* captures the mentality beautifully: "It was the proud boast of the grandest Anglo-Canadian mansions that not a stick of furniture in the house, not a knife, not a single painting of Highland cattle in a gloomy brownish glen, was home produced — all came, as they liked to say, from the Old Country."

No matter how hard the Commanding Generals tried to work for the greatest good of Canada, in the end they were still foreigners.

Even if, like Herbert, some of them were more sensitive to the French Canadians than were many local officers and wished to see the development of homegrown Canadian military institutions instead of aping British ones, their loyalties were inevitably split between Britain and Canada. Their overriding objective was Imperial defence. Canadian security came second.

Despite their divided loyalty, some of the British generals, like General Herbert, did see the Canadian military problem in clear perspective. General E.T.H. Hutton, who was in Canada from 1898 to 1900, neatly analysed the problem, but not the solution:

> If Canada will only determine upon looking on its present militia force as its "National Army," the remodelling and reconstruction necessary for enabling a Defence Force thus designated to perform its role will be comparatively easy — moreover the political interference and petty log rolling which hitherto have crushed the very life out of Canadian troops will cease.

As today, the fledgling Canadian military had to struggle against the deeply held conviction that the country had no enemies, and that should one show up, someone else would come to the rescue. With the realization that mother Britain was no longer capable of or willing to protect her giant offspring, the rebel sibling, the USA, became the new protector. Prime Minister Sir Wilfrid Laurier summed up this growing perception in 1902, when giving advice to Major-General the Earl of Dundonald, the newly arrived General Officer Commanding: "You must not take the Militia seriously, for although it is useful for suppressing internal disturbances, it will not be required for the defence of the country as the Monroe Doctrine protects us against enemy aggression."

This was at the same time that President Theodore Roosevelt was using the big stick on Canada over the Alaska Panhandle and other boundary disputes. Canada had to concede to virtually all the American claims after a joint tribunal ruled in favour of the Americans. This was just as well, for Roosevelt had assured the US Senate that he would only accept a favourable verdict.

Although Laurier was a Liberal and French Canadian, then as now the Conservative point of view of Canadian defence was, in essence, the same as the Liberal one. As General Herbert wrote of Sir John A. Macdonald:

> His views were very peculiar. Whilst upholding in the strongest manner politically the idea of integrity of Canada, as a portion of the British Empire, he would do nothing practically for the defence either of the Dominion or of the Empire. He looked upon money voted for militia purposes, only as a means of gaining political ends.

Part of the original reason why Canadians failed to come up with homegrown defence solutions was that there were no Canadian institutions for training officers or men. To rectify this, in 1876 the Royal Military College was opened in Kingston to train Canadian officers. During the same period, a small cadre of non-commissioned officers and men were taken into full-time service to train the militia and to maintain technical and tactical expertise. Unfortunately, both developments took an unusual twist, the results of which are still with us today. The regular soldiers never managed to control the militia and the products of the RMC did not, for the most part, become regular Canadian officers.

The political roots of the militia and the power of the parliamentary colonels prevented a confident professional officer corps from developing. The problem was not helped by the close ties which the newly established Canadian regulars maintained with their British counterparts, partly as a result of the preference shown by the British General Officers Commanding for the better-disciplined regulars over the politically connected, upstart militia. After all, this was the system that still worked to rule the Empire.

In the period leading up to the First World War, the militia, although not efficient by professional military standards, had become a firmly established Canadian institution and an important part of the local political process. It functioned, as it was supposed to, in its role in the defence of Canada, both from internal problems and from external threats. A good example was the incident which culminated in the Battle of Ridgeway in 1866. In this minor skirmish, a force made up largely of militia repulsed a force of Irish republican Fenians made up largely of Civil War veterans. The Fenians' somewhat blarney aim was to take over Canada and join it to the United States.

It was not a very serious invasion and the militia did not cover themselves in glory in repulsing it, both sides running away after the first shock of contact. The raid was not officially sanctioned by the American authorities, although they did nothing to stop the free-booting Fenians from recruiting and forming on American soil. Had the raiders met with initial success, their incursion most probably would have been exploited by local Irish sympathizers and the external pressure could have set off internal resistence. The small external jab could have developed into a major internal problem. Nothing further happened because a few partially trained citizen soldiers stood up to the veterans of the Civil War and thereby demonstrated that Canadians were serious about their independence.

There were other instances where the militia played its role, perhaps the most serious were Louis Riel's rebellions, the first in 1870 and the second in 1885. In both instances the troops had to travel across huge tracts of the wild Northwest. (The second trip was done partly on the new, yet-to-be completed railway.) Although much more serious than the Fenian Raids, the action may also seem a storm in a teapot in retrospect; it was soon over with very little loss of life. Yet the response by the civil authority was the right one and helped ensure that the development of the Canadian West was orderly and peaceful.

An epitaph to the calibre of the Canadian citizen soldier of the period was later written by one of the participants. At the time he was a corporal in command of a latrine-digging detail at Swift Current during the campaign:

Forgive my mention of the circumstance
It's just because in retrospect I see
What men of note my party, picked by chance,
Were destined all in later life to be:
A doctor, judge, professor, bishops twain
Got started right trench-digging on the plain.

Quoted in W.T. Barnard's *The Queen's Own Rifles of Canada,
1860-1960* — Colonel Barnard does not "right record" if the corporal's latrine-building skills were better than his later poetic structure. When he wrote the poem in his *Versified Memories of a Corporal*, he was a full professor of German at the University of Toronto, as well as a Major in the Regiment.

In the late nineteenth century, rudimentary mobilization plans existed, but these were not designed to turn the militia into an expeditionary force for the waging of foreign wars, but for defence of the homeland against invasion or general insurrection. So when the Boer War broke out in 1899, it brought to a head the question of to what extent Canada was to participate in Imperial defence. Although the cause was dubious and Britain was not directly threatened, in the end jingoistic sentiments prevailed and two contingents were raised for service in South Africa.

It was a strange foreshadowing of the raising of the troops for Korea fifty years later and points to the need for two types of troops. Reserves for home defence and regulars for foreign wars. (This does not mean that reserves on a short full-time engagement cannot be used for peacekeeping or NATO commitments, it merely means that if casualties are expected in a war short of a major one, they had best happen to professional soldiers.) For it is politically dangerous and often impossible to order reservists en masse to full-time service for anything but home defence.

In the Boer War there were no militia units mobilized, although most of the recruits came from existing militia units. The first contingent was formed into a new battalion, the 2nd (Special Service) Battalion, The Royal Canadian Regiment. The second contingent also consisted of specially raised troops. Although some again came from the militia, as mounted troops were asked for by the British, the majority came from the Permanent Cavalry School and from the North-West Mounted Police. These units, called Canadian Mounted Rifles, later became the basis for Canada's first regular cavalry regiment, the Royal Canadian Dragoons.

After the Boer War the special service force was disbanded and the majority of the veterans returned to civilian life. The militia with its small permanent force of instructors and its British General Officers Commanding was still developing into a national army at the onset of the Great War. In 1910 Sir John French, who was to command the British Expeditionary Force which went to France in 1914, visited Canada in his capacity as the Inspector General of the Imperial Forces. As a result of his visit, a general mobilization plan based on six divisions was developed. Although not specifically designed for service overseas, this plan would have given the Canadian army a workable structure for the integration of regular and reserve forces.

How well the mobilization of the militia would have worked will never be known, for when war was declared in August of 1914, Sir Samuel Hughes, by now the Minister of Militia, scrapped the existing plans based on mobilizing existing militia regiments and, instead, mobilized Canada by means of an emotional call-to-arms. Volunteers were put into newly formed battalions without proper complements of trained officers and non-commissioned officers, equipment or logistical support. Chaos resulted and was straightened out only with the help of the British Army, on Salisbury Plain, after the Canadians arrived in England.

Hughes, who had been rightly snubbed by British professional soldiers during his short period of irregular service in the Boer War, harboured a deep resentment against all professionals. Now he further aggravated the problem by wasting what small professional resources were available. His dislike and vindictiveness for the one professional infantry battalion, The Royal Canadian Regiment, is demonstrated by the fact that instead of using it in the Expeditionary

Force for Europe, he sent it to perform garrison duties in Bermuda.

The Canadian Expeditionary Force eventually grew into a Corps of some one hundred thousand men and performed magnificent feats-of-arms. It was a great fighting formation, but not a national force. For although its Commander, Lieutenant-General Sir Arthur Currie, had the rights of a national commander, it was for all intents and purposes an integral part of the British Army. There was no staff machinery in Ottawa to translate Canada's national aims into actual military practice. The headquarters in Ottawa, as well as a headquarters in England, were merely administrative and logistical organizations. They simply ensured that a steady stream of young men kept flowing to the sausage grinder of the Western Front.

Hughes, the Minister of Militia, did not know his place and thought that his brief service in the Boer War in a junior capacity gave him the expertise to operate as a commander as well as a politician. He had no understanding that there must be thinking military professionals between the troops in the field and the politicians.

Without a properly functioning military headquarters in Ottawa, Lieutenant-General Currie, himself a prewar militia officer, had to fight on two fronts. In addition to his tactical command on the Western Front, he was constantly battling for the integrity of the Canadian Corps. For the British commanders would have preferred to use the Canadians in divisional or smaller increments to feed into the front wherever weaknesses existed. Only the development of a balanced army could keep a Canadian identity and give the nation the credit it deserved for the lives expended. It was the independence and integrity of the Canadian Corps that was to become the proud legacy of an independent postwar Canada.

To understand how difficult a task this was, one must understand the military organization of armies in the field. The Canadian Corps was one of several belonging to an army, which in turn was only one of the four in the British Expeditionary Force, which in turn was part of the overall Allied command of the Western Front. Therefore, Currie was the military subordinate of the British Army commander, who in turn was the subordinate of the British Commander-in-Chief, who in his turn, eventually, was subordinate to the French Supreme Commander on the Western Front.

As a result of this situation, Currie had to have the confidence of his British military superiors and also retain the backing of his Canadian political masters. This was tricky because the British did not like the idea of his going directly to the Canadian Prime Minister, who had direct access to British Prime Minister David Lloyd George. For their part, the Canadian politicians got angry if he carried out his military orders without consulting them, orders which inevitably resulted in the deaths of Canadian soldiers.

The commander of a field formation, whatever the size, must execute policy, not assist in its formulation. Policy is the precinct of a military strategist close to the political centre who has a say in the grand strategy of the nation. Eisenhower and Marshall, Montgomery and Allenbrook — behind a successful tactical field commander there must be an equally competent and respected general to guard his political rear and to translate political goals into military aims. There was no George C. Marshall behind Currie. There was a headquarters in England, but the senior soldier there, Lieutenant-General R.E.W. Turner VC, was subordinate to a civilian appointee. Although Hughes was finally fired midway through the war, his malignant influence never did permit a proper chain of command to develop in England or in Canada.

The position from which the army could influence policy in the Canadian and British systems was that of the Chief of the General Staff. During the First World War, that position was held in Ottawa by the British Major-General Sir Willoughby Gwatkin. While he was a great promoter of a balanced Canadian Army, he was still a foreigner. There was no Canadian military voice in the Canadian capital to advise on the overall conduct of the war. Furthermore, there was no proper staff in Ottawa to advise Gwatkin and through him, the government. In the end the only Canadian advice that Prime Minister Sir Robert Borden trusted on matters concerning the Western Front was that of Sir Arthur Currie, who had his hands full commanding the Canadian Corps in the field in France.

The public did not know this and did not care. During the First World War, the majority were quite content to have the Canadian Corps march to the beat of a British drummer. Canada still had not emerged fully from colonial status and had no independent voice in foreign affairs. As one result of this, the Canadian Army concentrated on producing field commanders while British officers held most of the staff positions. For the greater portion of the war, this was true even within the field force. There was no Canadian air force and only a token little navy.

To the end there was no Canadian soldier even remotely connected with the British Chief of the Imperial General Staff Sir William Robertson. And it was "Wully," the first "ranker" of common birth to rise from Private to Field Marshal, who, far more than Sir Douglas Haig or any other commander, influenced Lloyd George and the overall conduct of the war.

In the First World War, Canada's defence production was also limited. For the most part the equipment for the army was of British manufacture. The most famous Canadian attempt at weapons production, the Ross Rifle, was a pet project of Sam Hughes and like many of his other projects, it ended up as a complete fiasco. As soon as the unfortunate soldiers got to the trenches, they threw away this untrustworthy weapon and picked up the reliable British short Lee-Enfield.

In sum, at great sacrifice, the first steps to an independent military had been made. In 1914, Canada, not yet a fully independent nation, automatically went to war with Germany and Austro-Hungary when Great Britain did. The war aims that Canada fought for were formulated by Great Britain. Canada went to war to save democracy and help the "Old Country," but she had no pressing national reasons for fighting. This fact should have become apparent when the casualties on the Western Front became so heavy that the enthusiastic flow of volunteers was no longer sufficient to stem the wastage of infantry in the Canadian Corps. Unfortunately, there was no part of the staff in Ottawa where such things as strategy and the morale and motivation of the troops were studied.

The emotional appeal to fight for King and country, practically drained the country of eligible British-born men, and caused many others of those who were English-speaking to enlist, but by and large the appeal for volunteers failed in the province of Quebec. There was no sentiment among the French Canadians to help an Old Country, for it was not theirs. Neither was there any great emotion generated to help the French, for France had long ago left the Canadians to fend for themselves.

Still, in the beginning, there were French-speaking volunteers. Young men who sought adventure, excitement and the chance to prove themselves or merely to escape their civilian existence flocked to the colours. But there was no sentiment for the war among people who could not share in the excitement of what was initially called "The Great Adventure." The social pressure to join up was not as great as in the rest of Canada where hysterical women often gave out white feathers to men in civilian clothing.

Even those French-speaking volunteers who did come forward were mishandled. The obvious method of getting the most out of them would have been to form entire units made up of, and led by, French Canadians. The military authorities did not take this step. It took great political pressure on the part of prominent French Canadians before even one French battalion was formed. When Sam Hughes could not find a Roman Catholic priest to take the job, he appointed an English-speaking Methodist clergyman to be in charge of recruiting in Quebec. When the all-French 22nd Battalion went to France, the very number *vingt-deux* came to signify the dashing and fierce bravery of the French Canadians; however, the appeal to the French on their own terms was not followed up.

As the casualties on the Western Front mounted and the infantry units became short of officers and men, the recruiting slowed up everywhere, but in Quebec it almost stopped altogether. Eventually, when conscription had to be introduced to keep the Canadian Corps in France up to strength, it was in Quebec, where the largest pool of young men remained, that it was most bitterly resisted. Men went into hiding and some of those who resisted conscription were arrested. There was great unrest and riots which had to be quelled by soldiers.

Troops of the Canadian Expeditionary Force waiting to go overseas, were brought down from Toronto to end the unrest. But the soldiers were not trained in internal security duties, only in the brutal application of sufficient force to do the job. Mounted troops charged rioters. Rifles and a machine-gun were used to return fire of rioters sniping on the troops from rooftops and from snowbanks. Civilians were killed and injured, and a tremendous anger welled up against *les Anglais* and their army. The fact that the troops were commanded by a French Canadian, Major General F.L. Lessard, made no difference. The anti-English legacy of the First World War as well as the antipathy of many Quebecers to their army remains to this day.

Yet there still could have been a chance of a proper maturing of the military if the whole of the period had not been dominated by the immensely powerful and megalomaniacal Hughes. Despite the fact that the Prime Minister had fired him halfway through the war, Hughes's influence lingered on. Morton shows how the personality of this one man shaped Canadian civil-military relations during this most important time in our history.

Nevertheless, the sacrifices and gallantry of the Canadian Corps in the First World War forged a nation from a colony. It was only after the end of the conflict that Canada began to have an independent outlook on the world. In turn, the world started forming an image of our nation as something more than a wheat-growing appendage of the mother country.

Paradoxically, while the men who died in Flanders Fields were the instrument of Canadian independence, the army failed to gain its proper place in the Canadian social structure. The reason for this was that it did not develop in two important dimensions. On the one hand, as in the mother country, there was no General Staff to do the strategic thinking. On the other hand, there was its lack of integration with society, another British inheritance. Had both these problems been corrected, this book might not have needed to be written.

# CHAPTER SEVEN

# Forgetting the Lessons (1919–1945)

*We are far from saying that a government should sacrifice everything to the army, for this would be absurd; but it ought to make the army the object of its constant care; and if the prince has not a military education it will be very difficult for him to fulfill his duty in this respect. In this case — which is, unfortunately, of too frequent occurrence — the defect must be supplied by wise institutions, at the head of which are to be placed a good system of the general staff, a good system of recruiting, and a good system of national reserves.*

Baron de Jomini

The thinking officers who came home at the end of the Great War knew what had to be done, but they were able to accomplish very little. As the army had failed to develop a head and a brain when it was at the height of power during the war, it was unlikely that it would do so in the peace that followed.

The great Canadian Corps demobilized and the army went back to its two prewar solitudes, touching, but not melding into one. The professional army reverted back to its prewar training role and retained its parochial outlook. The quickly re-politicized militia were again virtually the sole contact between the military and mainstream society.

The regular army was slightly larger than before the war, its expansion based on the addition of two further infantry regiments: the famous 22nd Battalion of French Canadians, now elevated to the Royal 22e Régiment, and the equally famous Princess Patricia's Canadian Light Infantry, forever to be known by the seniority-conscious Royal Canadian Regiment as "the other English-speaking regiment."

Although many of the returning veterans joined the militia, the pressure of starting civilian careers did not leave them much time for militia politics and control of the militia stayed with the political colonels.

With a few exceptions, the best and most experienced surviving officers went back to civilian life, finding no place in the postwar military establishment, even if they had wanted to stay on. Milton Gregg, for example, who had won two Military Crosses in addition to the only Victoria Cross ever awarded to a member of The Royal Canadian Regiment, was not offered a regular commission after the war. The British and Indian Armies were both interested in his services, but he wanted to come home and get married, and therefore left full-time service. In the 1920s, the command of the Regiment went to a regular who had been a prewar lieutenant, but had only managed to get briefly to the front in late 1918 as a major.

Sir Arthur Currie, the prewar insurance agent and Saturday soldier, who rose to command the Canadian Corps, was in the best position to effect any reforms. He was unable to do anything, because shortly after his return, he was brought down by a peculiar Canadian strain of the virus of mediocrity. This disease ensures that native genius remains unrecognized at home and discounted if it blossoms overseas.

During the war, Currie was recognized as one of the most capable British generals, not only for his military virtues, but for his grasp of the political strategic picture. It is a measure of his stature that he was respected by Sir Douglas Haig, the Commander-in-Chief, at the same time that Lloyd George, Haig's nemesis, was considering him as Haig's replacement.

Currie's wartime fame caused great envy back home, particularly with Hughes, who had failed to make real soldiers respect him. The shy, ungainly Currie, whose reputation had always been higher with the brighter officers who had served under him than with the rank and file, was discredited after his return. It was said of him by Hughes and his cronies that Currie had wasted men's lives needlessly. He became the goat for the general revulsion with war.

It was a younger war veteran, Brigadier-General Andrew

McNaughton, who had the greatest influence on Canadian military affairs between the wars. McNaughton did not return to his civilian career as an engineering professor, but stayed on in the postwar regular army in increasingly responsible positions. He was appointed to the top army job as Chief of General Staff in 1929. But despite his efforts, the final results were limited. Many of the things he wanted to accomplish are still awaiting action.

Above all McNaughton made a plea for a properly thought out, balanced force. He argued that "thought costs little" and with proper planning, the armed forces could concentrate on developing those aspects of defence which were necessary for war, but lacking in the civil sector. Those already in existence merely had to be mobilized, not duplicated. As a result of his farsightedness, the emerging Air Force piggybacked on the newly formed Trans-Canada Airlines. The symbiosis was so beneficial that the army general became known as the father of TCA.

He also wanted some form of universal service obligation, so that the army would be more fully integrated into society, with all men helping to bear the burden of defence.

One of McNaughton's positive achievements in trying to get the officer corps to think for itself was the founding of an Army Staff College in Kingston. Here young staff officers would get the theoretical foundation to prepare them for senior rank. Unfortunately, it failed to develop a tradition of strategic thinking and never rose above the tactical level.

Another positive postwar development welcomed by Currie, McNaughton and other thinking officers was the establishment of a French-Canadian presence in the regular force by the addition of the Vandoos to the regular order of battle. Until the First World War the only institutional French presence had been in some militia regiments. McNaughton and Currie were aware of the need to integrate the French Canadians into the military, as had been some of the British general officers who had gone before. Good communications are essential to leadership and the more intimate the communication, the better the leader's chances of achieving his aim. But when General McNaughton attempted to have all the officers in the army learn French, the political Anglo rednecks sneeringly asked why they should not be taught Latin instead.

The need of French institutions for French-Canadian soldiers was as foreign to the pilots and engineers running the newly founded Canadian Air Force as it was to the British-thinking naval officers and the civil servants who had the ear of the political leaders. Neither air force nor naval officers have the experience of leading large numbers of ordinary men in the fog of the battlefield. Air combat is an elite and far more individualistic form of fighting. The flight crews are all carefully selected and highly motivated volunteers, while the ground crews comprise technicians who do not fight. Therefore, air force officers do not have to inspire much trust in other ranks. Actually it is more necessary for the trust to flow in the other direction: officers must rely on the other ranks to give them the best possible chance of bringing their aircraft home.

Even naval officers do not understand as fully the need for complete trust and understanding between officers and men. A far tighter control is possible over sailors, who are all confined to a ship, where no man except the captain is able to exercise much discretion as to whether he will do his duty in a battle or not. In the chaos of infantry combat, there are many opportunities for each individual soldier to let down his unit. A private can keep his head down and not provide aimed fire; a corporal can abort a patrol and cook up the results. Infantrymen must believe that their own and their buddy's best chance of survival is to follow and obey an officer whom they trust. If they are not properly led to fight, they have countless opportunities to avoid contact. A unit without effective leadership is quickly reduced to a group of demoralized individuals, each seeking personal survival.

For the navy and the air force it was easier to operate only in English, and made sense both from the technical side and in order to fit better with the parent RN and RAF. Therefore, to have a career in either the Royal Canadian Navy or the Royal Canadian Air Force, the French Canadian first had to learn English. However, as the air force and the navy were both much smaller than the army, and did not have their own reserves, for the sake of the nation's unity the important thing was to establish French in the army. (Later in their history both of the junior services got small reserves; neither is called the militia.)

The result was that between the wars and again following the Second World War, the Vandoos were the only French-Canadian presence in the regular forces. The regiment became an enclave within an enclave, an alienated fraction within an already alienated minority. For protection they ruled all their members by a regimental organization of senior officers, serving and retired, known throughout the army as *La Régie*.

The Vandoos protected their own, but woe to the officer who transgressed against the strict tribal rites. The regiment's fierce and protective hierachy became known by the rest of the army as the "Vandoo Mafia." This was fine when the bullets were flying, and the Vandoos have produced splendid field commanders, but it can not be relied upon to nurture innovative strategic thinkers.

And so the lesson in unity and cohesion, learned at such cost in the fields of France by the soldiers, was never absorbed by the population at large. On one side, the jingoists sneered that the French Canadians were unpatriotic and unmilitary; on the other, the Quebec hyper-nationalists insisted that *les Anglais* were trying to kill their boys in useless foreign wars.

Problems with the French language were only a small part of a more general malaise which set in following the disbanding of the Canadian Corps. Not only did the regular officer corps fail to gain control of the militia, but they were also denied any say in co-ordinating the two new services into a Canadian whole. The inter-war military remained split into a small, alienated professional force; a larger, more politically powerful, but militarily poor, militia; and a navy and air force who looked on themselves as adjuncts of their parent British services far more than as being vital parts of a co-ordinated Canadian defence force.

Sam Hughes may have been instrumental in the failure of the

formation of a national army before and during the Great War, but William Lyon Mackenzie King, Canada's longest-serving prime minister, was as responsible for blighting the army's development in the peace that followed. His was also the dominant influence in the next war, extended into the postwar period. King was prime minister for thirteen of the twenty inter-war years, remained in power for the entire Second World War and stayed for three crucial years following the end of hostilities in 1945. During all this time, there were some Ministers of National Defence who understood the military problems and who themselves had good war records, but King, who disliked and mistrusted all things military, so dominated his cabinets that there was no progress possible in the development of the army.

In terms of the relationships of the military to Canadian society, the Second World War was something of a replay on a larger scale of the First. Again, Canada mobilized men and matériel out of all proportion to the direct threat to the nation. Again, this effort pushed the country's economic and social development at a great rate, so that by 1945 Canada was one of the leading industrial powers in the world. And again, the flower of Canadian manhood was sacrificed for strategic goals determined by her allies.

The lack of place of the military in Canadian society and the lack of understanding of things military by the general populace was once more graphically demonstrated by the conscription crisis of 1944. As in 1917, the flow of volunteers was not sufficient to keep the ranks of the infantry up to strength. This was due more to a lack of integrated planning than to a real shortage of volunteers, for there were great numbers of men willing to serve overseas in combat who were in other arms and services. In fact, while the army was having its conscription crisis, the RCAF was discharging aircrew volunteers or giving them menial ground positions.

In 1944, after much heated debate and a great deal of fence-sitting by King, conscription was again introduced and again caused a crisis which threatened the unity of the nation. This time it was not only French Canadians who objected to being conscripted; there was a small mutiny in a Western holding camp, indicating a rift in the West as well. There the anti-conscription sentiment came from the sons of poor immigrants who felt that if young men were to be conscripted, the wealth and property of the old and the rich should also be appropriated for the war effort. Fissures started opening between ethnic groups, between generations, between classes and along occupational groupings. It was yet another example of the necessity for some form of universal militia service and for the strengthening of the French factor in the forces.

During the Second World War, the officer corps again failed to develop any strategic planning capabilities. Although there were others who agonized over the problem, only General McNaughton had the stature to give Canada its proper place in the Allied structure. As it was, he was neutralized by a combination of British military jealousy and lack of Canadian support and understanding.

When McNaughton had been the Chief of the General Staff, he was not in fact head of a Continental-style General Staff. The title merely signified the senior serving position in the army and corresponded to the Chief of Naval Staff and later to the Chief of Air Staff. In 1935, the Conservative Prime Minister, R.B. Bennett, realized that Mackenzie King and the Liberals were about to come back to power and would not reappoint McNaughton in the top army job. In order not to lose his talents just as the war was approaching, Bennett made McNaughton the President of the National Research Council. From this position he made comprehensive plans for an industrial mobilization in case of war.

When war came, McNaughton accepted King's offer to become the Commander of the 1st Canadian Infantry Division, which was the initial Expeditionary Force for Europe. The appointment of Chief of the General Staff went to a series of officers who were junior to McNaughton and who proved easier to manipulate. Meanwhile, McNaughton's industrial strategy plans were slow to be put into effect. The industrialist C.D. Howe became the minister responsible for co-ordinating the production of matériel for war. Because of his foot dragging, it was not until the summer of 1940 that

Canadian arms were made for the Canadian Army. Nevertheless, largely as a result of McNaughton's prewar farsightedness, in the end Canada's war industries were better co-ordinated than those of any other nation on the Allied side. In popular history, it is C.D. Howe who gets the credit for this and, ironically, it is also he who is known as the "father of TCA," not McNaughton.

In England, McNaughton's unremitting struggle to maintain the integrity of the Canadian Army eventually proved his undoing. He not only wanted Canadian control of the troops, but also wanted at least to have Canadian monitoring of the strategic plans for the theatres of war where Canadian troops might be deployed. But this was unacceptable to the Imperial generals.

Overseas, with the British in operational command, was the wrong place from which to fight the battle. Eventually, senior British military commanders, including Generals Brooke, Paget and Montgomery, ganged up with some of the politicians in Canada to convince Prime Minister King that McNaughton needed to be removed from commanding the Canadian Army in the field.

General Alan Brooke, who was eventually the Chief of the Imperial General Staff, was particularly persistent in politicking for McNaughton's removal. His memories of the Canadian went back to the First World War when McNaughton had proved to be the most innovative and brilliant artillery officer on the Western Front. This must have been difficult to swallow for young Major Brooke, who had been appointed to the Canadians to give them some professional depth in gunnery.

The only evidence used to support the drive to get rid of McNaughton was that his performance on a major exercise was deemed faulty. There are various versions of this event. According to some, McNaughton merely refused to panic and tried to give his junior commanders as much practice as he could. At any rate, King was easily convinced to remove McNaughton from command. The General returned to Canada and retired from the army. He did not give up the cause of Canadian security.

As for the British Army, it was busy purging older men from

command positions. All battalion commanders old enough to have fought in the First World War were replaced by younger men. With no minds of their own, the Canadians followed suit. This was an unfortunate move. As there were almost no Canadians with postwar operational experience, the army was denuded of officers who had experienced war.

Men such as Milton Gregg, who by 1940 was commanding the West Nova Scotia Regiment, were sent home to train and prepare others for the fight. He was bitterly disappointed at having to hand over his beloved West Novas to other hands just before they went into battle. At the time, he was only in his forties and as fit as any of the young men under him.

The young officers who were promoted to fill the vacuum left by the departing veterans were not as conscious of the need to Canadianize the army as were those who had already experienced the frustrations of serving two masters — the Canadian political one and the Imperial military one — two decades earlier. And the Canadian Army had no institutional memory of its own in the form of a general staff system to replace the experience of individuals.

The officers who had to grow up in combat were so young that a pub on Salisbury Plain is reputed to have had a sign saying: "No Canadian Colonels under the age of 21 will be served." Most of those youngsters who survived the initial shock of combat performed well enough, some brilliantly as commanders. But they did not have the experience to properly question the right of non-Canadians to decide the military strategies of the war. As had their predecessors during the First War, they learned by bitter first-hand experience the intricacies of Allied military politics.

Meanwhile, back home, none of the wartime Chiefs of General Staff was strong enough to show Mackenzie King the need for military input into the Canadian planning of the war and Canadian input into the overall strategies of the Allies. The Prime Minister clearly revealed through various actions the small importance that he and his civilian advisers placed on military advice and their low opinion of its calibre. Although the Chiefs of Staffs were not in fact excluded from the War Committee, King did not think that a soldier was even needed for its deliberations. He wrote in his diary:

> I ruled out having the Chief of Staff present . . . It had been Heeney Clerk of the Privy Council] who had arranged for these meetings himself as he says, just to give the Chiefs of Staff a "look in" and let them feel important . . . The procedings made it apparent that they were not needed, and by their not being present, the discussions were shortened.

And so, as in the previous war, for lack of military and political acumen, Canada had no say in the strategy which sent so many of her young men to their deaths.

In the Second World War, Canada's greatest total losses were in the infantry, but proportionally, aircrew casualties were the worst, with Bomber Command losing the most. A great number of the young men who died flying the Lancasters, Wellingtons and Halifax bombers on the saturation night bombing raids of the RAF were Canadian. Yet, the highest RCAF formation outside Canada was a group, an organization which did not even function as an independent tactical entity. Despite the fact that more than a quarter of all aircrews in Bomber Command were Canadian, it was totally run by the Royal Air Force. The RCAF, whose officers did not have the benefit of the army's experience of the First War had very little to say even at the tactical level.

This meant that senior RCAF officers did not have operational command experience past the equivalent of an army brigade. The brightest and the best volunteered for operational aircrew duty, yet their courage and intelligence could not be developed for the service of Canada. Some of the best Canadian officers ended up serving in the RAF. In fact, at least one postwar British Chief of Air Staff was one such transplanted Canadian. The policy of integration with the RAF made sense from the overall viewpoint of the Allies, but meant that the RCAF developed far less institutional strategic sense than did the army.

If anything, the navy had even less strategic independence than the air force. The RCN concentrated on anti-submarine warfare in the North Atlantic, and while they in fact ran the whole convoy protection operation in the North Atlantic and thus became tactically independent, they did so within the British naval strategies. Strategic thinking as well as the more glamorous tasks were left to the Royal Navy. As with the air force, many of the best Canadians simply served in the parent service. One such officer, Lieutenant Robert Hampton Gray VC, earned Canada's only naval Victoria Cross while flying with the Royal Navy's Fleet Air Arm in the Pacific theatre.

Again in this war, Canada started badly. The mobilized militia was little more than an enthusiastic rabble when it sailed for England. Again, it was the British Army on Salisbury Plain who made soldiers of the civilians in uniform. In the two first significant actions in which Canadians lost their lives, there was no strategic reason for their commitment. At Hong Kong, two untrained militia battalions slated for garrison duty were slaughtered in a futile defence of the colony. At Dieppe, a Canadian division was committed to a doomed raid. It is debatable whether with better planning the lessons learned could have been bought at a cheaper price. What is certain, is that the lives were used to teach Allied, not Canadian, strategists.

Not only was there no Canadian say at a level higher than division in the Dieppe raid, but the later invasions of Sicily and Normandy were again planned without Canadian strategic input. Eventually the Canadian Army managed to achieve tactical independence to one level higher than the Canadian Corps of the Second World War. The 1st Canadian Army took part in the invasion of Normandy as part of the Army Group commanded by Field Marshal Sir Bernard Law Montgomery.

Nonetheless, there remained no Canadian input into the overall strategy of the alliance. The Free French under the farsighted General Charles de Gaulle was only a tiny fraction of a defeated nation, which was content to collaborate with the Germans.

However, it had much more input into strategy during the war and far more global influence after it, than did the loyal Canadians.

Perhaps the wartime development most illustrative of the lack of thought and semi-colonial status of the army was the CANLOAN scheme. As a group, the CANLOANers were the most experienced of all Canadian infantry officers. They had seen more action in more different theatres of war than any other group of officers in Canadian history and their enormously high casualty rates were the payment for this experience. Their story demonstrates as well as any how badly Canada, and especially young Canadians, have been served in the past by our lack of strategic planning and proper defence policies.

Except for the Hong Kong and Dieppe disasters, the Canadian Army did not take part in the fighting until the 1st Division went to Sicily in 1943. The bulk of the army was not committed until the Normandy invasion of 1944. Meanwhile, the British Army was fighting on many fronts and suffering large casualties. The ensuing manpower shortages were most acute among junior infantry officers. In January of 1944, Canada agreed to loan the British Army hundreds of infantry subalterns for an indefinite period. The scheme was called CANLOAN.

The best and bravest of young Canadians volunteered to help the British. Some even reverted in rank in order to get into action ahead of the rest of the army. Eventually there were 623 junior infantry and 50 ordnance officers who possessed one of the coveted regimental numbers with the preface CDN (Canadian). The infantrymen became platoon commanders with British regiments across the world. But the majority of the CANLOAN officers went to the divisions which landed in Normandy. After the final tally, they had suffered 75 percent casualties. Of the less than seven hundred who had gone, over one hundred twenty were killed or died of wounds.

The British were, naturally, slow to promote the Canadians, who were there to command troops in action not to go to staff appointments. So when the chance of a staff appointment came along, it would usually go to an officer who would be useful to the regiment after the Canadians went home.

When a CANLOAN lieutenant earned his promotion on the battlefield the hard way, by being the only one left to promote, he was given temporary rank, then acting rank. If he was promoted again, he would perhaps have brevet rank on top of his temporary and acting ranks. Thus a lieutenant-colonel could actually be a substantive lieutenant, acting captain, temporary major, brevet lieutenant colonel. This strange way of promoting was not discriminatory against the Canadians, it was the British system. However, it did not fit in with Canadian procedures. Whereas the majority of British got to keep their acting ranks once the fiction of paperwork caught up with the fact of battle, the CANLOANers went back to their substantive rank on return to Canada. With the exception of three who stayed on in the British Army, the CANLOAN survivors all came home. Only a very small handful ever made senior rank in the Canadian Army after their return. The majority ended up the way that they had started, as lieutenants.

Most of them gladly returned to civilian life when the war ended, together with the great majority of the other young men who had matured in the cauldron of war. By and large, those who stayed on in the postwar permanent force were content merely to keep the machinery bright and help train the militia.

# CHAPTER EIGHT

# The Uncertain Call to Unification (1945-1968)

*. . . we believe that determination proceeds from a special type of mind, from a strong rather than a brilliant one. We can give further proof of this interpretation by pointing to the many examples of men who show great determination as junior officers, but lose it as they rise in rank. Conscious of the need to be decisive, they also recognize the risks entailed by WRONG decision; since they are unfamiliar with the problems now facing them, their mind loses its former incisiveness. The more used they had been to instant action, the more their timidity increases as they realize the dangers·of the vacillation that ensnares them.*

Carl von Clausewitz

Canada came out of the Second World War with some of the makings of a first class power. The raw industrial and military effort which the nation put into winning the war was only exceeded among the Western Allies by the USA and Britain, yet Prime Minister Mackenzie King had been unable to turn this into real power and influence. At the Quebec Conference where the fate of the postwar world was being decided, he was reduced to petulant grumbling.

After the war, King's dislike and distrust of all things military, ensured that the forces were quickly returned to their prewar impotence. During demobilization, General Henry Crerar, who commanded the First Canadian Army after McNaughton's removal and who brought it home to Canada, wanted to visit all his troops across Canada to raise their morale. King vetoed the trip; he was afraid that Crerar might use the occasion to organize a military seizure of power. At the same time he authorized a cross-Canada victory tour for British Field Marshal Montgomery.

The young officers who had risen so rapidly during the war now became the senior military leaders. They had helped to defeat Hitler, but when they got back to Canada, they found that they were no match for those who had stayed behind. The civil servants, who had spent the war years running Ottawa while the soldiers were overseas fighting, were so entrenched in the corridors of power that there was no chance for the military to get a proper hearing. The men in grey suits were also impeccably educated, many of them with postgraduate degrees from Oxbridge or the Ivy League. If the young generals who stayed in the service had any post-secondary education at all, it was of the engineering type favoured by the Royal Military College.

More importantly, as with all the other Allied powers, serious and far-reaching inroads had been made into the governing and mass influence institutions by Communists and their supporters. As the Gouzenko affair of 1946 demonstrated, Canada was an easy field for Soviet agents to operate as there was no one in the Canadian polity equipped to counter this subversion.

Igor Gouzenko, a junior officer entrusted with the encoding of messages concerning the Soviet subversive network in Canada, defected from the Soviet embassy in Ottawa with documentary proof of the enormity of the subversion. He had great trouble in getting the RCMP to take his story seriously and even when the authenticity and serious nature of his evidence had been verified, Mackenzie King was in favour of returning him and his documents to the USSR so as not to upset our wartime friends.

In this new spirit of "see no evil, hear no evil," the postwar generals failed not only to influence national affairs, but were not even able to put their military house in order. The three forces had separate headquarters in Ottawa reporting directly to the Minister of National Defence. Eventually a Chiefs of Staff Committee with a small staff and a chairman was established to provide at least some co-ordination. But this arrangement did not give the Chairman any executive power and the staff any reason for forgetting their parent service loyalty. As there was no genuine General Staff, they knew their careers lay within their own service to which they would eventually have to return.

Not only was the Department of National Defence quickly reduced in importance, but it was also evident that King saw no distinction between the military staffs and other civilian officials. To him they were all simply civil servants, and the armed forces was merely another government department. But even so, he could see that some form of co-operation and economy of effort was needed. In his diary of November 1946, he wrote that he was thinking of amalgamating "the three departments into one with a single Chief of Staff and three deputies."

After the defeat of the Axis powers, the fourth-largest remaining military machine in the world was rapidly demobilized. With the army reduced to almost its prewar posture, the regulars again quickly lost control of the reserves and the militia returned to the tribal collection of regiments which it had always been. Although until the early 1960s many militia officers did their initial training with their regular force colleagues, by and large, as before the war, training and military proficiency were rapidly displaced by politics, mess life and ceremonial parades.

The two newer services, although tactically never as independent as the army, had grown into large, powerful organizations, backed by efficient industries. As a result, inter-service rivalry became more intense than ever in the postwar years.

The senior naval and air force officers, to a greater degree than even the young generals, only had experience working as junior partners in an alliance. At no time during the war did they take part in any operations calling for the co-operation of the three Canadian services without support and leadership from senior Allies, and they saw no reason for exercises to practice such co-operation now.

Whereas the army had Canadianized the British regimental

system, the navy's total subordination to things British was detrimental rather than helpful to morale. The senior naval officers all had pseudo-English accents. This "wardroom accent" was expected of all those who aspired to be naval officers and gentlemen. An artificial social distance between officers and men, which was copied from the British, but did not reflect any Canadian class difference, was greatly resented and helped to foster some of the small, but nasty, postwar mutinies among the demoralized sailors.

The forces settled back into a posture which was very similar to the years before the war, while the public once again thought that it could not happen again. Thus after only half a decade of uneasy peace, the outbreak of the Korean War in the East and of the Cold War in the West, found Canada again unprepared.

After making the political decision to participate in the passive defence of Europe and in the small shooting war in Korea, military strategic planning could have advised the politicians how to best commit Canadian men and weapons to these two distant theatres. Instead, the decisions of where to send our troops and what the nature of the commitments should be was made with no thought of the consequences to existing military structures and the future consequences of the upcoming expansion.

Canadians were committed to Northwest Europe and Korea without an overall Canadian strategic plan. A brigade had to be raised to serve in the Commonwealth Division of the United Nations force in Korea. Another brigade and an air division of jet fighter aircraft was sent to Europe.

The commitment by the Western democracies for the defence of these two disparate fronts was necessary because there was a need to show that, despite the massive demobilization of Western armies, violent Communist takeovers could and would be resisted without resorting to nuclear weapons. In Europe, this demonstration of resolve took the form of the new North Atlantic Treaty Organization (NATO), which indicated in a more comprehensive way, the solidarity between Western Europe and North America. Korea was reactive, NATO proactive.

In fact, NATO was a brilliant political application of Clause-witz's theory of the strength of the defensive position. The West's nuclear weapons provided the necessary threat, without which NATO would have been merely another Maginot Line, inviting attack, with the time, place and method all of the attackers choosing. Instead, it has kept the peace for almost forty years, but the strategic concept behind it has yet to be satisfactorily explained to the Western public. And without the broad, intelligent support of the citizens of the democratic nations, all long-term Western strategies are vulnerable to the indirect attack.

The eventual raising of the Canadian soldiers for the non-shooting war in Europe was completed successfully on existing mobilization plans based on the militia infrastructure. The infantry brigade group for Korea was another matter; it was needed as soon as possible and had to go straight into action. It also had to be replaced each year with a fresh brigade. Unfortunately, the well-planned mobilization plans which were used for raising the NATO brigade, were politically unusable for Korea. There was not sufficient national will to mobilize the militia in order to send them to a dangerous little war fought over a little-known peninsula.

General McNaughton's son, the late Brigadier-General Teddy Leslie (he had changed his name by deed poll for family reasons), had as a major commanded an artillery battery in Korea. He summed up the problem many years later in a letter to the author. As opposed to volunteers raised off the street, he wrote, militiamen were part-time soldiers, who could only be mobilized for overseas service in a war which the whole nation supported and perceived as a direct threat to the nation. Therefore, each militiaman had to be a volunteer just like the man straight off the street. The militia units, each belonging to a community, would be an enormous political liability as soon as they started to take casualties. As General Leslie put it, "militiamen tended to have mothers."

Lieutenant-General Guy Simonds, the Chief of the General Staff, refusing to take the political implications into account, would not consent to a modification of the basic mobilization plan to suit the

Korean situation and in the end had to be overruled by the Minister. Brian Brooke Claxton, the Minister of National Defence, overruled Simonds, and then hurriedly ordered the improvised recruiting of men off the street, thereby bypassing the existing channels entirely.

Fortunately, there were still quite a few officers and men left from the Second World War who had not found a niche on civvy street. So, after a fashion, the mobilization worked. As during the Boer War, instead of mobilizing militia units, new active service battalions were raised for the regular force infantry regiments. The whole episode pointed to the fact that the militia was an instrument for home defence and for mobilization in major wars threatening the existence of the nation. While volunteer militia could be used for peacekeeping, in the case of small foreign, shooting wars, professionals were politically the safest instrument. The actual raising of the active service units was reminiscent, on a smaller scale, of the fiasco of Sam Hughes's call to arms in the First World War. Once again there was no strategic planning, once again the professional soldier was not in tune with the political nuances of the society at large.

To make matters worse, the RCAF jet fighter aircraft division sent to Europe was totally separate geographically and by mission from our ground troops. While there was a need for Allied fighters, the reason why Canada responded was mostly because the air force and the air industry wanted their share of the expansion. Raising a modern fighter aircraft formation is a far more complicated problem than the raising of an Infantry Brigade. The officers and men were highly skilled technicians, who were not as readily available and took a longer time to train, while the provision of the aircraft themselves took even longer. In a monumental irony, the air force, which towards the end of the Second World War was releasing men while the army was simultaneously going through the conscription crisis, was now expanding at the same time as the army was releasing soldiers.

The soldiers were released as the Korean situation cooled,

because in the meantime the Americans had invented the concept of "trip-wire deterrence." To make up for the lack of will for a universal national service, short-range tactical nuclear weapons had been substituted for conventional strength. Now the threshold for deterrence had been lowered and supposedly any war would escalate to the exchange of nuclear weapons long before reserves could be mobilized and reinforcements reach far battlefields.

In the late 1950s, this concept had filtered through to Canadian defence policy and spelled doom for the militia. As any future war would quickly escalate to a nuclear exchange and as the need for reserves in an internal security role had been forgotten, there was no further need to train the militia as combat arms soldiers. In this strategic scenario, the proud militia regiments became "re-entry columns," whose job would be to clean up the domestic mess following a nuclear attack. At armouries and parade grounds across the nation, ropes and ladders replaced Bren guns and mortars, while junior militia officers ceased to train with their regular force counterparts. The gap between the regulars and militia grew ever wider.

This demoralizing trend continued. In 1961, the government attempted to use the militia as a means of countering winter unemployment and ordered the enrollment of large numbers of the jobless to be trained in civil defence as members of the militia. Such an expansion of the militia could have been used to strengthen the reserves and bring them into closer contact with the regular force. But it was mishandled and instead of closing the ranks of the militia and the regular force, served to move them further apart.

As a result of all these developments since the end of the Second World War, in the 1960s, the structure of the armed forces had no Canadian defence rationale behind it. To an outside observer the most obvious irrationality would have been the fact that Canada was the only country in the world whose largest service was the air force. And to make matters worse, it was an air force which could only give very limited support to the army. It contained only enough tactical transport to lift some one thousand men and their equipment, the equivalent of one airborne battalion group, while one squadron of T-33 jet trainers was all that was left of ground tactical support. The rest of the air force effort in Canada was integrated with the USAF as part of the North American Air Defense Command. The Canadian air division in Europe had no connection with the Canadian Army brigade group.

In the 1950s, a large and efficient aircraft industry was one of the legacies of the war and the NATO expansion. In combination with the powerful RCAF, it planned to make Canada a leader in fighter aircraft design and manufacture. The result of this determination was the world-beating Avro Arrow. Unfortunately, it was built on the assumption that the RCAF would order at least 500 of the aircraft and that other air forces would flock to purchase the plane as well. But this assumption was not based on any long-term perspective due to Canada's lack of co-ordinated strategic planning.

The Arrow was unveiled just as the manned bomber was in the process of being replaced by the intercontinental ballistic missile (ICBM) as the number one threat to North America. It quickly became obvious that there was no profit to be made from the Arrow and Prime Minister John Diefenbaker's Conservatives cancelled its production. Canada's supremacy in fighter aircraft design and manufacture disappeared overnight as brilliant young engineers emigrated in droves or became high school teachers.

The Royal Canadian Navy in the 1960s continued with its wartime role as primarily an anti-submarine force. When a choice had to be made, it chose this task rather than deplete its resources in the less warlike ice breaker jobs which were needed for the Arctic. While it stayed practically indistinguishable from the Royal Navy, unlike the RN, the RCN had no role and no capability outside its NATO commitment. Sailors continued to think as cogs in the alliance. They had no strategic concept of what their role should be, or how the RCN interacted with the other two services in the preservation of Canadian sovereignty. Evidence of this was, and is, that the small fleet on the West Coast merely acts as a training squadron for the more operational vessels in the Atlantic. Or in the words of Brigadier-General Bud Taggert, the current commandant of the Canadian Armed Forces Staff College, from an operational point of view, the West Coast navy "is no more than a sailing club."

When the Korean War had ended, the army's prime focus became its NATO role. The regular army had one domestic airborne battalion group, which sometimes exercised in support of the joint Canada-Alaska defence treaty, while the three Canadian-based brigades all trained for Northwest Europe. The units in the three Canadian-based brigades all longed for their three-year rotational tour with the elite formation. For me it was a chance to view firsthand the Canadian contribution to the defence of Europe.

In May of 1960, I was sent as a platoon commander to the 1st Battalion of The Black Watch of Canada, a part of the 4th Canadian Infantry Brigade Group, stationed in the Ruhr Valley of northern Germany. This brigade group was a key formation in the British Army of the Rhine.

The Black Watch was garrisoned in Fort St. Louis, a barracks in the small town of Werl in the Ruhr. The economic recovery of West Germany was in full swing and life for the young Canadian soldiers was delightful. The physical scars from the war had mostly been repaired. The Mohne Dam, which had been demolished by the RAF's dambusters, had released a raging flood on the valley below the camp, but this could not be guessed from the neat copses, farms, suburban villas and small hamlets which covered the landscape. Even buildings that had been completely destroyed had been rebuilt to look like the originals, and in the lake behind the dam, sailboats and swimmers made the war seem like some ancient, bad dream.

The Canadian military were well tolerated. Beer cost one mark per bottle, there were four marks to the dollar, and the Canadian Army was reputedly the best paid in the world. And even if the girls for whom they bought the beer were not of the highest social standing, they were pretty and gay. But the military situation of the army itself did not present such a rosy picture.

Instead of the armoured personnel carriers which the tactics of the day called for, the Black Watch had ¾-ton Dodge trucks. In these, they bumped across country behind aging Centurion tanks of the 8th Canadian Hussars, eight or nine men in the back of each truck. Although the ¾ ton was designed to travel off the roads, it had not been built to do this at speeds fast enough to keep up with tracked vehicles. So every now and then a soldier would fly out of the open back.

This transport was not comfortable, but the infantry took pride in keeping up with the tanks. Certainly, the Black Watch could soldier. The men were nearly all Maritimers, in for a career and content to serve without promotion. There were still private soldiers in the battalion who had wartime service, and the unit stacked up well against the best regiments of the British Army of the Rhine.

More worrying than the inadequate and outdated equipment were the nagging contradictions in the Canadians' actual strategic role. In case of a raised degree of preparedness, the battalion had preplanned positions to which it would deploy and where it would make a stand against the invading Soviet Army, if war did break out. The troops practiced deploying at the most unlikely times, sometimes just as a long mess dinner was drawing to a close in the officer's mess. But the positions to which they rushed, still wearing formal mess uniforms, were all in West Germany. If there were any plans to counterattack into East Germany, we did not know about them. It seemed that for land forces the Iron Curtain was only permeable westward.

NATO intelligence briefings made the situation seem even less encouraging. My platoon of thirty men was expected to dig in around a little bridge crossing a narrow stream where we could face quantities of attacking Soviet armour that would have made Horatius's bridge defence look easy. And like Horatius, we would have no reinforcements. The official reason for this was that the war would not last long enough for any reinforcements to reach Europe. The doctrine of trip wire deterrence neatly camouflaged NATO's and Canada's lack of mobilizable reserves and equipment.

Although outnumbered and outgunned, the soldiers of the Canadian Brigade were serious about stemming the hordes from the Soviet bloc in the event of war. No one told them that their political masters believed there was no chance of their having to do the job for which they were trained. In the decade since the end of the Korean conflict and the organization of NATO, the Western alliance had settled into a fairly comfortable pattern. This pattern would soon be given a sharp jolt by what came to be known as the Cuban Missile Crisis.

Despite the numerical and conventional superiority of the Warsaw Pact forces in Europe, (the Warsaw Pact Treaty Organization of Soviet and satellite forces was the reply to NATO), in 1960 the USSR was not yet a global military power. The USA still had overwhelming nuclear, naval and air superiority. The Soviet nuclear build-up and the flight of the Sputnik in 1957 were clear indications that there was no change in Communist aims, but the concept of nuclear deterrence had lulled the Western public to the dangers. Then in 1959 under the guise of genuine reform, Fidel Castro's Communists took Cuba from the corrupt Batista regime. Soviet strategists soon attempted to exploit this success and make Cuba into an impregnable Communist bastion close to the heart of the democratic world. They started to arm the Cubans with modern technology.

Finally in 1962, while clandestinely attempting to deploy some of their own nuclear weapons to Cuba, the Soviets got caught. Ostensibly they were shipping the missiles to Cuba for protection against air attack from the USA. But as a consequence, which they must have planned, the deployment also replied in kind to the more intimate nuclear threat which NATO posed to the Soviet Union. As opposed to the intercontinental ballistic missiles and long-range bombers which threatened both homelands, NATO tactical nuclear weapons threatened Russian territory. The Warsaw Pact's theatre weapons did not however threaten North America.

The Americans acted quickly and put the military on advanced alert status. Although Prime Minister John Diefenbaker was kept fully informed, he was not prepared to follow suit. Therefore, the Canadian Forces were not readied for action as were their American counterparts.

The RCN and the RCAF, which were fully integrated with their larger alliance partners through the NORAD and NATO alliances and therefore received all the military communications ordering the increased readiness status, were particularly restive at this seeming failure to live up to our treaty obligations. They knew that they should be going through the same motions as the Americans in order to keep the military and tactical integrity of the alliance, but they had not been kept up to date on the political net.

Minister of Defence Douglas Harkness, who was an army combat veteran of the Second World War and who shared the military's concern, finally ordered the naval commander on the East Coast to put his fleet to sea. Apparently, the RCAF, even without orders from Ottawa, also jumped the gun, but this was not as publicly apparent. Naturally, a great furor resulted from this apparent lack of political control of the military. Unfortunately, the conclusion drawn was the wrong one.

The lesson that should have been drawn was that there was a great gap in communications between the political leaders and the senior fighting officers. The reason for this was an old one: the senior officers did not know enough of national political imperatives, Canadian-American relations and the fine nuances of gunboat diplomacy as practiced by the superpowers. In short, the whole crisis was caused by lack of clear strategic thinking and planning.

Instead of moving to rectify the problem, the situation was made worse. Since senior officers and the ex-soldier Minister of Defence had acted against the Prime Minister, there were calls for more "civilian" control of the military. And communications between the elected leaders and the professional military became even more distant.

Even before the missile crisis, the Glassco Royal Commission, named after its chartered accountant commissioner, had been charged with recommending the reorganization of the Department of National Defence. In 1963 the commission suggested restructuring that in future would make civil servants control military policy, in effect placing a further bureaucratic layer between elected leaders and the professional military. This error was to be greatly reinforced in the 1970s.

By the mid-1960s, the decline of Canada's militia, the isolation of her military from mainstream society and of the three regular forces from the militia and one another, was matched by the country's complete inability to develop strategy appropriate to a new and complex international environment. A move to break down the independence of the army, navy and air force would have been a move toward solving part of the problem. Instead, the government of Lester Pearson, more interested in promoting national unity during the rise of Quebec separatism than worrying about global strategic concerns and the details of national security, embarked on a policy of unification of the forces. It was a policy that almost destroyed the weakened Canadian military altogether.

# CHAPTER NINE

# The All Green Force (1968-1974)

*Nemo Me Impune Lacessit*

(Black Watch Regimental Motto)

In 1968 when unification of the armed forces became law, Canadian military leaders failed to convince the decision makers of how vital existing military traditions were. The military and civilian bureaucrats, who were rapidly becoming indistinguishable and interchangeable, wished to do away with the regimental system altogether. They did not understand the fine nuances which Kipling called "the unwritten things" that go into making up an effective army.

At that time, dropping the regimental system was one of the more reasonable proposals. When totally interchangeable servicemen were seen just around the corner, the numbering of units as a substitute for the names and traditional trappings of the regiments was not a radical thought at all. It was one which not only made sense to the civil servants, but even to those tidy military minds who had never been to war in that mysterious organization known as The Regiment.

On June 1, 1970, I was an unhappy participant in a memorable event in the making of the Green Machine, as the unified armed forces in the new green uniform came to be derogatively known. This was the striking from the regular army's order of battle of my regiment, the Black Watch of Canada. The day was damp and cold, and the mist that filled the Saint John River Valley was almost a drizzle. It turned to moisture where it came into contact with the bayonets and rifle barrels of the men standing rigidly to attention on the parade square in Camp Gagetown, New Brunswick. It beaded on the camouflage-painted surface of the armoured personnel carriers which were drawn up behind the ranks of kilted men. The two regular battalions of the Black Watch (Royal Highland Regiment) of Canada were parading their colours for the last time before laying them up. The regiment was being struck off the regular army's order of battle with the closing down of the two regular battalions and the regimental depot. Only the 3rd militia battalion would remain in existence.

The sound of the pipes in the drizzle, combined with the whiskey taken to combat the raw dampness, all raised the level of grief among the spectators. Officers on parade and off it all wore black armbands on the right sleeves of their uniforms to denote mourning. This, as well as the whiskey, was in defiance of regulations which strictly prescribe when the signs of mourning can be worn.

Regular officers of the regiment, who were temporarily serving away from the home station, had come from all parts of Canada and from overseas to be present on this last family occasion. Indistinguishable in their kilts, tropical summer worsted jackets and Sam Browne belts were the officers from the 3rd militia battalion. Practically the whole membership of the Montreal mess had come for the weekend to assist at the wake.

Looking the same as his Canadian brother officers was the lone British exchange officer from the Imperial Black Watch. He had just served for two years as a platoon commander in one of the rifle companies of the 2nd battalion, while his Canadian counterpart commanded a platoon in the parent regiment. Superficially, the regiment had about it far too much that was British, too much that smacked of the old colonial relationship.

This was one of the underlying, unstated reasons why the Black Watch was one of the three regular infantry regiments that were being "reduced to Nil Strength" as part of the Liberal government's massive cutbacks in defence. Superficial was all the knowledge that the Prime Minister and the Minister of National Defence who had engineered unification had about the army. Pierre Elliott Trudeau was as prejudiced against the armed forces as had been Mackenzie King. This was compounded by the fact that Paul Hellyer, who was the architect of unification, but had by 1970, moved out of the Defence portfolio, had never reached a rank higher than corporal during his own time in the service. (He was a ground crewman of the Royal Canadian Air Force during the Second World War.) Not only was Hellyer's understanding of things military limited, but he also seemed to harbour a contempt for senior officers, which must have been born of his wartime service. He rode roughshod over military advice in a way not seen since the heyday of Sam Hughes.

The most visible sign of unification at the Black Watch funeral were the new green uniforms worn by a few of the onlookers. The new design of the uniform was an attempt to cleanse the forces of their Britishness, which in the era of bilingualism and biculturalism was deemed contrary to the cause of Canadian unity. This attempt to Canadianize the forces only cut off their roots; it ignored the positive elements of the Canadian military tradition. The result was a major loss of identity for Canada's soldiers.

Of all the changes wrought by unification, this deep psychological wound may have been the most harmful. A major part in maintaining morale of an army is what is loosely called tradition. Young soldiers, untried and unsure of themselves, draw strength and courage from those who passed before, and win or lose, have stood the test.

In the case of Canada's armed forces this identification with past battles is inescapably tied to the British tradition. This is just as true of the French-speaking units, where the British forms and style blended with the earlier colonial French-Canadian traditions. It is equally true for Canadians of all other ethnic origins. The heart of Lieutenant Filotas, a first generation Canadian of Hungarian origin, responded to the pipes and drums of the Black Watch as readily and deeply as that of Sergeant MacKenzie, a fifth generation Haligonian of African descent.

Until 1967, there were thirteen infantry battalions in the regular army. The five English-speaking regiments had two battalions each and the Vandoos had three. As part of the reductions and in order to man the newly formed Canadian Airborne Regiment, five battalions had to be disbanded. It was anticipated that two English-speaking regiments would disappear and the Vandoos would lose their third battalion.

In the initial cut, the Queen's Own Rifles and the Canadian Guards each lost a battalion. Both had been having problems with recruiting and retention. The economy was booming and soldiering was not a popular pastime, especially in Ontario and the West, where the two regiments had their home stations and recruiting bases.

The Canadian Guards, although an excellent regiment, had been formed more or less on the whim of General Guy Simonds, who was the Chief of General Staff during the expansion of the 1950s. The regiment had no traditional or geographic base from which it could draw recruits and only a tenuous connection to the militia through the Governor General's Foot Guards in Ottawa and the Canadian Grenadier Guards in Montreal.

The troubles of the Queen's Own Rifles were caused by the military bureaucrats' lack of sensitivity to the great possibilities of having regiments from the militia finally incorporated into the regular army. The logical thing would have been for the regular Queen's Own battalions to recruit in Ontario and for the regimental home to remain in Toronto, where it had been an important part of the community for almost a hundred years. Instead, the regiment's regular battalions and depot were transplanted to Alberta and British Columbia, while the militia remained in Toronto.

In 1970, during the next phase of the infantry reorganization, the Guards and the Queen's Own disappeared altogether, but inexplicably, both battalions of the Black Watch were also disbanded. At the same time, The Royal Canadian Regiment and the Princess Patricia's Canadian Light Infantry each gained a third battalion, and an entirely new organization, called the 3rd Mechanized Commando of the Canadian Airborne Regiment was brought into the regular force establishment.

Then in the mid-1970s the pendulum started swinging. The reaction against the homogenization of the fighting units had set in and the three remaining regiments — The Royal Canadian Regiment, the Princess Patricia's Canadian Light Infantry, and the Royal 22e Régiment — were saved. On the political scene, there was no further mileage to be made out of reorganizing and reducing the military.

But already great damage had been done. The regiments that were strengthened by the addition of extra battalions had no real roots in the militia, whereas the Black Watch and the Queen's Own Rifles, which could best bridge the gap between the regular force and the militia, had gone with the stroke of a bureaucratic pen. Although among the oldest militia regiments in Canada, they had only been activated as units of the regular army during the reorganization in the early 1950s, which resulted from the expansion for NATO and Korea. The three remaining regiments had all been part of the prewar permanent force. It made some sort of limited sense to first disband the three units that were newest in the regular army's order of battle, but this deed only widened the already yawning chasm between the regulars and the militia, and further distanced the army from the surrounding society.

Nowhere was this more evident than on the East Coast. The Black Watch, which in the 1950s, unlike the Queen's Own, had been successfully transplanted from Montreal, had its home base in New Brunswick. The Atlantic provinces were its greatest source of recruits. At the time of disbanding, its two battalions were up to strength and had the highest retention rate in Canada. With Camp Aldershot, Nova Scotia, and later Camp Gagetown as its home station, the Black Watch had become in the twenty years of its regular army existence an institution that fitted well into the four eastern provinces. It was easier to come home from Gagetown than from Calgary, and to those "downhomers" who wanted to remain on the East Coast, it was the only regiment to join.

Unification destroyed the traditional pattern of regimental indoctrination for both officers and men. Under the old system, the recruit went straight to his regimental depot for his training, so that his loyalty from the start was to his regiment. Unification brought centralized, standardized training, most of it having to be undone and retaught by the infantry regiments, whose standards of physical toughness, endurance and weapons handling had to be much higher than that of air force tradesmen and service support troops.

With the traditional regimental system, the newly joined subaltern (junior officer) was subjected to the same kind of almost childish humiliation as the new recruit, until he became atuned to all the finer nuances of regimental life and custom. Only then would he be accepted. The term "brother officer" meant just that. The young officers worked together, and lived and socialized together in the officers' mess. They got to know one another so that in later life they would still know who was good for what, particularly under pressure.

This system worked well, and was ruthless in sidetracking and eliminating those who did not fit and especially those who could not be trusted. One of the serious results of the loss of the unwritten regimental codes was that there was no longer any way of weeding out all of the unsuitable officers. Under the old system, they would have been stopped from progressing up the ladder of command. A regiment was small enough that each member was well known to everyone. No elaborate reason had to be given for the refusal to promote an officer or give him command of men. It was sufficient to say that "the chap simply wouldn't do." Or in the words of a famous confidential report written by a British cavalry colonel about one of his officers: "I would not breed this man." With tradition replaced by paperwork, some of the bad eggs that have slipped through are now in very senior positions.

The loss of tradition was hardest on morale. Gone was a soldier's sense of being grounded in the past, and with it much of the fierce loyalty and cohesiveness characteristic of our regimental system, qualities which had been envied by larger, more powerful armies. Once upon a time the uniform distinguished every man whose "unlimited liability clause" in his employment contract was liable to be called. Soldiers, unlike accountants and lawyers, are sworn to carry out any legal order to the point of death. The traditional uniforms and trappings gave status, regardless of rank, to those belonging to the units that were most at risk.

This elitism favoured the infantry, the most underprivileged soldiers, but also the most likely to die. A soldier wearing the eight-pointed star and shoulder flashes of the Royal Canadian Regiment could identify with Milton Gregg winning his Victoria Cross at Bourlon Wood. The maroon beret of the parachutist set him apart from the lesser breeds who did not have to jump out of aircraft behind enemy lines.

The new green uniform made everyone the same. And the homogenization it represented was a major step in the demilitarization of the forces, a process which had already begun in the 1950s and the '60s. Recruitment advertising for officer candidates now showed young men and women in the bland green outfit, stepping off a passenger aircraft, briefcase in hand. To attract other ranks, the advertisements used photos of good-looking young men and women running through the grass together. These could have been selling deodorant or a new brand of beer. Nowhere was a weapon to be seen, nowhere was there an appeal to patriotism, to duty or to regimental pride.

A survey conducted a decade after unification came into effect showed that a great number of young soldiers and officers in the support trades had no intention of fighting. Even the percentage of those in the combat arms who were prepared to fight, was slipping. This came as a great surprise to senior officers and politicians alike, but little was done to counter the trend.

Not only was the psychology of a successful force forgotten in the process and its aftermath, but the survival of the three parts of the armed forces became a matter of internal politics even more than it had been before.

The air element, as it was now called, not only continued to have the most people and the largest budget, but it enjoyed a much greater rapport with the civilian bureaucrats. Like them it had no overall philosophy of defence; the air element merely wanted to maintain jobs for as many of its specialists as it could. For example, when the de Havilland Crown corporation needed a quick sale of their new, and incidentally very good, Dash 7, the government easily persuaded the air element to acquire a few of the aircraft, which it fit into its structure. Similarly, when the Chief of Reserves (a new post-unification position for the senior reserve forces adviser to the Chief of Defence Staff, a part-time political post) was an air reserve officer, Major-General Richard Rohmer, he pushed through the replacement of old light transport Otters by small reconnaissance helicopters. These had no role in the overall force structure at the time and did not fit into the structure which was being planned for the future.

This flexibility of the air element coupled with the lobbying power of the largely foreign aerospace industry, ensured that the pre-unification asymmetry remained. This was aided by the fact that the navy, traditionally the most silent and the smallest service, was also least able to adapt to the idea of integrated forces. But it was the army's intricate internal divisions, which had been an important morale booster before unification, that now prevented the soldiers from presenting a united front in the silent internal battle for supremacy. The army generals were continually outmanoeuvred by the smoother, less military-sounding air force senior officers.

This was one of the reasons why, following unification, equipment became more important than people. In the navy and the air force, weapons tend to have a greater importance than in the army. The airman and the sailor man the weapon, whereas the soldier is the man armed. Even within the army, only in the infantry is this distinction most clearly evident. It is a basic principle of all armed forces, but it was forgotten by the post-unification leadership. Inevitably, when the technology is put ahead of the man, it leads to many costly investments with no overall strategic rationale. More importantly, it eventually obscures the real heart of any military organization, the unit of men prepared to obey orders to the ultimate, their own death, or preferably, the death of the enemy. When those supporting the fighting man not only outnumber him, but also have more leverage with the decision makers, the combat role, instead of being the *raison d'être* of the armed forces, becomes an archaic specialty.

In addition, the logistics, administration and engineering functions of the three services were much easier to unify than were the
fighting elements. This new union gave them power proportional to
their total numbers, and it began to overwhelm the combat elements
of the three competing "elements."

At the same time, the service colleges, which had never served
purely military needs, began to produce fewer officers for the
regular force infantry than ever. The numbers of pilots and
navigators were now equalled by engineers, logisticians and other
non-combat trades. Some years there were fewer than ten infantry
cadets out of an intake of well over one hundred.

One of the permanent casualties of unification was the system of
honours and awards. The Victoria Cross and all the other gradations
of courage and devotion to duty, which were instantly recognized
by all military personnel, were discontinued as being too British.
They were replaced by a new Canadian system, in which there was
no longer any exclusive decoration for courage in the course of
military service.

Under the old system there were decorations for bravery shown
when not in face of the enemy, such as the George Cross, which
could be won by civilians and military personnel alike. But the
majority of awards were only for military virtues. The new system,
with its Order of Military Merit, rewarded efficiency, but no longer
recognized military valour. The new Cross of Valour, Star of
Courage and Medal of Bravery could be won for acts having
nothing to do with war or even service to the country.

Worse still, with unification, service in the combat arms ceased
being a criterion for promotion to higher rank. Under the old
system, 90 percent of the generals had come from the combat arms
of the army, and they accepted the combat training of all ranks as
normal. Similarly, the admirals had mainly risen from the executive
branch of the navy. But though they valued the need for discipline
among all ranks, they saw no need for training all personnel as
infantry, because in their narrow world, there was never any need
for it.

The senior air force officers came largely from the aircrew classifications. These ex-pilot and ex-navigator bureaucrats saw very little reason for wasting time in training their technician groundcrew for infantry combat. And it was the air force officers who were the most numerous and the most influential with the very civil servants who made the final compromise decisions.

Now came a proliferation of generals with little or no operational experience. (With the first rigid orthodoxy of unification came unified ranks, the army's. This was fine with the ever flexible air force, but the sailors were horrified with the thought of green colonels commanding ships, and when the dogma of unification started easing up, went back to their old ranks.) The senior ranks filled with officers for whom the ability to operate in the bureaucracy became more important than the military virtues. These new leaders had no experience of war and no education in military philosophy and psychology. They easily fell in with the demilitarizing process being planned by the government and executed by the civil service bureaucrats.

"Modern management" became fashionable to the extent that one of the three military colleges started to specialize in "administration." This was ironic, because the study of administration as a university subject in the USA received most of its impetus from businessmen who had served in the armed forces during the war and had been impressed with the military's methodical way of managing the chaos of conflict. Now, twenty-five years later, the Canadian military was throwing out its war-tried methods and replacing them with a diluted version, much simplified and changed to suit commercial enterprise.

One of the trendy management techniques of the early 1970s was "management by objectives." This was a method by which management attempted to judge subordinates by results. For a firm selling widgets, this was fairly simple to do. However, for a squadron commander training his pilots for war, the easily quantifiable factor was invariably one which was the least relevant to the real needs of conflict. For example, the objective might be the number of successful interceptions during training. The squadron commander who would only fly missions during perfect conditions, would have better "objective" results than one who made the training as difficult as possible. Of course, it was not usually as simple as that, but the point was that the officer who played the management system would show up better than the one who was playing by the old rules of leadership. The unquantifiable factors of morale, courage and endurance were not on the curriculum of administration faculties.

The new management thinking permeated all aspects of military life, and nowhere was it more pervasive than in training. For example, the new managers would demonstrate that technicians of various types spent all their time in technical tasks, therefore it was a waste of time and resources to train them as infantrymen first. Furthermore, it would be more difficult to get recruits of sufficient intellect if they had to face physical hardship before learning to be electronic wizards. Therefore the centralized training system cut out much of the military training and made what was left soft enough so that no future technician would fail to pass. As a result, the infantry was forced to retrain the soldiers coming to it from the unified training depots to get them up to combat standards. Infantry training, instead of being a common entry experience, became a barbaric speciality.

Thus the opportunity for a psychologically integrated force was killed before it had a chance to start. And, ironically, its defeat was ensured by the very army officers who were most aware of its importance. The original military need for integration had not been forgotten by a few senior officers who had survived Paul Hellyer. They were keenly aware of the potential disasters and waste which would happen in a shooting war if Canada again lacked national strategies and a unity of purpose. In the increasingly isolated world of the infantry, the lessons of Dieppe and Hong Kong were still remembered and nowhere more so than among the Vandoos Mafia.

General Jean-Victor Allard of the Royal 22e Régiment, who had served with distinction in the Second World War and commanded the Canadian brigade in Korea, became the first commander of Mobile Command, the operational portion of the "land element." In effect, he was the army chief of staff. But as there was only a unified headquarters left in Ottawa and as the government was pushing the regionalization of federal functions, General Allard's Mobile Command Headquarters was located in a suburb of Montreal. At the same time, the air headquarters went to Winnipeg and maritime command was set up in Halifax.

This was a time when Prime Minister Trudeau wanted to cut our European commitment to NATO and a time when peacekeeping activities for our armed forces were at the height of their popularity. On the strength of the peacekeeping concept, General Allard and his staff dreamt up a new integrated force which could deploy anywhere in the world and be self-supporting. The transport would be Canadian, the air support would be Canadian and the strategic planning would be Canadian. Unfortunately, although the underlying motivation was sound, the idea was not. It had no logical strategic basis. This dream for an all-purpose integrated force for the 1970s became known derisively as the Global Mobile force. For many reasons it never came to pass.

The idea of Global Mobile never had much appeal to the air force and the navy, and it soon proved to be totally counterproductive even for the army. Under peacetime budget and manning levels, such a self-supporting force could have been at best only big enough to capture the island of Grand Manan against very light opposition.

Unfortunately, the Trudeau government also saw the establishment of Global Mobile as a means of reducing the expenses and sophistication of the forces weaponry to the point where they could no longer operate on a modern conventional battlefield in support of the NATO alliance. Although the idea never got past the early stages, it fit conveniently into the policy shift towards operations outside Europe. The government knew that peacekeeping operations in the Third World were predicated at a much lower level of intensity than conflict in support of NATO operations on the Central Front in Europe. Therefore, it argued, the army would not need sophisticated weapons such as heavy armour and self-propelled artillery, nor the air force state of the art interceptors and other aircraft which would have to survive against the most modern of Soviet equipment.

In 1966, General Allard was promoted from Commander of Mobile Command to Chief of the Defence Staff, and the armed forces started to re-equip so that they could operate as a national force instead of separate adjuncts to larger allies. But there was no attempt to place Global Mobile within the context of the alliance. Therefore it became easy for those wishing to save money on defence budgets to further reduce the forces. The future tasks for the forces were mere concepts and not actual alliance commitments, so they did not have to pass any credibility tests. Whether we had thirteen battalions or nine to help keep order in the Third World was academic when the government wanted to spend the money on matters of direct concern to Canadians. There were no hard-nosed allies to complain that the planned force levels were insufficient to deter the enemy, because there was no identifiable enemy in the brave new world for which Trudeau seemed to be planning.

The new emphasis on operations in the developing world gave the government the opportunity to cut Canada's European-based contribution to NATO in half. Now with the Brigade Group reduced from three battalions to two and each battalion's four rifle companies to three, the formation was no longer fit to hold its old blocking position in a key part of the British Army of the Rhine. So it was moved from the Ruhr to an undefined role in the rear area of the Central Army Group near the French border. The cuts and the move were completed by 1970, just as the army could no longer operate with its worn-out Centurion tanks. Now it was easy to avoid the expenditure, for there was no place for a heavy main battle tank in light operations in the Third World and our NATO role had become very unclear. Since no one in the military was able to give a philosophically sound strategic reason for maintaining a well-equipped conventional military force, Canada was unilaterally disarming.

After General Allard was outmanoeuvred in this way, even the combat arms officers who had been the greatest supporters of peacekeeping because of its operational training value, began to shy away from it. They saw our commitments to NATO and NORAD as the only justification for modern equipment. Lacking a Canadian defence strategy, the alliance became the only real *raison d'être* of the armed forces.

In the late 1970s, this survival tactic, coupled with a slow reawakening of public and political support for defence, eventually halted the budgetary and manning cutbacks. However, this new tactic of survival ultimately proved the most dangerous of all. While our alliances had loose strategies for the collective effort, our allies could not plan for our inner security and defence.

In the light of past experience and the probable future, structuring our forces on the basis of our alliance commitments was very short-sighted. Indeed, Allard's basic idea of an integrated, mutually supporting national force was good, but its translation into Global Mobile, which permitted Trudeau to carry out such deep unilateral cuts in our defence forces, proved disastrous. It was one more example of how by a lack of clear thinking and straight talking, the politicians, the bureaucrats and the military in Canada work at cross-purposes.

The unification of the forces between the mid-1960s and mid-1970s, coming at the same time as the deep cuts in budgets and force manning levels, was a serious blow to our defence capabilities. It continued with accelerating demilitarization of the forces and a civilianization of the headquarters and the senior officer corps. This coincided with the last of the officers with wartime experience retiring from service.

It was in this climate that I was to have my first experience of National Defence Headquarters in Ottawa.

# CHAPTER TEN

# Scribes and Pharisees (1974–1980)

*I have undergone a pitiable experience as prompter at headquarters, and no one has a better appreciation of the value of such services than myself: and it is particularly in a council of war that such a part is absurd. The greater the number and the higher the rank of the military officers who compose the council, the more difficult will it be to accomplish the triumph of truth and reason, however small be the amount of dissent.*

Baron de Jomini

By 1974, with unification complete, the demilitarization of Canada's military was so far advanced that it had reached crisis proportions. This problem was evident at every level of the "all green force," but it was most serious at the highest echelons of the military hierarchy. In effect, Canada's defence policies were stagnant and whatever changes occurred were not influenced by honest professional advice from experienced field soldiers. As a result, our country's lack of strategic planning became even more obvious.

In the period between the wars when Andrew McNaughton was Chief of the General Staff, he had written:

It is essential that in matters of policy as distinguished from routine civil administration, that the heads of the Fighting Services should not be required to present their advice through and to take their instructions from a civil servant who has not had the benefit of the special training and professional experience in these matters which a senior officer of the Fighting Services who is selected for appointment as Chief of Staff may be presumed to possess.

Experience with Ministers and Governments since the war has emphasized that in policy matters they invariably and rightly insist on direct advice from their professional advisers, and that whenever an acute situation has arisen the Deputy Minister has only functioned in his proper role as an administrative officer.

It has been amply borne out by experience that to be effective the civil control of the armed forces, which is essential, must be exercised directly by a member of the cabinet and not through a civil servant.

In 1974 the situation was far worse than in the 1930s, but no officer in a senior appointment was complaining to his political masters about the subordination of the military to the civil service. (In the Canadian federal usage the civil service is confusingly called the "public service." This semantic subtlety has made the necessary separation of the military more difficult: while the military is obviously not a "civil service," the soldier by definition "serves the public good.") In the 1974 Summer issue of the *Canadian Defence Quarterly*, two colonels, out of all the senior officers stationed at the headquarters in Ottawa, had the courage to write:

Military policy makers are not only not selected by military officers at large, they are in large measure from the civil service. The Canadian Forces are therefore not self governing in any sense, and there cannot be said to be a profession of arms in Canada.

All military policies are now in whole or in part prescribed by civil servants and one can expect the Canadian Forces to take on the coloration of a civil service, at least until it comes to the shooting and the suffering. This may be fine if we don't expect to fight; but of course, if we could confidently predict the end of wars, we wouldn't have armed forces at all.

Colonel Neelin and Colonel Pederson went to their retirement shortly thereafter, their criticism unheeded. During the crucial period from 1969 to 1972 when the civilianization of the military hierarchy had been planned, the air element's General Freddie Sharp, who later became an armaments consultant, had been the Chief of the Defence Staff. Although he was in the best position to make a strong public statement, he did not do so. Nor did any general officer feel strongly enough about the total subjugation of the military to the civil service either to resign or make a public declaration of protest. They had all been promoted to senior rank since Hellyer had decimated the officer corps of those who had cautioned against his unification policies. They knew the value of political expediency, but had forgotten the "unlimited clause" in their unwritten contract.

In the decade of civilianization following unification, the institutional importance of the officer corps greatly deteriorated. During much of this time, the crucial position of Deputy Minister of Defence was held by C.R. "Buzz" Nixon, now a defence consultant. Nixon had been a junior engineering officer in the Royal Canadian Navy before he began his civil service career, and this had left a deep impression on him. Although he never appeared in uniform on horseback, he seemed to think of himself as a strategist and commander, in the grand old manner of Sam Hughes and the political colonels.

In 1975, having read of General McNaughton's struggles to maintain military input to the elected leaders on defence policies, it was with a deep sense of foreboding that I heard Nixon address the cadets at the Royal Military College. He said, as though stating the obvious, that he and the Chief of Defence Staff divided the duties of running the armed forces in such a way that while the CDS was responsible for maintenance of the day-to-day routine, he, the Deputy Minister, looked after the long-range plans and the policy end of the shop.

There was no doubt of Nixon's sincerity. He wanted to make the forces as strong as possible. Unfortunately, to his civil servant, engineering mind, strength meant bigger budgets for equipment.

Strategically, he was still thinking of preparing for a "come as you are war" in Europe. He appeared to have no concept of the need for public support for the military, of the need for viable reserves or of the importance of the "unwritten things," such as morale and tradition.

By then General J.A. Dextraze had succeeded General Sharp as Chief of Defence Staff. "Jadex," as he was known throughout the army, had been a great infantry officer. During the Second World War, he had risen from private to Lieutenant-Colonel commanding a battalion and had returned from civilian life to lead a battalion of the Vandoos in Korea. In both wars he had been decorated for gallantry. He was decorated a third time during the UN operations in the Congo in the early 1960s. After the demise of so many senior officers during the Hellyer purges and because of the new emphasis on promotion of French Canadians, he had risen in rank with great speed.

I had been an officer cadet when Jadex had commanded the Royal Canadian School of Infantry in the late 1950s. Together with all the other cadets of that time, I retained a deep admiration for him. He had changed the training of infantry officers so that a minimum of time was spent on the parade square and in lectures and the maximum in the field and on weapon ranges. And he was there watching, encouraging and going on the toughest patrol exercises with his "boys."

As soon as possible after listening to Nixon at RMC, I asked General Dextraze how the armed forces could possibly work with a civil servant being responsible for what in effect were military strategies. Jadex replied that when he wanted it, he had access to the very top, meaning if things were really going astray, he would use his prestige and influence to set them straight. I suppose he meant that he had a special relationship with the Prime Minister. At the time, I was still in far too much awe of the old warrior to confirm if this is what he did mean and to follow it up with the obvious question, "Et après vous, mon général?"

Jadex was the last officer with combat experience from the

Second World War to be CDS. When he retired in 1977, to become the Chairman of Canadian National Railways, he was replaced by Admiral Robert Falls. Although originally a naval pilot, the Admiral had never been to war or had any strategic training. He was the quintessential military bureaucrat who, teamed up with the equipment-minded Deputy Minister Nixon, ensured that the human factor in the nation's security was pushed further and further into the background. The two top men were only symptoms of the problem; there were many other reasons why the equipment side of defence was getting priority.

As the defence budget shrank in the 1960s and '70s, equipment also deteriorated. Major weapon systems became obsolete, wore out, and were not replaced. Also, because the quickie war in Europe was thought to be the only thing that we had to prepare for, the war stocks of weapons, ammunition and equipment were happily allowed to be used up. They, too, were not replaced. For these and more ominous reasons, the once thriving defence industry also fell into neglect. By the late '60s, the Canadian Forces were spending the major part of the budget on personnel and on operating costs. So little was being spent on the purchase of new equipment that massive expenses were inevitable.

When at last towards the end of the 1970s the political climate started to change slightly and the military began to receive more money, the obvious deterioration and obsolescence of old weapon systems and the lack of bullets were easier to argue for changing. The army's main battle tank had been designed in the Second World War, the fighter and the maritime patrol aircraft were becoming dated, and by the time that it was the navy's turn, the anti-submarine destroyer escorts would be reaching the end of their useful life. As a result, the proportion of funds spent on personnel, overhead and maintenance were proportionally decreased and more money allocated to capital expenditure.

There were other more subtle reasons for the decision to spend money on equipment. With the civilian public service in ever greater control of the policies of the armed forces, the criterion of success for the Department of National Defence was becoming the same as for all other government ministries: how much money was in the budget? So, to the defence bureaucrats, it did not really matter what the money was to be spent on. If it was allocated to the military, this was victory enough. The money for replacement of hardware was easier to substantiate than for the increase of manpower. More men in uniform would be a far more visible sign of revival of the military, and this was not high on the list of priorities of either the Liberal Pierre Elliott Trudeau, or the Conservative Joe Clark, who briefly replaced him as prime minister. Also, by increasing the budget for equipment, the existing balance between the three components of the forces would be unaffected. Thus capital expenditure was the easiest way for the civil servants to adjudicate the clandestine war of survival among the three services, now being fought under the ubiquitous camouflage of the green uniform.

To the rosy-visioned politicians who saw in the world of the 1970s no threat to our democracy, the advice to re-equip was easier to accept than any plan for putting more young Canadians in uniform. Ostensibly, this was still the time when armed forces were unpopular. Yet we were being pressed to make a better contribution to the defence of North America and Europe. Equipment was the easy answer. Canadian industry was promised spinoffs from the offshore purchases, our allies were pleased with the solution and no extra young Canadians would be asked to don uniforms.

In all this no one asked the obvious question. Was replacing old systems with new ones of the same kind and in approximately the same numbers strategically sound? Were our security requirements so static that we could afford to go on doing the same thing into the twenty-first century? The officer corps, having no capability for strategic thinking did not have any coherent proposals for a change in direction. All that they were interested in was that a good deal be struck among the three services.

First, as the primary and least expensive step, the army would get a replacement for the obsolete Centurion tanks. Following this, the airmen would get replacement maritime patrol aircraft for the ancient Argus and new fighter aircraft for the CF-101 Voodoos and CF-104 Starfighters. Finally the navy, the weakest of the three services, would get desperately needed new ships.

By replacing existing systems, the same ratios and numbers of specialists could be kept in uniform. The forces would stay as they had been and there would be no further cuts in personnel. The carefully structured career progression pyramids would remain and a happy pension could be looked forward to by all those then serving. At a time when the very existence of the military was being questioned, these were pure survival tactics. The officer corps had no confidence in its ability to justify continuation of the armed forces if fundamental questions about policy and strategy began to be asked.

Allied support for the re-equipment policy was automatic, and once given, was in itself used in lieu of strategic planning. It was understood that NATO had practically ordered us to take the direction in which we were heading. Of course, no allied general would dare to criticize supposed Canadian strategies, and as Canada was attempting to maintain and even increase the proportion of its GNP that was spent on defence, the NATO bureaucrats were happy.

It was at this time, in 1978, that an extra commitment was made to Norway on NATO's Northern Flank. This was done without any analysis of whether it could possibly be honoured. Presumably, extra commitments prevented future defence budgets from further cuts. By a strange coincidence, after the Canadian commitment was made, the Chief of Defence Staff, Admiral Falls, instead of retiring, replaced a Norwegian general in the plush and prestigious job of Chairman of NATO's Military Committee in Brussels.

The weapons manufacturers of our allies were more than content with the new policy. Canada did not now have the industrial base to produce the majority of the equipment on the shopping list. Thus huge amounts of money would have to be spent offshore. When eventually it came time to let the contracts for the ships, it appeared as though this, at least, was mainly a Canadian venture. But this too was illusory, for now that the ships are being built, it turns out that we are able to construct only the hulls, which represent only a small portion of the cost. The more expensive detection and weapons systems are mostly of foreign design and manufacture.

Even the maritime patrol aircraft were foreign made. Although de Havilland of Canada proposed building a patrol version of its Dash-7 commercial aeroplane, this aircraft would not have been able to carry out the NATO antisubmarine function. So the old Argus was replaced by a custom-designed Canadian version of the American Orion. Named the Aurora, it was built in the USA to different specifications from the Orion that is used by the US Navy and other allied forces. Since the number of planes we wanted was so small, the cost for each aircraft was considerably greater than it would have been had we simply bought Orions.

Not surprisingly, the industrial offset benefits to Canadian industry were not what they had been cracked up to be. Eventually de Havilland, by then a Crown corporation, had to have massive infusions of taxpayers' money to survive and was finally sold to the American firm of Boeing. Bureaucratic compromise and lack of vision had once again managed to find the solution that was the most damaging to Canadian independence.

By the start of the 1980s, the perception that Canadian defence was in poor shape had begun to reach the public and the politicians responded. In the seven fiscal years since 1981-82, the real increase in defence budgets has never sunk below 2 percent. But this has done nothing to reverse the disarming of Canada.

Since the Second World War, the Canadian military had not only lost any capability for giving direction from the top, it had also frittered away the only solid social base from which it could communicate with the political leadership of the country. The meddling of the militia "Political Colonels" had always been resented by the regular force, and it had often done more harm than good, but it was a once powerful link between the military and the political leadership. By the 1980s even that was mostly gone. In the

Autumn 1980 issue of the *Canadian Defence Quarterly*, Professor Terry Willet, a soldier turned sociologist, summarized a three-year study that he had conducted into the militia:

Units seem to have become virtual non-entities in their communities, and their once prominent civic role has almost disappeared. While there is no evident hostility towards them, ignorance and apathy are marked. The once close relationship between units, civic leaders, and such organizations as the Royal Canadian Legion has weakened, and it is common to find mayors and police chiefs whose contacts with the Militia are confined to occasional visits on formal occasions . . . . . . the Militia is no longer a citizen force in which all sectors of the community are represented. It seems that the prestige of being an officer or senior NCO, even in old-fashioned regiments, has declined greatly since the 'Fifties. It seems also that the Militia has been tailored to suit schoolteachers, minor civil servants and students, as they are the only people who can afford the time to attend long courses and spend upward of twelve days monthly in training. Such demands deter people who are building demanding civilian careers.

Another important link to society, which had been lost since the Second World War, was the army's Canadian Officer's Training Corps and its naval and air force counterparts. All were disbanded in the 1960s. Under the COTC, university undergraduates became officer cadets of the reserve forces and during the long holidays each summer undertook training together with officer cadets of the regular forces. On graduating they became commissioned officers and could serve either with the reserves or with the regular force. Thus for a very small cost, the forces had a ready supply of young officers. At the same time, the civilian academic establishment kept an informal but strong link with the military.

In order not to sever all links between civilian academe and defence and to try to offset the lack of in-house strategic planning in Canada's armed forces, a few centres for strategic studies were started at selected universities. But the tradeoff was not a good one. The COTCs had given practical military training to a wide variety of undergraduates, whereas the new centres are creating graduates with theoretical knowledge, but no basic military grounding. What is called strategic studies is actually a mixture of political science, international relations and economics, with the occasional breath of military history. There is no expertise in the psychology of conflict and Carl von Clausewitz, premier among theorists of war, gathers dust on library shelves, most often in the bowdlerized version.

These civilian institutions cannot provide the strategic thinking which should be done by a General Staff. In order for them to be effective, there would have to be clear leadership from the officer corps on the one hand and financial independence on the other. As it is, direct funding from the Defence Department only makes the academics cautious. They tend to produce studies which they think might be what the bureaucrats want.

In the years following unification, the strategic planning capability of Canada's military — which from Confederation onwards was never properly developed — has been allowed to wither even further. Now officers get posted into senior strategic positions with no previous background or suitable practical experience. A classic example is Major-General Leonard Johnson. A high school graduate, the majority of whose career was spent as a transport pilot and staff officer, he was posted into National Defence Headquarters as the Associate Assistant Deputy Minister, Policy. His next, and last posting, was as Commandant of the National Defence College. He is now much quoted and interviewed as a member of "Generals for Peace."

The last attempt to put strategic planning into the defence establishment in Ottawa had been made during the chaos of unification. The Canadian Forces Headquarters had become the new unified military headquarters of the Defence Department. After the initial unification was finished, it was amalgamated with the small Deputy Minister's cell, to become the hybrid National Defence Headquarters. The civilians who had been on the Deputy Minister's staff and who up till then had duties which consisted mainly of auditing, now became major players in the command and control of the forces.

It was in this new NDHQ that a Directorate of Strategic Policy Planning (DSPP) was established. The Director who headed it was originally a military officer; however, he was under the civilian Chief of Policy Planning, who in turn reported to the civilian Assistant Deputy Minister, Policy. The directorate, manned by a mixture of military officers and civil servants, was to become the monitoring and supervising body for the civilian strategic studies centres.

The directorate never had a chance of becoming a true focal point for strategic planning for several reasons. To start with, although the officers and civil servants posted to it were supposed to have postgraduate degrees in War Studies or a related subject, there was no requirement for a background of experience in strategy or a previous record of strategic publications. Furthermore, very few of its members were combat arms officers. To my knowledge, during its existence there have been only two infantry officers in the directorate.

Even if the properly trained personnel had been available for the Directorate of Strategic Policy Planning, its positioning deep within the policy group of National Defence Headquarters ensured that any suggested strategy would be modified beyond recognition before it came to the decision makers. It had to pass through several layers of senior career bureaucrats who would grind any hard edge from the message to make it politically acceptable.

As a result, no researched professional military strategies could ever reach the elected leaders, only those ideas which the bureaucrats thought that their political masters wanted to hear. Of course a forceful senior officer like Dextraze or Allard, or Currie and McNaughton before them, could develop a personal relationship with the elected leader that bypassed the structure, but this is no substitute for systematic strategic planning. In such a case, the ideas are only from one person, whose prime job is command or administration, and who does not have the time or perhaps the aptitude for thorough research.

The desk officers in the directorate were not encouraged to write the stark truth. Their papers were returned countless times for changes and then, even when the carefully phrased papers passed muster, they usually saw them put into permanent pending files. They therefore would cloak any real message in so many coats of innuendo that no one except an expert in the deciphering of Soviet and Chinese press releases could divine what the original thought had been.

I had the opportunity to experience this sad state of affairs at first hand when in late 1977 I joined DSPP as one of its five desk officers. For the two years that I was there, I was also a member of the Strategic Assessment Team. It, in conjunction with a one-man directorate called Socio-Economic Strategic Planning, with co-operation from the Department of External Affairs, was the group responsible for writing the Strategic Review. This was an annual document which gave a summary of the world from the point of view of military strategy and was made available to other departments.

My job in the directorate and on the Strategic Assessment Team was to assess the latest secret intelligence and open media records and interpret them in terms of strategy for the Department of National Defence. My two chief areas of responsibility were terrorism and the Soviet Union and its allies. I was to write the portions of the annual Strategic Assessment dealing with these subjects as well as write independent "occasional papers" when I felt they were necessary.

The Strategic Assessment was never what it should have been because we were never permitted to suggest any Canadian strategies as a result of our deliberations. And nowhere in the department was there any other group so charged.

The half a dozen officers and civil servants who made up the Strategic Assessment Team were encouraged to write individual "occasional papers" on their subjects of expertise. I started to research the impact of the Soviet Union and the possible consequences of the psychological war and indirect attack on Canadian defence and Western security.

My analysis of the strategic situation of the Soviet Union and the Warsaw Pact countries suggested that terrorism and the indirect attack were among the best options for the Communist powers in the future. How ready was Canada for this form of conflict and what strategies would we have to adopt in order to be better prepared for it in the future? My education in bureaucracy now began. I learned the hard way why our defence policies were so unrelated to what I perceived to be the obvious needs of our security and how difficult any change would be.

The FLQ crisis of 1970 had demonstrated vividly that even for low-intensity operations of the most primitive kind we were desperately short of combat arms soldiers. Now, seven years later, I found that there were still no plans for expanding the infantry and that the few soldiers we had were no longer to be trained for internal security operations. The equipment that had been found wanting during the October Crisis and made available in its aftermath was nearly all gone and was not being replaced or updated.

I discovered that the decision not to train for insurgency warfare had been made for reasons which had nothing to do with strategic analysis or threat assessment. It was a part of the bureaucratic compromise made among the competing services to fit in with the single-minded drive for new major equipment.

Even though the October Crisis of 1970 should have been still fresh in everyone's mind, it was a non-subject at National Defence Headquarters. Planning for possible internal security operations might have entailed the allocation of extra funds from the limited defence budget to the infantry and thus would have risked losing momentum from the capital equipment project whose turn had come — the new fighter aircraft.

Of course a pseudo-strategic rationale had to be found to cover up the absence of real strategic planning and justify the fact that 90 percent of the capital expenditure for the next decade was going to cover what was then widely estimated to be 5 percent of the threat, that of the manned Soviet bomber threatening North America. And this while much more immediate dangers were not being addressed at all.

The whole fake rationale behind this policy posture was never put into one document, but the first, implicit part of it was to deny that there was any non-nuclear threat to Canada. The politicians, the bureaucrats and the press were easily persuaded that Canada was a fireproof house from everything except a full-scale nuclear exchange between the superpowers. Next it was said that internal security operations were not the proper job of the army but should be left to the police. The Solicitor General's Department and the RCMP had even less strategic analysis and planning capability than the Defence Department. There was no co-ordination between the two departments and no clear line had been drawn to indicate where internal security ended and military operations began.

The last part of the rationalization was still being written in 1978 in a military planning directorate with no connection with the strategic directorate. The author was a smart young engineering major with no infantry experience. The argument was that the army should only be used as a force of last resort. But because it was the last resort, once committed, it had to conclusively win. For such decisive action it would operate with essentially the same deadly weapons and tactics designed for its NATO role; i.e., for a major conventional war. Its lack of men would be made up by weight of firepower and offensive tactics. All the principles of conventional war would apply: maintenance of the aim, surprise, economy of effort and, above all, concentration of force. Hit them "fustest with the mostest" would be the order of the day. This force of last resort policy neatly took care of the fact that there were not sufficient infantrymen in the forces to maintain security in a future crisis and that there was no time or equipment to train even those we did have.

It also took away from the military the ability for graduated response, essential not only in internal security operations, but also in all warfare. If you can only strike at the high end of the continuum of conflict, the war may be lost in the process of winning the immediate battle. The same inflexibility was the Achilles heel in the American "trip wire" concept of the 1950s and the Mutual Assured Destruction of the 1960s and '70s. Now, as I listened to the bureaucratic reasoning for the new policy, I found the whole process devoid of strategic thinking or of an understanding of the principles of war. I became convinced that Canada was building a similar potentially fatal flaw into its defence policies. The Canadian military was being condemned to inaction or disaster in any internal security operation of the future.

There was no input from our directorate into these policies of "last resort" and "win at all costs." Their strategic justification came from a book written about the FLQ crisis by the respected military commentator, John Gellner. The book, called *Bayonets in the Streets*, clearly revealed that the author was not a soldier, and had no practical understanding of internal security operations and little of Canadian police structures. (Gellner, an international lawyer by training, had in fact been a decorated wartime RCAF bomber pilot.)

The philosophy of *Bayonets in the Streets* was based on the fact that Gellner, like the French Baron de Jomini 200 years earlier, believed that internal security operations were distasteful for soldiers and could ruin good armies. But instead of analyzing the problem and suggesting how the army should cope, as had de Jomini, Gellner's solution was for the military to simply stay clear of such war.

In *Bayonets in the Streets* Gellner compares British and French methods of handling internal security. The British use of troops much earlier in a situation than the French he ascribed purely to false economy. Apparently the British failed to provide sufficient police forces for these emergencies because of cost, and therefore the army had to be brought in at a comparatively early stage. The French were lauded for having much more extensive centralized police forces, including special police battalions trained and maintained exclusively for internal security duties.

No matter what the reason for the differences between the British and the French approach to internal security, the different effects are noticeable to anyone who has any knowledge of the two societies. The British policing system makes for far less pervasive police powers and presence, whereas France is probably the most heavily policed of all the major democracies.

There is a basic difference between the philosophy of a soldier and a policeman. The soldier's ethos is to defend his country against the enemy from without, the policeman is trained to look for the enemy within. The army can train without having to justify its existence by finding a specific enemy of the moment. Therefore the social implications of having greater numbers of police than short-term soldiers are great and can be seen in restrictions of personal freedom.

John Gellner of course did not suspect that his book would be used to justify policy. When I mentioned to him years later that it had been so used, he bristled at the idea. The book, he said, was intended only as part of a strategic debate. Unfortunately, in Canada there is no debate. Since his book was the only one around and since his ideas suited the decision that had already been made, it served in lieu of strategic planning.

Even had the philosophical justification been sound, the policy did not make sense. The Canadian system with its three levels of policing does not lend itself to the French example. As a result, apart from a small increase in strength for the Royal Canadian Mounted Police after the troubles of 1970, nothing much was done to prepare Canada for future insurrection.

Canadians have little fear that their country will become a police state. However, in the intervening years since that silly, dismal October, the army had done away with all centrally scheduled and controlled internal security training and had bought no new equipment appropriate to such a task. Those officers and non-commissioned officers who had training and experience in this highly specialized form of warfare had mostly passed out of active soldiering in infantry battalions.

This was the state of affairs which I encountered as I was preparing to write a background paper on internal security in the early days of 1978. In order to do it properly, it seemed like a good idea to go to Northern Ireland, where British troops had been fighting a low-intensity war for twelve years.

Internal security operations do not require too much expensive equipment, but if such operations are to succeed, large numbers of basic combat soldiers are needed. The Ulster problem had put an intolerable strain on the resources of the British regular army. I knew that they had used as many as eleven battalions in the city of Belfast alone, which is two more than the total number of battalions in Canada's regular force. What could Canada learn from the situation?

My request for an Ulster visit was denied. The notion that there had to be a practical core of experience or direct observation as a basis for the strategic planning process, had disappeared from Ottawa. Fortunately, I was sent to a Foreign Office conference in England and while there I took some leave. While on leave, some friends in the British Army, arranged for me to conduct a lightning inspection of the troubled province. When I returned to Canada, I was able to complete my paper on low-intensity war.

I then concluded that the possibilities of internal security operations in Canada had to be put into the context of the superpower struggle and the state of affairs in our own forces. So I talked with as many officers and civil servants with inside information as I could, both in the Department of National Defence and the Department of the Solicitor General. Drawing on this information, I wrote a draft of Strategic Assessment Team Occasional Paper, 2/78, "Crisis in Canadian Defence." Throughout, I kept checking with Major-General Dan Loomis, who although not in my direct chain of command, was then the senior infantry officer in the Policy Branch of the Department of National Defence and incidentally had been the other infantry officer to pass through DSSP, as its original director.

When I was finished I circulated some twenty drafts of the paper around my directorate and to other senior officers whose judgement I valued in National Defence Headquarters and in the field. After incorporating criticism, comments and suggestions, in December of 1978 I put out the final edition, and having made it unclassified in order to give it the widest circulation, spread it to as many officers in the forces as I could. I then handed the paper to every senior member of a conference at Mobile Command in Montreal. This conference was attended by 90 percent of the army generals then serving. Not a single one ever acknowledged that he had read the paper. My gallant director, Captain Bernard Thillaye, a wartime naval officer, who together with his deputy Lieutenant-Colonel Don MacNamara, had encouraged the writing of the paper, passed the finished product to his civilian superior, the Chief of Policy Planning. And then, nothing.

Fearing that this would happen, I had used only publicly available knowledge in writing the document and given it an "Unclassified" security classification. Even so, I could not give a copy directly to the press without going to jail, or give one to the Minister without being instantly posted to Yellowknife as the butterfly control officer.

Many of the military officers up to the rank of colonel who had read the paper and had agreed with my summary of our defence problems, had made extra copies for further distribution. I could only hope that one such copy might be read by someone with sufficient influence to turn the criticism into positive action. In the end Douglas Fisher did two thoughtful, helpful columns in the *Toronto Sun*, and the CBC did a dramatic "leaked document" piece which came very close to getting me court-martialled under the Official Secrets Act. And then silence again.

Meanwhile the government was working up to a decision that would eventually cost the taxpayer some $10 billion. It was 1978 and the replacement of the existing fighter aircraft was about to be made. Both the Voodoo, which was used in Canada in the interceptor role, and the Starfighter, used in Europe as a strike and low-level photo reconnaissance aircraft, were reaching the end of their useful life.

There were any number of other options which should have been examined, including a complete renegotiation of our NATO commitments. None were. Instead, we made the new commitment to the Northern Flank of NATO for a Brigade Group that would deploy to Norway on a first priority basis. I wrote a memo protesting this decision as well, but this time there was no way of making the problem public without going to jail, for it exposed the fact that the commitment could not be met.

Once it was announced that the new fighter would be bought, the pressure for the government to keep to its decision became very strong as all the contending foreign manufacturers started pushing their wares. In the end the air force project management team recommended that two contenders fit our specifications best, the General Dynamics F-16 and the McDonnell Douglas F-18 Hornet. The final choice, the F-18 Hornet was made in 1979 during the short time that Joe Clark and his Conservatives were in power. But as with the Aurora, the last aircraft to be purchased, it was not to be an off the shelf buy. The original F-18 was redesigned to fit both the NATO role in Europe and the NORAD task in Canada. (In the end it became the most expensive fighter aircraft in the world, at around fifty million dollars per plane.) All that remained was to let the contract.

Many people inside the bureaucracy had watched helplessly as the decision was made and knew that it would be disastrous. My boss Bernard Thillaye, the Director of Strategic Policy Planning, wrote a desperate memorandum to his superiors, outlining the lack of strategic planning in the upcoming decision. I wrote a covering memo elaborating on the theme. As usual, there was only thundering silence in response.

Once again, on purpose, I failed to give my memo a security classification, but this time there was a very close deadline for the information to reach the Minister. So I worked out a scheme to lessen my chances of being court-martialled but still ensure that the Minister saw how serious the situation was. I leaked the memo to Peter Ward, an Ottawa freelance writer who understood the situation. Peter has attempted for longer than anyone in Canada to be an independent, full-time defence correspondent. He was also then a reserve naval officer, still on the supplementary reserve list. As a regular officer, I would have been guilty under the Official Secrets Act if I gave even an unclassified memo to the press, but perhaps I could get away with talking to an officer on the supplementary reserve, who also happened to be a journalist. Peter was less liable to go to jail than I was, or so he hoped. And we agreed that the situation warranted some risk.

Peter phoned The Honourable Allan McKinnon, the Minister of National Defence of the day, and asked him if he was aware of the concern of the strategists within the department about the wisdom of committing ourselves to the F-18 Hornet. When the Minister said that this was nonsense, Peter mentioned the memorandum.

Allan McKinnon had won a Military Cross during the Second World War and retired from the regular army as major. He is a man of honour and was deeply concerned with his new portfolio. He now got very angry with Peter and told him that it was impossible that a memo of such importance could exist in the system without it being brought to his attention. When Peter insisted that the memo did in fact exist and that he had seen it, McKinnon told him that he would find out very quickly if this was the truth. When the Minister phoned back several hours later he assured Peter that there was no memo.

Peter then went to the Minister and showed him a photocopy of the unclassified memo. Still no action. So, putting on his journalist hat, Peter wrote up the whole affair in an article which was published in the *Globe and Mail*. The article elicited absolutely no reaction from the rest of the press or the great Canadian public.

I then wrote a private letter to the Hon. Walter Baker, who was the Deputy Prime Minister and my Member of Parliament, and dropped it through the letter box of his home, stating in it who I was and why I felt compelled to write. Again, I received not even an acknowledgement. As one last attempt, I had a private talk with Arthur Mathewson, the Chief of Policy Planning. He said that it was far too late to do anything.

The decision to purchase the aircraft was duly made. Shortly after, the Conservative Government of Joe Clark was defeated and the Liberals continued with the policy which they had started before their brief sojourn in the political wilderness.

Neither Peter nor I went to jail, but a short time later I was summoned to the Director General under whom our directorate fell. I was told that I was to be posted from Ottawa to some as yet undetermined place. Until I left, I was not to use the telephone, write anything, or talk to anyone. However, I did have to come to work.

Later, many of the civilian and military bureaucrats in the long, one-way channel of communications between the Directorate of Strategic Policy Planning and the elected government were promoted. Many of them went to their just rewards as consultants, brokers between the weapon manufacturers and the government. The officer who was the new Fighter Aircraft Project Manager has since had three promotions and is the current Chief of Defence Staff.

Nothing much has changed since I left Ottawa. There is still no machinery to ensure that strategic advice reaches our elected leaders. In 1987, Canada is a virtually demilitarized state in a world where all levels of conflict are constantly raging. In the event of any kind of attack on our country, or any raised level of demand on our forces in Europe, our military would be unable to respond. This was graphically demonstrated by the October Crisis of 1970. Nearly a decade after making the NATO commitment to Norway, we are about to cancel it, in tacit acknowledgement that we have bitten off far more than we can chew. In the process of cancelling the commitment, we are once more dealing a psychological blow to the unity of the Western alliance as well as to the morale of the weakened Canadian Forces themselves.

# CHAPTER ELEVEN

# Ceremonies of Innocence: Two Cases of Canada Disarmed

*We must carry out political instruction directed toward the resurrection of our people (stimulate the soldiers' national consciousness, their patriotism, and their love for the people and for the masses) and to see to it that every officer and soldier in a guerrilla unit understands not only the national tasks for which he is responsible but also the necessity of fighting in defense of our state.*

Mao Tse-tung: *Basic Tactics*

The 1987 White Paper on Defence tacitly admits that Canada's forces are bankrupt and unable to meet their NATO commitments. No matter how good the individual soldiers are, no matter how well trained the infantry battalions and fighter squadrons, we can no longer add to the strength of our allies. Without restructuring our forces and renegotiating our part in the Western alliance, common action is nothing more than an empty promise.

Fortunately, the alliance of the Soviet Union is in disarray, while our own larger partners such as the USA, West Germany and Britain have lately become more confident. This gives Canada a breathing space. But before we can again become effective participants in the defence of the West, we must ensure our own security.

In the years since unification, there have been numerous signs that Canada was unable to defend itself from any form of attack at any level in the continuum of conflict. Should we be attacked directly, we would at least have the help of our giant neighbour, with all the penalties to our independence which that entails. However, only we can defend ourselves against the indirect attack which I believe is today's greatest threat to Canadian security.

This chapter explores two cases of indirect attack in detail. The first, known as the October Crisis of 1970, was a local, premature and unexploited act of terrorism. It failed, but demonstrated clearly how ill equipped our military was in the event that the civil power required help to retain social order. It is very fortunate that the "apprehended insurrection" of 1970 was more imagined than real. We learned nothing and failed to capitalize from the lessons.

The second, which I call the November Happening of 1986, was a political attack mounted by an opinion-manipulating fifth column within our system. It aimed to change the direction of our defence policies and pull us out of NATO. Because it was ill timed and did not attract the support which it was supposed to it too failed and passed in a moment. But unless we learn from its lessons, we may fail to get a third chance.

CASE 1:

At 08:15 hours on October 5, 1970, James "Jasper" Cross, the British Trade Commissioner in Montreal, was kidnapped by members of the "Liberation" cell of the Front de libération du Québec (FLQ) from his residence on Redpath Crescent in Westmount. At 18:15 hours, October 10, 1970, the "Chenier" cell of the FLQ kidnapped a Quebec provincial cabinet minister, Pierre Laporte, from outside his home in the Montreal suburb of St. Lambert. The following morning the Director of the Quebec Provincial Police told his military opposite number that he was recommending that the Provincial Cabinet request the deployment of troops "in aid of the civil power." A state of apprehended "Armed Insurrection" was declared, and the Federal Government of Pierre Trudeau put into effect the Emergency War Measures Act. Without prior planning or preparation, Operation Ginger and Operation Essay were initiated. "Ginger" was the code name for the deployment of troops under the federal power in the National Capital Region, "Essay" for the larger operation under control of the provincial authority in Quebec.

A few days later paratroopers who had deployed from Edmonton, boarded Huey helicopters at St. Hubert near Montreal. After a short flight across the predawn Laurentian skyline, the helicopters landed and the troopers leapt out, their FN semi-automatic rifles loaded with live ammunition at the ready. Ducking under the still-whirling rotors, they ran to surround a lone farm. A waiting group of Quebec provincial policemen broke down the door of the farmhouse and rushed inside. As they swept through the house, the old farmer and his wife jumped from bed, terrified. There was no one else in the farmhouse.

In the ensuing days, similar scenes were repeated time and again. At one such predawn raid, another group of soldiers isolated a shop in downtown Montreal and as the armed police burst through the door, they were greeted by the raucous squawks of rudely awakened parrots and the squeals of a frightened monkey. This was the raid on Louis' pet shop, destined to become a legend in the unwritten annals of the Canadian Airborne Regiment.

In the search for Pierre Laporte and Jasper Cross, thousands of houses, farms, factories, apartment buildings and nightclubs were cordoned off by troops and searched by the police. Laporte was eventually found dead in the trunk of an abandoned car and his killers were later captured. The other terrorist cell released Cross in exchange for safe passage to Cuba. With that the "Oktoberfest" of 1970 was over. Its nickname resulted from the fact that Canadian soldiers were more familiar with autumn deployment in Germany during annual NATO exercises, than putting down apprehended insurrections at home.

Canadians, when they remember at all, regard the events in Quebec during the autumn of 1970 as an isolated aberration. But terrorism knows no boundaries and can spread very quickly. During the emergency in Canada, there were threats against the military attaché in Paris and bomb scares at the High Commission in London. As with all revolutionary violence, there was a rift in our society which was being exploited by the same visionary malcontents with the same ideological background and training. And there were other nations prepared to fish in troubled waters. Into the unrippled backwater of Canadian complacency came the sudden chilly squall which often precedes a storm.

There were many lessons to be learned from 1970. While the nightmare of armed revolution disappeared with the end of the emergency, the problems of the French-English schism in Canada remained. As usual, the troops saw and reported the military weaknesses which became apparent as the operation unfolded, while the senior officers, the politicians and the bureaucrats seem only to remember the relatively happy ending.

The weaknesses were obvious to those on the scene, but in true bureaucratic fashion, the higher that the message got, the more muted was the criticism. Had just one of our other military commitments been called, such as deploying the battalion dedicated to Norway in the event of heightened tension on NATO's Northern Flank, we would have been bankrupt. The reserves were too weak to take up the slack; there were no means of producing reinforcements.

Such added trouble would not even have had to be on the East/West axis. A disturbance among NATO allies would have been quite sufficient. Had the Turkish invasion of Cyprus taken place coincidentally with Oktoberfest, instead of three and a half years later, we would have been unable to send even the modest reinforcements needed for a UN situation which had gone wrong.

The after-action reports only hinted that "the operations were extremely costly in terms of manpower." And in the corridors of power was heard only the sound of self-applause, while the soldiers went back to their barracks and married quarters in Gagetown, Petawawa, Val Cartier, Winnipeg, Calgary and Edmonton and joked about Louis the angry pet shop owner and his disturbed livestock. They wrote off their autumn in *la belle province* as just another snafu.

In the end there was no expansion of the regular infantry corps and the militia were still deemed unusable for internal security operations. Although the regular army trained for low-intensity operations for a while and a small amount of equipment was made available for this task, this soon stopped and it was decided that this was not a job for soldiers. The RCMP got a slight increase in manpower instead.

A major reason why the Federal Government emerged relatively unscathed in Quebec was because the Canadian legal apparatus for the use of troops in aid of the civil power is an excellent tool for such an emergency. Unlike the state-controlled National Guard in the USA, the Canadian provinces do not have their own military forces. For internal security operations in Canada, federal regular and reserve troops can be deployed at the request of the provincial authorities and legally become provincial troops for the duration of the operation.

In 1970, the soldiers guarding installations and politicians in Ottawa remained under federal control, but the majority of troops were in Quebec under the direct control of the Quebec government. Their titular allegiance to the Crown now went through the Lieutenant Governor of Quebec rather than directly through the Governor General of Canada. There is a clever clause in this form of arrangement, guaranteeing federal retention of control. Although the Chief of the Defence Staff must provide troops when a provincial government requests them, it is his decision, subject to Federal Government direction, how many men and resources will be allocated to the task. Thus if the provincial authority needs soldiers for something of which the Federal Government disapproves, instead of providing resources appropriate to the task, they could send a military band.

This simple but sophisticated legislation not only makes the best use of resources, in that the provincial authorities do not have to maintain their own back-up for aiding the civil power, but more importantly, it puts the troops in the hands of the local government. This permits more sensitive handling of the issue and also leaves the senior power less open to propaganda attacks. In 1970, no matter how hard the mud was flung at the Federal Government, little of it stuck, as the handling of the emergency in Quebec remained in Quebecois hands.

The other good things about the handling of the FLQ Crisis can, unfortunately, be said very briefly. The troops were deployed with speed and efficiency. Soldiers from Val Cartier were in Montreal one hour and twenty minutes from the time that Jerome Choquette, the Quebec Minister of Justice, sent a formal request to Ottawa for military aid. During the six weeks that most of the soldiers spent on the operation, there was not one serious incident involving the public. The still high discipline of the troops showed. They remained good-tempered and polite despite the fact that during the six-week operation they worked around the clock and were subjected to more than the usual irritations of unnecessary foul-ups.

Although the duty itself was not dangerous or particularly strenuous, the hardships were considerable. For example, the soldiers of the 1st Battalion of the Royal Canadian Regiment had just rotated from Cyprus after six months away from home, and were immediately committed to Operation Ginger in Ottawa, some without even seeing their families.

The faults in the handling of the episode were numerous and could have led to major disasters if there had been a skilled enemy. Fortunately, the wielders of violence, no matter how many supporters they had, were only an undisciplined, inept handful. They remained isolated and ineffectual.

Why did the whole episode catch Canada flat-footed? To start with, the tenor of the times had made no impression on military bureaucrats. The majority of soldiers had little training in internal security operations and techniques. Although the disaster at Kent State University, where Ohio National Guardsmen panicked and opened fire on demonstrating students, was still a very recent memory, and despite what was then happening in Northern Ireland, the Canadian Forces were unprepared.

There were pamphlets for riot drills, but they were replicas of British training manuals dating back to the Second World War. The methods in them had been developed in the heyday of empire when rioting was something associated with unruly natives. The line drawings in the pamphlets showed troops in shorts using shields woven from rattan. The drill was to beat their batons against their basket shields as they advanced in step and in precise formation. Loud noises and steady drill were sufficient to scare unorganized natives in faraway countries in days when propaganda could be better controlled. Before the days of television, the violence could be quickly escalated and the odd protester shot "pour l'encouragement de les autres" without immediately providing a winning propaganda weapon to the other side.

This form of simple "aid to the civil power," known then as "wog bashing," had also worked well enough in its day even in Canada, usually to break up what would now be regarded as legitimate strikes. Usually it was enough to call out the militia to restore order. In many instances, the young men most likely to cause their employers trouble were also in the militia and their sudden appearance in uniform left the strikers without leaders.

But not even the outdated drill from the old Imperial pamphlets was being taught to Canadian regular or militia troops prior to the FLQ Crisis. Our combat arms troops were preparing to fight a high-intensity war that could turn nuclear. The location of this war was invariably Europe, where they would be part of a larger NATO force. In the event of such a war, someone else would tell us what to do.

Fortunately many of the infantry officers and soldiers had experience of peacekeeping operations and thus they were familiar with the concept of minimum use of power, non-violent confrontation and the defusing of nasty situations by good humour and steadiness. It was this unplanned benefit of peacekeeping, as well as the fact that there was no concerted exploitation of the situation by the Soviet Union or its Cuban surrogate, that saved us in 1970.

Even the best troops in the world, if untrained and not properly led for internal security operations, can turn a small insurrection into a civil war. Most of the main principles of war, by which all officers plan their actions, have totally different applications in internal security operations. Selection of the aim, offensive action, concentration of force, economy of effort and surprise are of the utmost importance in all military operations, but they mean very different things in the two types of conflict. Without proper retraining from one form of war to the other, this can spell disaster.

According to the principle of offensive action, one attacks whenever possible. This way the enemy is kept off balance and is unable to launch an attack of his own. But such use of offensive action during an internal security operation would lead to disaster, especially if done without proper knowledge of what the enemy intentions were.

Concentration of force, surprise and offensive action all combine to make for the type of thinking which dictates to strike first with maximum effect. While this is very good practice in open warfare, it is the very antithesis of internal security operations where the terrorists have the initiative. As their tactics change, the defending troops have to constantly keep updating their own response. In a democracy, internal security operations short of civil war cannot end in a military victory, only a political solution.

Therefore the principle of offensive action is replaced by a principle which Brigadier Maurice Tugwell, a leading authority on low-intensity operations, calls contact. By staying in contact at all times, knowledge of the enemy is obtained and processed by the intelligence apparatus of a military organization.

The Canadian Forces have little experience or knowledge of intelligence operations in low-intensity conflict situations. Intelligence, or the gathering, collating and disseminating of knowledge about the enemy and his intentions in order to forecast his actions, is a very different matter in conventional war. The only recent experience of low-intensity operations that Canadians have is in peacekeeping. But even having the intelligence parts of the staff system in place is specifically prohibited in most peacekeeping operations. Although intelligence gathering is still carried out, it goes under a different name and is far more low key than in other operational situations.

It is very dangerous for local police to be involved in political intelligence. In Canada this function was carried out by the RCMP and led to great attacks on that organization in the years following the crisis. It is now the purview of the Canadian Intelligence Service and remains a very vulnerable chink in our defences. Sophisticated, experienced use of intelligence was another of our great deficiencies in 1970.

There were also organizational lessons that should have been learned from the FLQ incident. For one thing the unification of the forces, which had recently come into effect, was not working. Putting everybody into the same uniforms did not make for operational efficiency nor for unified action.

For example, the managers of the air force had forced their own preferred method of control on the unified whole. This was called functional command. It made for a certain centralized efficiency and lack of duplication by having specialists control their speciality regardless of geographic location. For instance, a senior transport specialist would be responsible for the running of transport units everywhere and the local commanders would request and receive transport as a "service."

This loss of control was anathema to the combat troop commanders who insist on controlling everything within their geographic area of responsibility. The functional command system meant that there were troops carrying out actions of which the local commanders were not appraised. This meant that one unit would be given the duty of guarding vulnerable points, while another would be responsible for providing protection to important people. Into this would come yet a third unit responsible for providing cordons for the police when a search was in progress. The subsequent loss of control made commanders very nervous.

But above all, there simply were not enough combat arms troops to handle even this minor Canadian emergency. In 1970, practically the entire field army was employed on Operations Ginger and Essay. These involved the National Capital area, Quebec City and the Montreal area; the rest of the country was denuded of troops. Although the battalion that had just been rotated to Cyprus was not pulled home, or the troops from Europe, the returning UN battalion went straight into the operation. The cupboard was bare.

Essential courses at the combat arms school had to be terminated and the students returned to their units. The army simply stopped doing anything else for the six weeks duration of the emergency. Yet not a shot was fired, the only casualty being a soldier whose submachine gun accidentally discharged and killed him as he jumped off a truck.

What would have happened if instead of a dozen amateurs there had been even a hundred well-trained and organized terrorists? At that time the British Army had eleven battalions of infantry operating in Belfast alone and the hard core provisional IRA did not number more than 250.

In the spring of 1971, less than six months after the October Crisis, I went to St. Jean, Quebec, on an intensive French course. One evening, I attended the showing of a separatist movie with one of my instructors, who was both a Vandoo officer and a devoted *indépendantiste*. Afterwards, over a beer, there was a discussion with the director of the film.

It was obvious that these people, who were overwhelmingly separatist, were not cowed by the events of the previous fall. Nor were they particularly angry at the government's reaction to the outbreak of terrorism. After half a dozen beers, I politely declined senior rank in the future army of Quebec and we went home singing "Alouette" through the warm spring night. The whole thing once again seemed to be on the level of a silly student prank.

Three and a half years later I attended another French course in St. Jean. By then the events of 1970, as interpreted by separatist intellectuals and artists, had become the official mythology. We were subjected to a stream of songs and articles about how freedom was crushed in Quebec by the jackbooted storm troopers of the fascist Trudeau. When the pendulum of Quebec politics swings again in the nationalist direction, the 1970 Oktoberfest will provide a rich historical lode to exploit.

Strangely enough, my fellow military students on the course did not object to this obvious propaganda, some of which was being used to teach us French. They did not seem to make the connection between themselves and the evil oppressors so vilified in the blood-stirring songs of Pauline Julien and other passionate Quebecois artists. Equally bizarre was the equanimity with which the separatist teachers happily cashed their federal pay cheques and conscientiously taught their oppressors French. Some of the best teachers, who also became my good friends, were the most separatist in their sentiments. In such an atmosphere, it takes an effort to remember that games can turn nasty and civil war make brother kill brother.

The FLQ's terrorism was premature and badly organized. There was no "armed insurrection" and, because of faulty intelligence, the provincial and federal governments overreacted. However, because the response was firm and prompt, there was no bloodshed and a rapid restoration of freedom. The terrorism which started the whole business did not spread and was effectively squelched before there was time for the Soviets or their Cuban agents to exploit it.

Fortunately for Canada and the Western alliance, the USSR was not then prepared to support an insurgency movement on the North American continent. Had the FLQ been as successful in direct action as they were in gaining passive support among the Quebec intellectuals, the situation might have evolved very differently. Just as the success of the Sandinistas in 1979 was the signal for the start of renewed support for Communist revolution in Central and South America, the Soviets, through their Cuban surrogates might have exploited success in Quebec in 1970.

CASE 2:

In November of 1986 there occurred a series of events which when viewed together point to a major concerted effort at influencing the defence policies of the Federal Government. The aim seems to have been to pull Canada out of NATO and cause a major crisis in the Western alliance. The psychological preparation for this had been evident for the past several years, but the overt, mass appeal started with the early fall, prime time showing of the National Film Board series "Defence of Canada" on the CBC television network.

The film's co-author/narrator Gwynne Dyer and co-author/ director, Tina Viljoen, cast doubt on the value of Canada's sacrifice in past wars with the theme that these conflicts had nothing to do with Canada. The historical perspective they took was that in the long term nothing was solved even in Europe by the World Wars and Canada was unwise to participate at all. The only sensible future option, they argued, is for Canada to be concerned solely with its own sovereignty. Accordingly, they advocated that Canada become neutral and extricate itself from NATO and NORAD. In the NFB series, the economic implications of neutrality were played down and the inevitable psychological damage to the cause of democracy was not mentioned. Throughout, a moral equivalence between democracy and totalitarianism was taken for granted. Finland was touted as the model for Canada to follow with no mention of the price the Finns continue to pay for their precarious independence from the Soviet Union.

A few weeks after the airing of "Defence of Canada," on the weekend preceding Remembrance Day, there was a conference in Edmonton called "The True North Strong and Free?" sponsored by the Council of Canadians and the Edmonton Chapter of the Physicians for Social Responsibility. It was attended by over five thousand people as well as most of the best-known figures in the Canadian anti-defence and peace movements. Trudeau himself was advertised as one of the panelists, although in the end he did not show up.

Of the twenty-seven listed speakers, debaters and moderators, only one strategist at all critical of the peace movement was invited. To give an appearance of balance, presentations were made by members of the Department of National Defence and External Affairs. However, in keeping with existing policies and so as not to cause a confrontation in the one-sided atmosphere of the conference, the main Defence Department speech did not even mention the Soviet Union as a threat. A resolution passed at this "public inquiry" called for making Canada a neutral country. Delegates also urged the government to make the entire country a nuclear weapons free zone and then uttered the ritual denunciation of the American Strategic Defense Initiative.

Next came Remembrance Day, when the theme that past sacrifice was in vain and future resistance pointless was echoed by peace activists across the country. Members of an organization called Veterans Against Nuclear Arms (VANA) wore white berets instead of the traditional dark blue of the Royal Canadian Legion. The white colour of the berets symbolized the spirit of surrender and thereby corrupted the very meaning of Remembrance. This was a similar tactic to that which was taken in Britain. There, large numbers of white poppies were introduced at the ceremonies by avowed pacifists in order to counter the traditional red poppies of sacrifice.

The Toronto branch of VANA is a good example of how a handful of dedicated activists with their own aims can infiltrate an organization and maintain the party line which the unsuspecting majority then follow. Four of the five members of the executive are listed by the Commission of Election Contributions and Expenses as having made donations to the Communist Party of Canada. While this in itself is not proof of membership and while many members are not financial contributors and although it is totally out of fashion with the main line media to mention communist connections, they are as important as ever. For the party always has been and remains one of the most effective conduits for the indirect attack against the democracies.

Not everyone can join the communist party, sympathizers are carefully vetted and once in, subject to very tight discipline. Unlike the members of democratic parties, the communists will take up and change careers, change location all on orders of the party. The career of one VANA warrior illustrates how much influence such dedication can wield, over long periods of time and in different areas of the struggle.

Ray Stevenson, now sixty-seven, "communist poet and writer" was the Northern Ontario organizer of the Labour Progressive Party (the name under which the Communist Party was running candidates during this period). He told the *Toronto Telegram* in 1949: "Our motto is 'get them young and then you have them for keeps.' Communism is the coming thing. We have at least 70 groups here in the north..." As Educational Officer in Camp Borden between 1944 and 1946, he taught "World Affairs" to the troops at the Armoured Corps School. After the war he ran unsuccessfully in the Federal Election as a Popular Labour Front candidate in Timmins where he was an executive board member of the Mine, Mill and Smelters Union. In 1978 he was on the secretariat of the World Peace Council and in that capacity moved to Helsinki in 1979. He came back to Canada in time to help run the eighties peace campaign. In December 1981 he was the guest speaker at a public meeting of the Toronto Association for Peace, a branch of the World Peace Council and the organization with which the Canadian Peace Congress got the eighties peace campaign going in Canada. In 1982 he is listed variously as the vice-president and secretary of the Canadian Peace Congress, the local affiliate of the World Peace Council. A frequent visitor to Moscow, he appears at all peace rallies and left-wing demonstrations at Toronto City Hall and the Toronto Board of Education in his white VANA beret.

The month of November ended with a national policy conference of the federal Liberal Party during which the membership resolved to make Canada a Nuclear Weapons Free Zone and to review our continued membership in the Western alliance. Although the Liberal Leader of the Opposition did not join in the clamour, it was led by two other past cabinet ministers, who, from their past access to classified information, must certainly have known of the dangers inherent in a neutral Canada.

Throughout November and the period leading up to it, there were stories in the media of the threat to our sovereignty in the Arctic and of the government's desire to be able to deal with it. A large new icebreaker was scheduled for production. The threat, which the great majority of military strategists agree is largely bogus, was supposedly coming mostly from the USA. The Canadian Institute for International Peace and Security released a major study which suggested the mining of our arctic waters. All this was taking place just before Brian Mulroney's government's first White Paper on Defence was due to be released.

The release of the White Paper was postponed and public opinion polls showed that there was a solid majority of Canadians who were in favour of continued membership in the alliance. The Potemkin illusion had passed, but not the danger. In order to understand the significance of the November Happening of 1986, one must go back sixteen years to the October Crisis.

After 1970, with the demise of the FLQ, subversion faded in Quebec. The main effort to split the province from Canada was transferred to the legitimate political arena, with the founding and eventual election of the Parti Québécois. Following this, and triggered in part by the final fall of South Vietnam in 1975, came a regrouping of the anti-establishment forces in the West. This was accompanied by the gradual start of a psychological reawakening of the will to win by the silent majority, first in America and then in the rest of the alliance. The surface manifestation of this was the election and domestic popularity of Ronald Reagan and Margaret Thatcher as well as the bold military initiatives in Grenada and the Falklands. On a more subjective level, it was felt by every NATO soldier wearing a uniform in public.

In the late 1970s, with the Soviets' development of their theatre nuclear weapon, the SS-20, they knew that the Western Allies would inevitably reply in kind with some form of European theatre weapons of their own. Therefore, in conjunction with the Kremlin's deployment of the SS-20s, the Soviet International Department, launched its peace offensive for the '80s. This new drive, co-ordinated by the Helsinki-based World Peace Council, signalled the reawakening of the grass-roots level attack on Western defences. This attack targeted the same groups in Canada as in the rest of the alliance: minorities, schools, universities, churches, women, unions and local governments. The tactics used in Canada were tailored to special local conditions.

Canadians were less concerned about defence matters and more oblivious of the threat than their European allies, but also less frightened of the Soviets and still opposed to pacifism and unilateral disarmament. Therefore, the measures advocated by the Canadian peace movement appeared fair on the surface and seemed only to aim at the mutual reduction in armaments which is universally desired. But when the peace movement was analyzed beyond its slogans and bumper stickers, its anti-alliance and unilateralist angle could always be found. This, however, was not noticed by the majority of the well-meaning people who joined the peace organizations. During this period, most peace activists, when publicly pressed, vigorously denied charges that they wanted Canada out of NATO. Meanwhile, with the help of many of the thousands of draft dodgers and deserters who had streamed into Canada during the Vietnam era, the activists exploited that perennial Canadian issue, anti-Americanism.

The federal political parties and the bureaucracy, as well as municipal governments and non-governmental institutions, mostly offered little resistance. So in some areas the campaign turned more blatantly unilateralist and pacifist. One of the campaign's more remarkable successes was the United Church of Canada, which issued a manifesto as part of its official policy, urging Canadians to: "reject the false gods of national security . . . and . . . the system of false values, which would lead us to believe that defence of possessions, territories or lifestyles is worth the sacrifice of human life."

One of the thinly disguised unilateral disarmament measures adopted by some non-governmental organizations and many local jurisdictions was the Nuclear Weapons Free Zone. This seemingly innocuous idea first surfaced from behind the Iron Curtain over thirty years ago. Initially, some international agreements were reached, such as making Antarctica and space nuclear free, but the main idea was for areas and governments to declare themselves either as being free of nuclear weapons, or, more drastically, free of all nuclear technology. Small units, sometimes even families and neighbourhoods, would declare themselves as nuclear free zones and then link up to make larger zones, thus eventually pushing the clock back and making the world once again free of the threat of nuclear annihilation. Since then, declarations of nuclear freedom have been made in the West by thousands of municipalities, local governments and some nations. But the first nuclear free zone has yet to be declared behind the Iron Curtain.

By 1985, Toronto and some one hundred thirty-seven municipalities had declared themselves nuclear free, while in 1983 the General Synod of the Anglican Church urged Parliament to declare Canada a Nuclear Free Zone. The small print which accompanies such declarations, although legally not binding at the lower government level, if passed at the federal level would make our continuing membership in the alliance very difficult. A similar case can be seen in the declaration of "Nuclear Freedom" by New Zealand, an event which has seriously divided the defences of the South Pacific.

Many of the same activists who favoured Nuclear Free Zones also became involved in the attempted twinning of Soviet and Western cities. This tactic became most evident in France, where the twinning of strategically important ports with Soviet cities led to espionage charges being made by the French government against a Soviet visiting group. In Canada, groups of people dedicated to end "misunderstanding between our countries" started travelling back and forth between Canada and the USSR. These naive idealists don't realize that such twinning is designed by the International Department of the Kremlin as a one-way propaganda and subversion method. The Western visitors to the USSR are always exposed to a Potemkin facade behind the Iron Curtain. Those who visit us from the East are carefully selected, briefed and controlled by members of the International Department.

Former Toronto mayor John Sewell, who became a columnist for the influential *Globe and Mail* newspaper, was a member of one such group. One of his columns was capped with the revelation that "the paranoia that some Westerners feel is because the Russian language appears too tricky for its own good . . . almost like a language in code."

Canadian peace organizations are now most active at the provincial level with a good deal of success in Saskatchewan and British Columbia, both provinces where the NDP has been in power. For example, the annual spring march organized by the peace organizations attracted 70,000 in Vancouver in 1987, while barely a thousand turned out in Toronto.

The one province with an NDP government currently in power, Manitoba, and the Northwest Territories each declared itself a nuclear free zone. Although the nuclear free zone campaign in Ontario failed initially, the second try in November of 1986 succeeded brilliantly. This was after a new coalition of Liberals and the socialist New Democrats gained power from the long-reigning Progressive Conservatives.

But Quebec has proved the most susceptible to the recent peace offensive. In the 1960s when the province was in the throes of its "Quiet Revolution," Communists with their history of highjacking revolutions, quickly attempted to exploit genuine issues to their own ends. During the heyday of the FLQ, pro-Soviet and pacifist sentiments quickly became fashionable with the majority of trendy intellectuals and much of the new bureaucracy and press. Now according to research by Maurice Tugwell of the Mackenzie Institute for the Study of Propaganda and Terrorism, the peace offensive is further advanced in Quebec than anywhere else in North America, with peace studies openly incorporated into the curricula of schools by direction of the provincial government.

The peace campaign has had a fair amount of success with so-called un-hyphenated Canadians, whose last experience of totalitarianism was during the Second World War. At the same time, federal policies have unwittingly ensured that the so-called "ethnic" minorities have remained divided and mutually suspicious. It is those escaping from communism who are in the best position to explain to their more innocent fellow Canadians what the dangers are. Unfortunately, the way that our multicultural policies have been used encourages the "ethnics" to remain noticeably "foreign" and therefore makes it easier to discount their opinions as to the dangers. This has been aided by an immigration policy which permits new Canadians to retain their old citizenship. Communist countries find this an ideal means of controlling and manipulating emigrant populations.

For example, any ex-Czechoslovakian is refused a visa if he wishes to return to Czechoslovakia using a Canadian passport. He is told by the Czechoslovakian consular authorities that he may, upon payment of a varying sum of Canadian dollars, sometimes in the thousands, do one of two things. Either he may "regularize" his situation by release from his Czechoslovakian citizenship, or he may ask for a "Presidential Pardon" and be reissued with a Czechoslovakian passport. Most old sins against the regime, such as escaping in the first place, are readily forgiven. Those who simply "regularize" their status by renouncing their Czechoslovakian citizenship, may or may not be given a visa as Canadians. Those with Czechoslovakian passports will be certain of permission to return. Thus the naive, the homesick or those with pressing family reasons for going back fall into the trap. Once the "citizen" concedes that he is Czechoslovakian, he loses the protection of the Canadian government, which does not even have a record of his visit to the country of his birth. Immediately he is subject to bullying and blackmail and only permitted to travel back and forth if he agrees to work for the Communists. All of this is well known to all Canadians of Czechoslovakian birth and the Czechoslovakian Association of Canada has made repeated requests to the Federal Government to remedy the situation, but nothing has been done.

The duties of such dual citizens can vary from reporting on other immigrants to the spreading of disinformation and actual acts of espionage. Much of the constant conflict of Czech against Slovak, Serb against Croatian and Jew against East European is fuelled and kept alive on orders from the homeland by such agents of influence holding dual citizenships. Attempts to warn complacent Canadians of the dangers are made even more difficult by the infiltration of many Communist agents among the real victims of suffering from

Central and South America. Other ethnic groups such as the Chinese and the Greeks are also greatly manipulated by agents of communism.

During the 1970s and '80s, there had been a steady campaign by the left to take over school boards and municipal governments. In Canada as in Britain, communism does not do well in the open. Therefore many Marxists vote for and often join the democratic socialist party, the New Democrats. In 1985 an NDP member of the Ontario provincial legislature estimated that in his riding a third of his support came from people who would vote Communist if there was a Party candidate running.

The results of this can be seen in the sort of issues which surface in local politics. An unattributed sticker, which often accompanies other bumper slogans of activism, has the message: "Think Globally, Act Locally," and this sums up the strategy. At the municipal level in Toronto, the NDP-controlled Board of Education established the Thinking and Deciding in a Nuclear Age Committee, TADYANA for short, to promote peace studies in the schools. Toronto has spent $540,000 on a Peace Garden in front of City Hall and another $12,000 for a suitable plaque. Jack Layton, the Toronto councillor and unofficial leader of the NDP caucus, became the chairman of the International Year of Peace Committee, with a budget of $75,000 for 1986. Ottawa City Council funded its own Peace Centre, while the Toronto Board of Education has made arrangements for student and teacher exchange visits with Soviet cities, incorporating the same built-in one-sidedness as the town-twinning described earlier.

Such gains at the local level have been made possible by the good organization of the left and the naivete and lack of interest of the majority of Canadians. Some of the initiatives are comparatively easy to overturn. A handful of people managed to block the turning of Ottawa into a nuclear free zone, and a new mayor immediately abolished the Peace Centre. However, many of the measures, together with strategically placed employees to enforce them, have become entrenched and are much more difficult to eliminate.

In 1985, Toronto voters, stirred from apathy to a large extent by the exposés of *Toronto Sun* education columnist Judi McLeod, broke the grip of the NDP caucus by electing a small majority of independent school trustees. But even then not very much improved. TADYANA changed its name to Critical Issues in Curriculum Committee, but was still dominated by the NDP and continued with its agenda of filling the curriculum with anti-defence, anti-Western propaganda. In 1987, another campaign had to be organized by irate parents to finally abolish the committee altogether.

The infiltration of teacher's unions by the far left makes the reversal of policies by newly awakened school boards doubly difficult. At the various government levels, the employee unions have also been targeted. In early 1987, Lucie Nicholson, the president of the Ontario division of the Canadian Union of Public Employees phoned Judi McLeod to tell her that she had just experienced classic Marxist tactics being used against her by activists in her union. She recognized what they were because she had read a McLeod column detailing a similar scenario at a local school board.

Another group with problems and grievances to be exploited is Canada's native population. A current tactic of the activists involved in creating problems among and between the various groups of native people has been the attempted creation of a climate of hostility to defence in the Arctic. Since the testing of the air-launched cruise missile over the Northwest Territories and northern Alberta has failed to scare or worry the natives, cruise-testing is being turned into an ecological issue. The overflight by a single, small, unarmed, relatively slow, unmanned jet is being made out to be a threat to everything from migrating caribou herds to rare plants. Recently the peace groups have started a campaign to undermine the proposed expansion of the military base in Goose Bay, Labrador, into a major NATO air training base. The line is the same, that low-flying aircraft will disrupt traditional native hunting lands. But the native people remain largely indifferent to these issues and to date have taken very little part in any of the protests.

Politicization of native people has proven a two-edged weapon for the Soviet Union, however. A much publicized trans-national conference of Inuit was remarkable for the failure of the delegation from the Soviet Inuit to show up, because their government refused them permission to come. In the same vein, in 1985 Canadian Métis leader Clem Chartier was ousted from the presidency of the World Council of Indigenous People because he visited the Mesquite Indians of Nicaragua to learn first hand about Sandinista oppression of Indian people.

Meanwhile, the small numbers of Canadians having access to military and diplomatic intelligence, who know of the Soviet threat as well as of the factual disinformation and one-sided nature of the peace campaign and the peace studies in schools, are silent. The small alienated professional military remains on the sidelines, while the Defence Department, even when conscious of the psychological war, is almost powerless to counter it. The Department of National Defence Office of Information has a smaller budget than the almost six million dollars the Federal Government contributed to peace and disarmament activities for 1986-87.

Five million dollars of this goes to the Canadian Institute for International Peace and Security, which, although supposedly de-signed to fund programs and research in security as well as "peace," gives most of its funds to initiatives such as the Edmonton confer-ence, and supports groups with anti-defence track records. This much money helps greatly to launch local initiatives and gives employment to many opportunists as well as dedicated misguided idealists. For example, the Ontario Peace Calendar was given $20,000 by the Canadian Centre for Arms Control and Disarma-ment, which in turn has an annual grant of $100,000 from the External Affairs Disarmament Fund, matched by a further $100,000 from Canada's largest foundation, the Donner.

Wider in scope, and much more effective, is the campaign that activists at the National Film Board have managed to generate under the guise of artistic freedom. The NFB proudly advertises a complete listing of its "peace" films with a special catalogue. The anti-Western defence films listed range from the Gwynne Dyer's series to the anti-American *If You Love This Planet* and the blatantly pro-Soviet *Speaking Our Peace*. Another NFB film attacks the psychological foundations of the forces by attempting to destroy the reputation of Canada's most famous airman, Billy Bishop VC.

A guide pamphlet called "Films for Peace Education," prepared and disseminated by the National Film Board, sounds more like a manual for political indoctrination than a film catalogue:

". . . prepared by Olga Denisko, an experienced teacher and a "student" of personal approaches to dealing with conflict . . . Ms. Denisko presents a number of the Board's films which can enlarge understanding and motivate the desire to seek peaceful solutions. Her proposals for the use of a number of the titles are truly imaginative, while remaining sensitive to an issue which is as personal as it is political."

For example, the Dyer films are:

". . . most obviously suited for social studies/history, and political sciences grades 10 through university, like the acclaimed seven-part War series (see NFB catalogue), their freshness of vision makes them also suitable for English and language arts, ethics, values education, and media literacy studies. As well, a teacher comfortable with a questioning approach could use them with a much earlier age group, selecting relevant portions to screen for the intermediate years."

A sign of the professionalism and success of this venture is the 1983 Oscar awarded to *If You Love This Planet*. The film medium is the most potent for indoctrination; the message can be put over simultaneously at many levels, most of them more emotional than intellectual. And there are no footnotes to keep the medium honest.

To round out the Potemkin Village front of apparent wide Canadian support for neutrality comes the infiltration and use of a whole network of "progressive" groups to support party line anti-defence resolutions. A clear example of this can be seen when the feminist movement is examined. More than sixty million dollars in federal funding goes to a multitude of women's programs, and this can buy a lot of influence. The umbrella organization designed to give direction and assistance to the women's movement is the National Action Committee on the Status of Women (NAC).

The NAC 1985 annual report shows that this influence is not limited to women's issues. According to NAC, Canadian women should be for:

- withdrawing Canada from NATO, NORAD and the defence sharing agreement;
- reducing Canada's defence budget by 50 percent;
- declaring Canada a Nuclear Weapons Free Zone; and
- rejecting any involvement by Canada in the Strategic Defence Initiative.

An umbrella group, such as NAC, gets its political clout by encompassing a great number of organizations whose members have some common characteristic, such as gender; or some common issue, such as the universal desire for peace; or some common injustice, real or perceived, such as racial or sexual discrimination.

Only a few activists are needed to put through policies that are totally unrelated to the real interests of a group. And because they are of little interest to many of the rank and file members, they are easy enough to incorporate into policy platforms. The activists need not be in key spots on the organizational chart, for the tactics used to whip the genuine single interest majority in an organization into conforming to the totalitarian minority are the time-honoured ones. The stalling, bullying and use of dialectic are all well documented in Marxist "how to" handbooks for subverting democratic institutions. An insight into the rationale used to explain to the naive the reasons for not following basic democratic majority rules was given to me, in all innocence, by an executive of the Canadian Peace Alliance during a chance meeting on an aeroplane.

She proudly told me that the alliance, instead of democracy, uses the methods of the Society of Friends. Apparently, the Quakers believe that a majority is not good enough; if men of good will sit down to debate an issue, they must eventually reach a consensus. And I suppose that if they really are godly and of good will, all working to the same agreed agenda, they will reach the desired consensus. But if someone in the group has a hidden aim which is not on the agreed agenda, and if this person is trained in the dialectic method of argument, then the hidden agenda will always carry the day. When the aim of the "good will" majority is to agree on the best way to achieve world peace, but a small minority secretly believe that this can only be achieved after the world is united under communism, every measure adopted will drive the program of the majority towards advocating the unilateral disarmament of the West.

This procedure of co-option was documented in a left-leaning Toronto entertainment magazine called *Now*. When, at a meeting in Toronto in November of 1985, Canadian peace groups unified under the umbrella of the Canadian Peace Alliance, the will of the small Canadian Peace Congress (a branch plant of the World Peace Council) ensured all future policies would only reflect the correct Moscow line. Some of the less tractable peace groups failed to join. Since then, among other signs, the Canadian Peace Alliance has made no mention of genuine Soviet peace groups, and criticism of the Soviet Union has been minimized.

Peace organizations are only one way of generating pressure and manipulating the political process. Peace activists, as well as the membership at large, can belong to many different organizations. Thus, an old, religious, black, Portuguese, handicapped, homosexual teacher, who rents an apartment, who is afraid of war, and who attends the University of Toronto part-time, can do multiple damage to Canadian defence.

She could belong to any number of women's organizations whose united voice on defence policy is the National Action Committee on the Status of Women. When the government launched NAC in 1973, the only requirement for membership was a commitment to the betterment of Canadian women. As a result, there are many strange bedfellows in the organization. The Imperial Order of the Daughters of the Empire and the National Progressive Conservative Women's Caucus snuggle uneasily with the Communist Party of Canada and the Voice of Women.

Our hypothetical teacher is in a union dedicated to teaching peace studies and belongs to various peace groups in her spare time. On Sundays, at church, she will of course support the neutralist position adopted by the Anglicans or the United Church of Canada, or support the liberation theology factions of the Roman Catholics. If, at the same time, she believes in communism or any other Marxist offshoot, she will see to it that the party line on the neutralization of the nation is pushed in her gay community, as well as in her ethnic language group, and her visible minority, handicapped, old-age, student and tenants' organizations. Her voice and presence are counted each time and in each organization as a different, indignant citizen, demanding that Canada be taken out of NATO.

A dedicated, hard line activist may well be a fit, young, Anglo-Saxon atheist, who owns a house in Rosedale. He can join most of the same organizations, offer his help as a volunteer worker, or even become a paid employee. He will probably remain well away from the Communist Party, and might well be a card-carrying Red Tory instead.

This networking through "Non-Governmental Organizations" (NGOs), many of which were good for the purpose for which they were originally created, puts enormous pressure on the government in areas totally removed from the one for which they were funded. Not only will an umbrella organization like NAC count each activist whose voice has been registered in other organizations, but also all the mute voices of conservative women and Daughters of the Empire, who have no idea that they are propagating the New Order in addition to their traditional charitable work.

The Soviet campaign to scare Canada into neutrality coincides with a time when Canadians who have personal memories of our nation as a vigorous, unafraid power, are fast retiring from positions of influence. War, and rumour of war, have taken on mythical qualities for the majority of the younger generation. Psychologically, our country is nearing a crisis of self-confidence. The idea that Canada is a helpless hostage in a nuclear sea of troubles with capitulation as the only possible option has no basis in fact, but war is won and lost in the minds of men.

After I originally wrote about the November Happening of 1986 in the British *Army Quarterly and Defence Journal* and the American *National Security Record*, several things have happened to show how much of the indirect attack is smoke and mirrors and how relatively easy it is to reverse in its early stages. At a convention of the federal Liberal party, the strong stand of the Leader of the Opposition, John Turner, swung the majority of his party firmly behind NATO and stronger defences. The latest opinion polls show that even most NDP supporters are against Canada's withdrawal from NATO, and the party defence critic has said that his party would strengthen defence even more than the Conservatives are attempting to do.

The long-awaited defence White Paper was tabled in early June. It unequivocally declared Canada's continuing commitment to NATO and NORAD and pledged the government to total solidarity with our allies. However, there was a great gap between the paper's stated aims and the strategies needed to secure Canada's defences. I shall address this in detail in the final chapter.

# PART THREE

# THE REARMING
# OF CANADA

# CHAPTER TWELVE

# The Citizen Armed

*. . . the first concern of defence policy is the national aim of ensuring that Canada should continue secure as an independent political entity.*

1971 Defence White Paper

During my time as a student at the Canadian Armed Forces Staff College in 1971-72, well before my tenure in Strategic Policy Planning in Ottawa, it was clear that Canada had lost sight of the most basic principles of defence. The 1971 Defence White Paper was the first to be produced by the demilitarized Defence Department. By then the senior serving military leaders were either those who had made the necessary compromise with their professional conscience, or those who simply did not understand what was happening.

The paper was written by one of the new breed of civil servant strategists, who came to the Staff College to lecture us on its content. While the document correctly stated the aim of national defence, as quoted in the epigraph of this chapter, the strategies for translating this aim into realistic defence measures were absent. There was no criticism of the paper's faults among the senior military hierarchy and no misgivings were publicly expressed. Apart from some criticism from lower-ranking serving officers, the most incisive critique of the white paper and advice on how to correct its faults came from a retired militia officer, Colonel Cecil Merritt VC.

While commanding the South Saskatchewan Regiment at

Dieppe, Cecil Merritt won one of the first Canadian Victoria Crosses of the Second World War. A prewar militia officer, he went back to his law practice and part-time soldiering after the war. In response to the White Paper, he wrote "The True Requirements of Canadian Defence: A Critique of the White Paper 1971" (*Canadian Defence Quarterly*, Winter 1971). It is so pertinent that it could have been written yesterday.

It is a fundamental principle that every commander is responsible for his own local protection at all times.

That is why every sailor, soldier and airman is trained in the use of a rifle; why, to go one step higher, in every military formation sentries are posted, guards mounted and outposts deployed; why, in fact, a nation maintains a military establishment. Such an establishment consists not only of trained men in formed field units, but also of such bases for military training, of such stores of equipment, and of such reserves of basic material and semi-trained men as will ensure that in time of war the country's dormant military potential can be expanded in a speedy and orderly manner.

If the principle of self-protection as one's own responsibility is sound, as it surely is, it must be concluded from Canada's present organization of her defence resources, and particularly from the most recent (August 71) White Paper on National Defence, that our country's defence requirements are being ignored; and that provisions made for our national defence are not only quite inadequate, but are wrongly conceived. In consequence, our inadequate resources are being wrongly applied.

Colonel Merritt identified the key problem. He pointed out that a country's defences can only work from the inside out and from the ground up. If they are organized from the outside and work in, they will collapse; the centre cannot hold. But his criticism went unheeded and by 1985 Canada had renounced responsibility for the planning of its own defence so completely that a release from the Defence Department stated:

Canadian Security policy consists of three fundamental and complementary components: collective security and membership in the North Atlantic Treaty Organization and by defence arrangements such as NORAD; the encouragement and pursuit of verifiable arms control and disarmament agreements; and commitment to the peaceful settlement of disputes.

A long time after Colonel Merritt's analysis of the problem, but before 1985, similar doubts started echoing from other sources. The Standing Parliamentary Committee on External Affairs and Defence and a more forthright Senate Sub-Committee on National Defence were both sounding the warning. This was welcome but came very late and from the wrong place, since timely advice must come from the military directly to the elected government. During a period of increased tension, there will not be time for basic facts to be brought to the surface and changes timidly suggested by a committee of politicians. The planning and strategic forecasting must be done by professionals and the results available to the elected government and the military chiefs on a continuing basis.

Since the end of the Second World War, the democratic nations have maintained their security with continually less effort. This has meant that their citizens have had to devote less and less time to defence. The English-speaking democracies, instead of distributing the reduced burden of service among as many citizens as possible, have tended to delegate it to a small number of professionals.

This abrogation of the duty to serve has advanced further in Canada than in any other nation. At the same time, strategic planning for defence has not been the responsibility of professional soldiers, a fact that has left Canada especially vulnerable to all forms of attack. The lack of familiarity with arms and armies means that the majority of citizens are ignorant of wars and conflict, while the professional soldiers are completely preoccupied with the techniques of defence. In short, no one in our society is now in a position to plan for overcoming these twin vulnerabilities.

To develop the intellectual side of the military will take time and will require the adaptation of some form of general staff system. But the familiarization of the population with arms and armies must precede even this. The citizen can only learn about defence by taking part in it himself or being connected with someone who is serving. In short, the military must be reintegrated into society.

Integration of the military with modern society will not be easy, because it is alien to the traditions as well as to current trends in the English-speaking nations. There are signs that in Britain and the USA attempts at broadening the popular base of defence will be successful. To date this has not happened in Canada.

I believe that in spite, or perhaps because of, the fact that defence is in such a critical stage in Canada, we can reverse the situation so dramatically that our nation can serve as a model of successful defence for the twenty-first century. In Canada the idea of the citizen soldier has strong roots. It is older than the regular force, going back to the French colonial militia, a tradition built on after the British conquest. Despite the fact that it was never developed to its full potential, it served this country well. These roots, coupled with what is still a highly professional regular force, better educated than at any time in our history, give us the foundation on which we can build a defence force which will keep us secure while aiding instead of detracting from the peaceful development of the nation.

The first priority must be to expand the combat arms of the army. This expansion must be accomplished by means of young reservists on a short full-time engagement, followed by a longer period in the reserves. In recent years there have been several attempts at establishing some sort of service which would give our forces the necessary manpower base. They failed because they did not have the political or public support necessary and because they were attempted in a half-hearted manner. I was involved in two of them.

Even though there is no professional body to write a program of military reform based on Cecil Merritt's clearly stated principles, an outline of such a program can easily be sketched out. The biggest problem is to generate the right climate of opinion in which the necessary changes become politically feasible. Only then will it be possible to overcome all the entrenched resistance to change.

As Merritt and other thinking soldiers know, national defence is based primarily on properly led and organized men and secondarily on their weapons and equipment. Unless there are trained and disciplined human beings to man them, no weapons can save a nation. The ideal would be to have as many citizens as possible feel that they are contributing to the defence of the nation without having to spend too much money on weapons or time in preparing for war. Unfortunately, as the psychological threat is only effective if there is a palpable military capability behind it, so the defence against it can only be effective psychologically if it is grounded in military fact.

An enthusiastic citizen militia without modern high technology weapons and proper training is as useless as weapons without an army to operate them. An example of this can be seen in the continuing bloodbath between Iran and Iraq, where countless Iranian boys have been hurled against a much smaller, but better armed and led army. Neither side is capable of winning the war. Security can only come from a proper mix of regulars and reserves, of men and equipment, of strategy and policy.

Senior soldiers, such as Currie and McNaughton, who had fought in the Great War, came back with a horror of war and apprehensive that the same mistakes of unpreparedness would be repeated. They wanted the burden of defence to be shared by as many of Canada's citizens as possible and advocated some form of universal national service as the answer. Their concerns were echoed by those who returned after the Second World War. But since the end of the Second World War, the system of alliances developed by the West has made universal military service unnecessary and wasteful. And because of the modern social climate, it is politically impractical.

Brigadier, the Honourable Milton Gregg VC served as a junior officer in the First World War and shared the ideas of Currie and McNaughton. Since he lived on into the late 1970s, he was able to develop the idea of a broader based armed service within the context of current realities. Gregg had been a federal cabinet minister in the postwar years and therefore understood the problem from the military as well as the political perspective.

After the First World War Gregg rejoined the militia and at the outbreak of the Second World War was a major in the Governor General's Foot Guards. On mobilization he became the Second in Command of his old unit, the Royal Canadian Regiment and later Commanding Officer of the West Nova Scotias. As part of the blanket purge of older officers, he was judged too old to command a battalion in action and was sent back to Canada from England.

On his return to Canada, he was put in charge of various infantry officer training schools. After the war he became President of the University of New Brunswick and then, for ten years, was the Federal Minister of Fisheries, of Veterans' Affairs and of Labour in the cabinets of King and St. Laurent. At the end of his political career in 1957, he became the U.N. representative in Iraq, then organizer of UNICEF in Indonesia, and then Canada's first High Commissioner to a newly independent Guyana.

The teaching of the young was one of the prime interests of Gregg's long life. Perhaps, he thought, with some modification, the methods he had used to train young men to persevere and succeed against the horrors, hardships and dangers of an infantryman's war could be used to train young people in peacetime. If only young men and women could be given a fraction of the self-confidence and leadership training which his infantrymen had, how much they could achieve.

A short while before his death, Milton Gregg saw his last chance for putting his ideas into practice. When he had commanded the infantry officer training school, Barney Danson had been one of his trainees. Danson, despite his impatience to go overseas, had been kept behind as an instructor, where he became one of Milton Gregg's disciples and life-long admirers. As it turned out, Danson did get to the war in plenty of time, but he was badly wounded almost immediately after joining his regiment, the Queen's Own Rifles, in Normandy and returned home.

After the war he became a successful businessman and eventually a politician. As he watched his own children grow up during the time of the flower children, he remembered his own youth, Camp Vernon and the training he got for later life under Brigadier Milton Gregg. He gradually developed a dream similar to Gregg's.

In 1976 the Honourable Barnett Danson was a minor cabinet minister in the Liberal Government of Pierre Trudeau. Early that autumn, following the resignation of James Richardson, he was appointed as the Acting Minister of National Defence. Immediately, he proposed a small pilot scheme for the national service that he, Milton and many other thinking soldiers had so long dreamt about.

He discussed it with Milton Gregg. Gregg knew that I shared his thoughts on expanding the opportunity for military training, and asked me to come to Ottawa to meet Danson. After I agreed to work on the plan, Danson ordered me to immediately leave the Royal Military College, where I had been doing graduate war studies. So in October of 1976, I commandeered a staff car, drove to Ottawa and installed myself and Captain Luigi Rossetto, whose services I had requested, in an office where we started to tackle the problem. We quickly worked out an outline of the pilot scheme and its implementation.

It was simple, but we believed effective. The young entrants would spend a period of six weeks in Outward Bound type of training, where their leaders would be young soldiers, just a little older than the recruits themselves. Here the young people's physical fitness and endurance would be built up. Above all they would learn confidence in themselves as a result of performing progressively more challenging and strenuous tasks. Having gained self-confidence, they would then learn to have confidence in their buddies by doing tasks which one man alone could not accomplish. At the next stage, they would be put into small groups to learn what a trained unit operating towards a common goal can achieve. All of this training would be done outdoors. Skills to be taught would include outdoor cooking, overnight shelter construction, use of map and compass, navigating through the bush, basic watermanship, and rudiments of mountaineering.

After the first phase of training, most of the young people would be sent off in groups to various non-military jobs involving national service. Some volunteers would remain and continue training to become soldiers. Subjects such as weapon-handling and the rudiments of military law would be taught in this brief second stage. Before the year of service was complete those young people would still have time to carry out a brief tour with an infantry battalion. Those who wanted to volunteer for extended service would serve for an extra year with the regular force or sign on for regular service. This military option could, in time, take the greatest number of recruits and finally break the reliance of the Canadian Forces on long-serving professionals.

Those who opted for non-military service would, after the initial six-week period, join their new organization for further training. Among the options which we had worked out and negotiated were jobs in wildlife and fisheries management, as youth leaders in various provincial and community schemes, and work with volunteer agencies of many kinds.

But it was not to be, for while we were laying out the details, a competing plan was submitted to the Prime Minister.

The competing dream for national service turned out to be that of Jacques Hébert. Hébert had not served in the military, but he was a well-known crusading journalist, author, university professor and an old friend of Pierre Elliott Trudeau. His idea was much more ambitious than that of the soldiers.

Hébert's young people, instead of helping Canadian society while training to fit into it, were going to transform it, and then, the world. Unfortunately, children's crusades usually end up crucifying the crusaders and this one was no exception. A draft of the plan which in its original version was passed to Danson and by him to me, was called Youth Camps For World Peace. While long on rhetorical idealism, it was totally lacking in common sense.

There were so many worthy things that the Youth Camps For World Peace crusaders had to do that they would have to have had a sixty-hour day and a twenty-day week to accomplish them all. They were to build their own geodesic domes to live in, have vegetable gardens to grow their own food, "a greenhouse, one or two beehives, chickens, a few rabbits, a goat, fishponds and so on . . . . Six mornings a week will be devoted to study sessions." The kids were to study languages and international development. They would also: "assisted by local resource persons and using available documentation, . . . train themselves in the various techniques which they will use in their practical projects, including market and greenhouse gardening, aviculture, smallscale breeding of animals, pisciculture, building windmills and geodesic domes." The geodesic domes are mentioned no less than four times in the outline.

They would "make their own electricity, . . . collect and recycle paper, glass, metals and plastic materials and so on." In their spare time "the volunteers must also work at the level of the region in which their camp is located. Rather than being theoretical work, this will involve direct contact with the people, participation in community projects such as pollution abatement, reforestation and the development of parks and recreation areas, cultural and information evenings and so on." The only significant difference between the proposal and Mao Tse-tung's plans for his disastrous Great Leap Forward was that it did not include a quota for the extermination of flies.

A short while later the government announced the start of a new program for Canadian youth, to be called Katimavik. It was to be run by Jacques Hébert and while we were not allowed to see the details, it took much longer to get off the ground than anticipated. Later I learned, from a Vandoo colonel friend of mine that he had been ordered to work on the program and had had to rewrite most of it, incorporating some of our detail, before the plan would work at all.

Although the fishponds and geodesic domes were out, some of the basic faults from the original scheme remained. The participants, who would have been paid the salary of a recruit in the forces in the original scheme, got paid only a dollar a day and then received a bonus at the end of the year. It made a great way of putting in a year for middle class young people who wanted to "find" themselves, but it did nothing for the unemployable youth from Glace Bay. He could make more money and be more useful to his family by taking welfare and stealing hubcaps.

There was a military option left in the Katimavik program, the sole sop to its beginning. This proved to be very popular, but was available to only 10 percent of those accepted and for only three of the nine months of the program's duration. Since there was no connection between Katimavik and any reserve unit, the militia did not get any value whatever out of the program. Finally, after a few years, the whole Katimavik experiment was killed off by the Conservative government of Brian Mulroney.

Soon after it became obvious that Katimavik was going wrong, there came another chance to get more young Canadians into the military. This one was seized by Major-General Dan G. Loomis, the grandson of Major-General F.O.W. Loomis who had commanded the Black Watch battalion in which Milton Gregg began his service in France.

Loomis had been the first Director of Strategic Policy Planning, and before me, the only infantry officer to serve in the directorate. In 1973 he had been my boss as the Chief of Staff of the Canadian Contingent in Vietnam. On promotion to Major-General, he became the Chief of Program at National Defence Headquarters and had been serving there when we were working on the aborted scheme.

In 1977, when the government called for departmental initiatives to ease unemployment among the young, General Loomis saw this as an opportunity to expand the infantry and reserves. He quickly drew up an outline of a plan and had me called off leave and seconded to his staff to co-ordinate it. It had all the essential elements for success and the final, staffed version did not vary much from his quick outline, which itself was based on the original plan written by Luigi Rossetto and me.

The basic scheme was to recruit up to 10,000 young Canadians the first year for one year of service. At the end of the year, a proportion of those finishing would then be retained for an extra year. From these two-year soldiers would come the numbers for new infantry units as well as the experienced junior leaders needed to train the recruits in subsequent years, the number of whom would grow with each year that the plan was in operation.

In this way, the annual number of recruits would rise until the base of trained regulars and reservists was again large enough to be capable of rapid expansion in time of need. Had the scheme for training 10,000 young Canadians been accepted, in the first year the infantry's share would have been sufficient to raise twelve extra full-time training battalions of 700 men, in addition to the regular operational nine which the army now has.

It is important to look in some detail at how the plan would have worked, since it was an eminently feasible idea for expanding the services. The new battalions were to become the second battalions of existing militia units. They would be located in areas which had a population high enough to easily support them and where un-employment was greatest. The areas had been picked with an eye on regional disparity as well as on the balance between French and English speaking recruits.

Going from west to east, Vancouver, Edmonton, Winnipeg, Toronto, Ottawa, Halifax, and St. John's were each to have an English-speaking battalion. There would be two French-speaking battalions based on Montreal regiments and one each on units in Quebec City, Chicoutimi, and Newcastle, New Brunswick. Com-panies and platoons would be formed in smaller population centres. Thus, the Princess Louise Fusiliers in Halifax would have had one or more companies in Cape Breton, the Seaforth Highlanders in Vancouver could have had sub-units in the B.C. interior and on Vancouver Island. These sub-units could be expanded into battalions as the scheme grew.

Each battalion was to have 600 trainees and a cadre of approxi-mately one hundred officers and men to train and administer them. This cadre was to come in about equal proportions from regular force and militia combat arms personnel. Where a trained militia officer or NCO was available and willing to serve full time, he was to be the obvious first choice for any of the available jobs. The other positions would be filled by regular army personnel. The regulars would be responsible for maintaining high training standards.

The course of training was to follow the time-tested cycle of armies everywhere. First individual training, then section training, followed by training as formed platoons and culminating with exercises involving full companies. Second-year participants were to be taught to operate the crew-served infantry weapons and to work in communications and other support trades. Some of them would also have been trained as junior non-commissioned officers, the best of them going on to officer training.

Ideally, the cycle would have worked as follows. During the summer, volunteers would be recruited, sworn in and documented. In cases where militia armoury space was insufficient, this could be done at schools and other suitable centres. In the autumn, to coincide with the start of the school year, the new entrants would move to small tented camps in the country where they would get their initial training. As the weather turned colder, the new soldiers would move back to their homes, for by now they would have enough self-discipline and self-confidence to be called soldiers and could be relied upon to turn up for training at the designated time. Those who lived too far from the place of training could be housed in portable trailers or other temporary accommodation. Thus the young people would be highly visible and part of the community, not hidden away in some remote area as though the country were ashamed of them.

During the winter, they would undergo training which could be done in town and be bussed out to nearby ranges for weapons firing, for field exercises and for winter indoctrination training. As the fine weather returned in the spring, they would move back out under canvas to do the section, platoon and company level work requiring larger areas and a greater concentration of numbers.

At the conclusion of the first year, the great majority of the participants would leave full-time service to become members of the part-time militia battalions. The financial, pension and other incentives to enter the militia would have to be good enough that most new soldiers would automatically do this and remain in the reserve system for a number of years. A selected number of volunteers with leadership potential would stay on for the second year of training to become officers and non-commissioned officers in the forces. Others could use their second year to fill out the units in Europe, do a peacekeeping tour in Cyprus, or take part in whatever overseas commitment the Canadian Forces might have.

As the years passed, the program could have been slowly expanded so that by now, ten years later, it would be taking in a great number of the unemployed young who have never had a start in the civilian job market, as well as all those who wanted to serve a longer term in the forces. Even if the program had not been expanded and had merely continued at the original rate of roughly ten thousand recruits per year, almost one hundred thousand young Canadians would by now have been trained. They would have given us substantial reserves which would have provided credibility to our defence structure.

So much for dreams.

The Deputy Minister of National Defence, Buzz Nixon, was lukewarm to the scheme and the Chief of Defence Staff, Admiral Robert Falls, was uninterested. Without the backing of our own chief bureaucrats, the plan stood little chance with the rest of the bureaucracy, let alone with the anti-military-minded Prime Minister. What hurt the most was that there was opposition to the scheme even among the people who should have welcomed it the most — the regular infantry officers.

An old friend of mine who later went on to command the Airborne Regiment was a senior staff officer at Mobile Command at the time. When he heard of the Loomis scheme, he muttered to me apoplectically through his greying moustache, "It will destroy the integrity of the regular army." His reaction was typical of many regular combat arms officers. A sudden influx of short-term reservists would certainly stretch the already overcommitted resources of the regular army to breaking point. Yet it was the regular army that would have ultimately benefited the most from the extra manpower in the combat arms, which the scheme would have provided.

At the time, even the most enthusiastic supporters of the plan feared that it would never be accepted. So at the eleventh hour on the suggestion of knowledgeable civil servants it was decided to put forward another scheme, called the Civilian Employment Option. It was the height of simplicity and the epitome of ineffectiveness.

Instead of learning to be soldiers, the participants in the Civilian Employment Option scheme would not be trained at all. They would remain civilians and merely do all the odd jobs around military bases that were not being done at the moment. These consisted of routine jobs such as snow clearance, grass-cutting and painting of the married quarters. The young people could also help in minor projects that had been shelved for lack of cash, labour or interest. Menial clerking and filing jobs, which can always be found around a large bureaucracy, would absorb still more of the Civilian Option entrants.

It turned out that the Department of National Defence could employ some seven thousand of these instant layabouts without disrupting the routine too much. The cost per participant, strangely enough, worked out to almost the same amount as for the Military Service Option. The Military Service Option was rejected, the Civilian Service Option was accepted. It was politically more palatable.

And so for a year, scruffy, demoralized teenagers wandered aimlessly around Canada's military bases, looking like orphans and being treated as the lowest form of life. No one in the forces took any real interest in them and at the conclusion of their year, they vanished like the fall leaves which some of them had been engaged to rake. They had learned nothing; they had no sense of having been a part of something worthwhile. The whole scheme was a waste of money and cruelly unfair to the young people who could have had a real start in life.

As I write these words in 1987, a decade later, there are more than half a million young people unemployed. To make our army a viable one and to make the percentage of Canadians with military training a little closer to that of most other nations, we would need a total force of half a million. There are great waiting lists of young people wanting to join the forces. The military cannot take them in. There are no vacancies, there is no money and there are not sufficient officers and non-commissioned officers for a training cadre even if the vacancies and the money became available.

In all the glossy pamphlets put out by the Ministry of Employment and Immigration explaining to young people how to get jobs and plan for careers, nowhere is the military even mentioned. One such publication, put out just before Katimavik was cancelled, listed 200 different jobs. These ranged from accountant, in which occupation we are told the working conditions are sedentary and the preparation that is required consists of professional accounting courses; to writer: working conditions — sedentary; preparation — varies. On the back of the publication is a full-page advertisement for Katimavik. Nowhere among the 200 jobs is listed soldier, sailor, airman, the armed forces, or the fact that there is such a thing as the Department of National Defence.

The time for rearmament is now. The only obstacles are the old ones: lack of knowledge and lack of vision. As long as Canada remains disarmed and defenceless, it will be psychologically unprepared for any current or future threat.

# CHAPTER THIRTEEN

# Canada Rearmed

*. . . no one who knew the Canadian Army of 1939-45 can doubt that it owed much of its effectiveness to the fact that it was Canadian. Many an observer has recorded how the pulse of the national life beat within the Corps of the First World War, more and more strongly as the conflict proceeded. The men of the Second World War inherited this national consciousness and to them their army was a living symbol of their country's position in the world. They were proud of it and its specifically Canadian nature. And to a country only too conscious of its internal divisions it is a matter of importance that they thought of themselves as Canadians and not as citizens of a particular province or local community.*

Colonel C.P. Stacey, *The Canadian Army 1939-1945*

On June 5, 1987, the Canadian Government tabled the first White Paper on Defence to be released in sixteen years. It comes at a time when the country needs a new vision of purpose and unity. The Canadian Army could help in providing both, but the White Paper failed to capitalize on the will of Canadians for renewal of national purpose. It fell prey to the same lack of vision, vested interests and inter-service rivalry which have always plagued the Canadian Forces in times of peace.

There is no doubt that the Minister of National Defence and his colleagues know from our allies and from public opinion polls that the time for a rearming of Canada is here. This has also registered with the opposition parties, for when the Liberal opposition critic rose to attack the newly tabled paper, he felt obligated to first defend his own party's commitment to the defence of Canada, while the NDP critic also spoke of the need for repairing Canada's run-down armed forces.

The great weakness of the paper was in its translation of this renewed national will into actual strategies. It ignored the fundamental principle that people must take priority over equipment. However, within the body of the paper can be seen the germs of the true needs of Canadian defence. It is these hints which must be developed, not only the more obvious and costly recommendations for more matériel.

With the 1987 White Paper, the government has committed itself to a Total Force concept for all three services, but failed to make the concrete recommendations necessary to its fulfilment. The establishment of a Total Force is a concept long talked about in the army. To the army generals using the term, it meant the integration of the regulars and reserves into one. Not a revolutionary concept by other countries' standards, but one which has never been managed in Canada. It means far more than bringing the reserves and regulars closer together, the goal mentioned in the White Paper. In this chapter I attempt to describe what our armed forces might look like in the future, if we are to keep the nation secure and united into the twenty-first century.

The broad outlines of a well-balanced, flexible defence are not difficult to describe. At the head of such a system, there must be a professional brain and nervous system in the form of a General Staff, while the body must be formed of ever replenishing cells consisting of young citizens spending a short period in the military and then staying on in the reserves. To sustain the two, the matériel needs of defence must be co-ordinated with the civil economy so that there is no duplication and so that we do not have to rely on other countries for our most intimate defences. The higher the level of conflict, the more will be the co-ordination and co-operation with our allies, principally the Americans.

How to get there from here is the problem. The current attempt to redress the decades of neglect of our defences by an increase in spending without an overall interim strategic plan, could be as dangerous as doing nothing at all. There must be some interim overall strategies to follow which will prevent our resources from being committed like so many buckets of water being poured into the ocean.

To begin with, the change in priority from weapons to people must be directed by the elected government. Once this is in motion, other changes will follow. In such a climate the outline of a national strategy based on Cecil Merritt's clearly stated principles can easily be sketched out.

Fortunately, there are excellent foundations on which to build. To start with, the stated direction of our defence policies have not changed for thirty years and are precisely what is needed today. They are, according to the Statement of Defence Estimates 1983-84, to provide forces for:

> • the protection of Canada and Canadian national interests at home and abroad; this includes the provision of aid to the civil power, and national development;
> • co-operation with the United States in the defence of North America;
> • a contribution, with our allies, to the security for the North Atlantic Treaty area; and
> • international peacekeeping.

First we must be capable of defending our own country with its huge territory, comparatively small population and a long, permeable common border with the United States. These facts set the limits on what we can and cannot do for ourselves.

Without question, our territory is difficult to defend, but because of the distances and harsh climate, it is even more difficult to attack. The sheer size of the land and the problems of moving over it and surviving on it are just as important to our defences as they have always been to the Russians. Unlike the Soviet Union, we do not have vast numbers of men, therefore we must develop the flexibility to move small numbers where they are needed.

Good surveillance and the capability of bringing even a few men armed with easily transportable, high tech weapons to any point in Canada would make any conventional breach of our territorial sovereignty tactically untenable. But we must then have the means of transporting them swiftly and precisely over land, snow, water and ice to all parts of the country.

As I pointed out in Part One, the NATO alliance contributes nothing to the intimate defence of Canada, yet our entire military structure is skewed so as to make it possible for us to fulfil our overseas commitments. In fact we could fulfil these much better by starting with our own defences as do all other members of the alliance, and renegotiating our NATO involvement to take account of Canadian realities. This would at the same time make us a much better ally for the United States.

The greatest contribution to the NATO or NORAD alliance that we can make is to guarantee our own national security. At the moment, should tensions increase in North America as part of an overall plan to destabilize NATO, the United States, in addition to worrying about the reinforcement of Europe, would also have to worry about securing the Canadian part of the home base of North America. And, as I have demonstrated, the long-term neglect of our armed forces has made us barely able to help in the defence of Europe.

What might the Canadian Armed Forces of the future look like? And how would our alliance commitments be realigned to reflect our true strategic concerns? Having resurrected the citizen soldier, what would be the military structure that would make best use of his growing numbers? While the seeds of the necessary structure are in the 1987 White Paper, priorities must be realigned before they can blossom.

The first principle must be that each recruit, before being trained as specialist must be trained to fight. Otherwise, rather than being part of the solution, he adds to the problem. Once trained he must be in a position to communicate his new confidence to the rest of the population. As I have already argued, to do this we must significantly increase the numbers of our citizens who have military training.

Canada should be able to mobilize approximately 2 percent of the population as opposed to the current 0.4 percent. This total mobilizable force of 500,000 is a modest target when compared to more than a million men and women, or almost 10 percent of the 1939 Canadian population, in uniform during the Second World War. (There is a need to make as many jobs within the forces available to women as possible, but only to the point where society is ready for this change. For example, there is as yet no way of integrating women into infantry units without drastic problems with morale and cohesion. Where this has been tried — in Israel, for instance — and such units were involved in close combat, apart from any problems with the women themselves, the men in the unit were demoralized at the sight of their women comrades being killed and often neglected their duty as a result.)

The figure of 2 percent would be close to the average of our NATO allies and about half the percentage of the mobilizable strength of the Warsaw Pact nations. It would be less than a fifth of most of the non-allied or neutral countries, such as Finland, Yugoslavia, Austria or Switzerland.

The second necessary step is the organization of the soldiers into units and formations; this is what converts an army from a collection of individuals into a cohesive force. It has long been recognized by combat officers that the functional command system imposed during unification (where specialists command specialists, regardless of location) is not appropriate for the army. This fact has now been given official recognition in the 1987 White Paper on Defence: "The Government intends to establish a geographically oriented regional command structure under the Commander, Mobile Command." (Although it is now again permissable to talk of the air force and the navy, the land part of the forces still goes under the name of Mobile Command.)

The army, organized into five geographic commands, could consist of five skeleton divisions, the most active of which would be the one committed to the Central Front of NATO. The Headquarters and half its fighting strength would be stationed there, the other half based in Canada, but spending the majority of its time in the field in Europe. The White Paper made tentative provisions for such an increase and consolidation of our commitment.

Each of the four other divisions would be responsible for its own geographic area as well as being tasked to protect and facilitate development of an area in the North or a sparsely populated part of the country. Each would also include a quick reaction parachute battalion capable of rapid deployment to any area of the country and smaller SAS-type units for the rescue of terrorist hostages abroad and at home. These two elite units, as well as many of the key and specialist positions in the rest of each division, would have a larger ratio of regular cadre. One battalion from each division, consisting mostly of second-year reservists, could be rotated to service with international peacekeeping missions. All the battalions making up the five divisions would belong to existing regiments. Thus the majority of soldiers, regulars and reservists alike, would again be rooted in time and space in the old regiments and in home locations.

Each of the four home-based divisions would also be responsible for providing large numbers of troops for guard, patrol and escort duties in aid of the civil power to back up the civil police. Again, timidly, the White Paper mentions our current vulnerability and the solution:

> Canada needs well-trained and well-equipped land forces, comprising both Regulars and Reservists, to protect military vital points and to deploy rapidly to deal with threats in any part of the country. Land forces now fall short of these requirements . . . in response we will create additional brigades, mainly from the reserves, to improve the land force's capability to undertake operations in the defence of Canada. There will also be a minimally trained guard force created to protect vital military installations.

Even without any internal security problems, the very existence of sufficient troops and reserves greatly decreases the danger of any such attack taking place.

The basic principle to follow would be that the higher the intensity of conflict, the greater would be the integration with our allies. The model is already available with the NATO arrangements for the new early warning aircraft systems. The costs for the large expensive aircraft are shared and the aircrews manning them come from all the allies who contribute to the cost.

The centrepiece and most expensive proposal of the new White Paper is the development of a nuclear submarine fleet to help us maintain arctic sovereignty and help fulfil our NATO anti-submarine commitment. There is no question that nuclear-powered submarines are the essential vessels in the high-intensity anti-submarine war. This is where the idea of shared defences is most appropriate. But the idea of using the same submarines to protect our underwater arctic sovereignty from the Americans is a red herring. The only way we can solve any disputes with our giant ally and protector is by legal means and negotiations. And the only weapon necessary in this is detailed knowledge of what is going on. Such knowledge is acquirable at a much smaller cost than the astronomical price of building our own nuclear submarine fleet.

The sum quoted for each of the submarines is half a billion dollars, providing we buy at least ten, in other words $5 billion for the proposed fleet. A more realistic sum, mentioned privately by defence officials is over $30 billion. This is what will be needed for the development of the entire infrastructure to put the Canadian Navy and the shipbuilding industry into the nuclear submarine business. Even with this amount of money spent, we will still not be on the leading edge of the technology. Therefore the entire effort would give some jobs to Canadian shipbuilders, but leave the main benefits to foreign manufacturers.

Allowing for inflation since I last had the opportunity to work out accurate figures (during my staffing of the Loomis military option mentioned in the previous chapter), I estimate that a part-time militia infantry soldier with equipment would cost some twenty thousand dollars per annum, one serving full time for a year approximately forty thousand dollars. A long-serving regular soldier, with pension benefits requires some sixty thousand dollars.* If in a division of 10,000 we had a mixture of 1,000 regulars, 3,000 national servicemen and 6,000 militia reservists, the cost for a five division army would be less than two billion dollars per year. This would be in addition to the defence budget now forecast only if we retain all the existing support staff as regular force members and proceed with all the planned capital equipment acquisition programs. However, there would inevitably be savings, because most of the other tasks in the military now carried out solely by regulars could be carried out by a similar mixture of regulars, short engagement full-time reservists and part-time militia.

As part of our new Total Force, the Princess Louise Fusiliers from Halifax would exercise in the area around Goose Bay twice a year, the Seaforth Highlanders from Vancouver, somewhere in the Yukon. Commercial airlines would get them up there; local firms would make the uniforms; Northerners would get jobs building and maintaining the airfields and the permanent infrastructure needed to make easy Northern deployment possible. We could also enforce sovereignty in places where there are no airfields and where we seldom even fly by holding small unit airborne exercises there. The list of possible spinoffs is endless, not least in terms of our ability to help the Western alliance.

At the moment, our contribution for the defence of Germany is an understrength Brigade Group (two battalions of infantry and one of tanks). These troops are long-serving regulars who are in Germany for a minimum of three years, without break. Therefore there are French and English schools, dependents' housing and a large non-fighting, peacetime administrative and logistic infrastructure. A good percentage of the money that we ostensibly provide for the defence of Europe goes to pay for all of this. The government

---

* The official figures given by the vice chief of Defence Staff recently are far smaller: $39,000 for a regular and $6,500 for a reservist.

now proposes to reinforce this commitment by establishing a divisional headquarters in Germany, pre-positioning equipment and tasking a Canadian-based Brigade Group with the responsibility of training for and exercising in Germany.

In order to do this, they propose to retrench our Norway commitment to the one quick reaction battalion which was originally tasked to the Northern Flank before the acceptance of the larger commitment. The 1987 White Paper finally admits the lack of realism of the current Norway commitment, without spelling out that it was irresponsibly undertaken at the very time when the troops who would have to honour it were being cut back. However, in the ten years of its existence, this promised Canadian help has become very important psychologically to the Norwegians, and although difficult to sustain, should not be cancelled. Under the five division concept, this commitment would become viable, providing that the Norwegians and other larger European allies were prepared to dedicate the necessary transport to get the troops to Norway, as well as the logistical and financial support.

With the reality of our priorities properly understood and presented, it could be shown to our allies that the new manpower-oriented defence was a far more valuable contribution to the Western alliance than all of our piecemeal efforts of the past. We could then work out the details of a revised alliance relationship while building the other parts of our strategy around the five division army.

The logic of these army reforms (looking after our own intimate needs at the lower end of the conflict continuum ourselves, while integrating more fully with our allies at the higher end) works equally well for the naval and air parts of our defences. At the moment our naval forces are less capable of unilateral action than even the land forces. Our sailors are totally committed to anti-submarine warfare in conjunction with other NATO fleets. This means that we have to have equipment capable of warfare at the highest, most intense end of the conflict continuum. The justification given for this by the Department of Defence is as follows:

Defence capability requirements are best built on the most critical and demanding of the tasks assigned to the Forces. The capability to meet a critical and demanding task, such as the protection of shipping in the hostile environment of the North Atlantic inherently provides the means to carry out numerous, less demanding tasks such as marine rescue and fisheries patrol.

This, of course, is patent nonsense. The anti-submarine NATO tasking in the North Atlantic which we have agreed upon means that we have to have enormously sophisticated, large ships. Now we are planning to acquire even more expensive submarines. Canada can afford only a token number of each. With our long coastline, this means that we cannot adequately look after marine rescue, control the drug trade or fight even a minor "cod war." We have no minesweeping capability; our ships for the NATO role have no capability for going in ice conditions; and we can train only a handful of naval officers in the most critical naval job of all, the command of a fighting vessel.

The White Paper talks of the purchase of new "mine counter measure vessels and aircraft," without mentioning numbers or giving the proposal any timing or priority. But for the same amount of money that we are spending on a half dozen of the new patrol frigates and for far less than we are proposing to spend on the nuclear submarines, we could have perhaps fifty of these smaller mine-sweeping vessels for the protection of our coastal waters. They would be capable of operating in ice as well as having some minesweeping capabilities and be armed with state-of-the-art missile systems which have the ability to turn them into modern Davids against any attacker Goliaths. As an important side effect, by concentrating on this sort of vessel, we could become world leaders in their production and stand an excellent chance of selling them to any nation with an icy coastline.

One of the rationales for keeping our sophisticated anti-submarine role is that our sailors must retain expertise in this most difficult of naval tasks. But there is a much cheaper and better way of maintaining our skills. This is to institute exchange programs with other NATO navies. We could employ their sailors and naval officers on our small coastal ships to give them expertise in arctic maritime warfare, and they could employ a like number of Canadians on board their ships so that we could keep up to date in the higher more intensive warfare methods of the NATO alliance.

The other major part of our anti-submarine warfare capabilities are our eighteen Aurora aircraft and some two dozen Sea King helicopters. The Auroras were bought from Lockheed for $2.1 billion, and the new White Paper proposes buying ten more as well as selecting a replacement helicopter for the Sea Kings.

Although there was enormous hype given at the time of the signing of the Aurora contract in the mid-1970s as to the benefits to the Canadian aerospace industry, to research and development, and to the Canadian economy generally, such benefits have for the most part failed to materialize. At the time, we could have bought Canadian-made Dash-7 surveillance planes from de Havilland for $10 million each. These aircraft would not have had the full capability for anti-submarine warfare of the Aurora, but they would have been better suited to the surveillance of our North. We could have bought fifty of them and still saved over one and a half billion dollars. And with the Dash-7 guarding the most arduous and empty territory in the world, de Havilland would have had a better chance of selling them abroad than it does now. Finally, with the Northern reaches of the continent secure, it would be considerably easier for us to convince our southern neighbour to add an extra two dozen anti-submarine vessels to its fleet of 160.

Finally, there is the air force, the most desperately mismanaged part of our forces on the one hand, yet the one which points most clearly to the future on the other. Currently we operate over thirty types of aircraft. Many of these are in the air force inventory merely to give employment to airmen. We have a tiny strategic airlift capability of seven obsolete Boeing 707s which take up an inordinate amount of resources and which recently proved to take an unacceptable length of time to transport our troops to Norway during the first and last test of the deployment of the Canadian brigade. Air Canada could provide this service at a fraction of the cost and in a much better approximation of how things would actually work in wartime. All that would have to be done is to make reserve military status a part of the terms of service of corporation airline employees. (Of this, more later.) The airlines would probably not need to increase their holdings of aircraft by more than one or two and their support systems, not at all, to guarantee the military its peacetime strategic airlift capability.

The future fleet of tactical air transport could consist of Canadian-made Buffalo aircraft, of which the military currently only owns a handful. These aeroplanes could, in their peacetime guise, be used to provide air services for the North. There is such a crying requirement for this form of government transportation that Ontario has had to start a special airline of its own for this purpose, Norontair.

Obviously, the defence of the air and space over the continent is an indivisible proposition. The North American Air and Space Agreement (NORAD) is a most sensible arrangement for sharing this responsibility with the United States. Canada's part is to provide several squadrons of interceptors, to man and operate those portions of the command, control and early warning systems which exist on Canadian soil, and to send officers and technicians to the Headquarters in Colorado Springs, where the deputy commander is a Canadian air force officer.

The lion's share of the interceptor fighter aircraft are manned and operated by Air National Guard Units of the USAF Reserve. The sensible and most economical manner by which we could fulfil our part of our NORAD obligation would be to lease from the USAF some of the same type of aircraft flown by their pilots. This would give us compatibility of equipment and cost far less than we are now paying to build our own version of the F-18.

But there would have to be strong government pressure behind such a scheme. It would obviously be strongly resisted by the US aircraft manufacturers, whose profits would suffer from the arrangements and who would have the US Air Force lobbying on their behalf. But there are precedents. For example, the South African Air Force leased French Mirage fighters for many years until they built their own factory in South Africa.

There is no panacea for the equipment problem. Our once thriving defence industry has practically disappeared. We have to build it up again, but in such a way that we can design and produce weapons and systems for the less intensive conflict where we might have to act without our allies. We should continue to specialize in equipment suited to our geographic and climatic conditions, which might then find buyers in other countries. Already we have a successful model for this sort of military industrial development: a number of aircraft made by de Havilland of Canada are sold around the world. For the more complicated equipment, we must try to get the best deal on the lines of the Auto Pact. There is a good precedent for this. In the 1960s and early '70s, until the drastic reduction in our defences and similar cuts by the American forces following the winding down of the Vietnam War, our defence production-sharing with the USA was one of the quiet economic successes.

But above all we must not be mesmerized by the benefits gained from spending huge amounts of money on a few complicated ships and aircraft. In the fiscal year 1985-86, Canadian defence spending accounted for approximately twelve billion dollars of the Gross Domestic Product. This generated 178,000 jobs in the private sector. Of those fewer than ten thousand were in the aircraft manufacturing and shipbuilding industries. Ten times that many were in the wholesale and retail trades, accommodation and food services, transportation and other personal services. The expansion of the army in or near population centres, where the majority of the support services would come from the local economy, would make for a significant increase of jobs in the private sector.

A five division army, based on a mixture of regular cadres, reservists on short-term full-time engagements and militia soldiers on weekend and annual training, would make for greater security at less cost. But this crucial step in the rearming of Canada will only be feasible if the appropriate legislation is accompanied by co-operation from all public and private sectors of Canadian society.

The White Paper states that in respect to the reserves: "Terms and conditions of service must be altered to make it easier for members to serve and employers will be encouraged to support Reserve service by members of their work force."

This timid approach will do nothing to improve the situation, for there is no easy way of making these changes. Individual employers beat their patriotic chests and agree that employees should have time off to train with the reserves, even unpaid time off. But when it comes to actually granting it, they quickly change their tune, if they have no economic incentive not to do so.

Some years ago when Barney Danson was the Minister of National Defence, letters were sent to hundreds of employers appealing to their corporate sense of patriotism and asking them to give unpaid leave for annual training to any of their employees who were serving as part-time soldiers in the militia. In response to the policy, the Royal Bank of Canada sent back a glowing letter agreeing with the concept and promising to put the policy into effect immediately. Everyone was happy — the Minister, because his scheme was so readily adopted, the bureaucrats in National Defence, because their planning was finally about to bear fruit, and the militia, because they expected to increase their numbers.

Unfortunately, there was a small rider to the bank's acquiescence. In accordance with the best of modern management practice, the final decision to grant unpaid leave was to be left to individual managers and supervisors. Understandably, supervisors did not leap at the opportunity to grant members of their staffs unpaid militia leave. A weakened department does not earn many brownie points. Not surprisingly, it appears that no one took advantage of the offer and, after a decent interval, it was dropped from the personnel managers' books.

For a scheme such as unpaid leave to work, it is not sufficient to appeal to a company's patriotism. It must first of all contain some clear economic incentive (or penalty) and be backed and understood by all governmental departments dealing with business and industry. For example, tax incentives could be granted to firms according to the numbers of their employees seeking unpaid leave for short periods of military service.

The reservist himself should also have more than a straight cash incentive for service. This could be in the form of tax breaks, the waiver of some post-secondary educational fees, or preferment for some government jobs. The US National Guard has a pension scheme for part-time service, which is an attraction not only for joining but also motivates reservists to stay for extended periods, thus promoting stability. In fact, the possible non-financial incentives are endless. The point is that more than lip service must be paid to the desirability of reserve service.

Any plan of incentives for employers and reservists must be based on a firm recommendation from the officer corps. Unfortunately, this still is lacking, as is the political support at the highest level for reform of the reserve system. Although some politicians are now making positive noises about incentives to serve in the militia, neither they, nor the regular officers who pay lip service to the concept, sound too convincing. A recent report of the Parliamentary Committee on External Affairs and National Defence called, "Action for Reserves," bravely attempted to do the job which should have been done automatically years ago by the military themselves.

Not only must private industry and business be given some form of incentive to give time off to employees who need time for reserve training, but all three levels of public service will have to re-establish lists of reserve occupations of those not eligible for service and grant time off for those not on the list. There have to be surveys, plans for the mobilization and emergency use of private as well as public equipment and plant, together with the personnel to operate it. For example, civilian air and surface transport would have an important role in an emergency. Private operators of planes, helicopters and mass surface transportation systems who undertook an obligation to serve in an emergency would be given some form of tax break as well as partial training in preparation. With all this in place there would be no necessity for the military to duplicate civilian holdings of equipment and training of personnel by the military.

The same principles apply today as when General McNaughton was planning the structure of the forces between the wars. But fifty years later, the civilian infrastructure is far more developed. For example, civilian air and surface transport would have an important role in any military crisis, but unlike in the 1930s, we do not need to train civilian pilots and develop airlines. All that would have to be done is to pay an annual retainer to private owners and operators of planes, helicopters and long-distance trucks, give them some tax breaks and provide their employees with some additional training. Publicly owned systems, such as Air Canada, and their personnel, would have an automatic reserve obligation.

As a result, the military could stop duplicating civilian training and education and concentrate on military matters, both basic combat skills for all soldiers and the military application of skills already learned in a civilian institution. For example, the Royal Military College should cease providing the same academic engineering courses available at civilian universities. If one of the three Canadian Royal Military Colleges became a military training school on the pattern of the British Royal Military Academy of Sandhurst, the resources of the other two could be applied to the formation of the academic and strategic parts of a general staff system, which is so lacking in the current military structure.

The task of basic helicopter and fixed-wing pilot training could likewise be taken from the military and only pilots already qualified to civilian standards considered for specialized military flying. In fact, the universities and community colleges could in future provide all technical specialist officers and men. Such trained specialists need not spend a lifetime in the forces. Some might even serve a stint in mid-career. Flexibility and interchangeability would be the keys to the system.

In sum, the principles for reordering our defences are simple. We must first of all plan our defences from the inside out and from the ground up. Our own needs must be met before we can give to collective security more than the peeling storefronts of our current contributions. In any high-intensity conflict involving the great powers, as well as any war in space and near space, we will never be more than a junior partner of the Americans. But to avoid repeating the mistake of the two World Wars in a future conflict, we must plan in such a way that we get as much of a say in the commitment of our men and resources as we can, while at the same time our industries and economy derive the maximum benefits possible from our contributions.

On the other hand we must realize that if we fail to look after our own ability to defend against conflict lower on the scale of intensity, or in disputes involving our territorial sovereignty, the end of Canada as an independent, unified nation is as certain as the extinction of the dodo bird.

There is terrible fear of war in the West which is fuelled by deep ignorance of human conflict. This fear actually weakens our society and makes war more likely. Unfortunately conflict is a basic part of human nature; it is impossible to eliminate, but not impossible to limit and resolve. Only by knowing and learning as much as possible about war do we stand a chance of resolving conflict before it reaches the stage where it can destroy us or transform our way of life from freedom to tyranny.

Our attitude to war is shaped by our own experience and by interpretation of the past, as well as by the manipulation of these perceptions by our enemies. Only a small percentage of our population has any direct knowledge of war and a smaller percentage yet any recent military training. To make matters worse we isolate those with expertise from the rest of society. In the English-speaking nations, which have set the pattern for the modern West, defence and security have become the domain of isolated professionals. In Canada and the West, security and defence must become again a normal, mainstream activity of society. It is for this reason more than any other that we must expose so many more of our young people to military training.

Until recently there was little danger of war on our continent and this gave Canadians a feeling of security and an aura of innocence that was envied by the whole world. With the advent of the nuclear threat, we started to realize that there was no haven from war. The feeling of security is now gone, but the innocence remains. As a result, we push for peace and disarmament while neglecting to study war and conflict. This limits our ability to defend ourselves and increases our insecurity.

The most potent and least expensive defence is the widest possible dissemination of knowledge. The strategies for our continued security and freedom must be all-encompassing. They must not be limited to the strategic theories of Euro-American thinkers, but must include those of other civilizations and cultures who did not work within the neat boundaries of war and peace, but rather with the understanding of the existence of a continuum of conflict.

The post Second World War era saw the development of civilian, non-governmental, institutions which attempted to fill the strategic vacuum in the English-speaking nations. These think tanks had the grave disadvantage of spawning theoretical ideas without having the responsibility of executing them. The civilian strategist was in little danger of having to lead men into machine-gun fire in some far-off jungle.

Recent developments threaten to confuse the strategic thinking process in the West even further. The study of war and conflict is being upstaged by the study of peace, some of this is undoubtedly through the adroit manipulation of our enemies who are masters in the art of psychological war. In the past the studies of the small American and Canadian segment of the academic community which seriously concerned itself with matters of security and defence have been limited. Its members have been distant from soldiers and from access to inside knowledge of the military and governmental machinery. Now, peace and disarmament institutions with even less knowledge of military realities are beginning to proliferate.

At a conference on peace and disarmament at Oxford University in September of 1983, the great British soldier-scholar, General Sir

John Hackett noted that by the dictionary definition, *peace* is "an absence of war." To concentrate, as we in the West increasingly do, on the absence of something, rather than on the actual subject, is to be dangerously ignorant. To be ignorant of war makes peace difficult, if not impossible to achieve.

If all those who call for peace in our time could be instilled with confidence instead of fear, then blessed again would be the peacemakers. To call for peace because of fear, as did Neville Chamberlain on the eve of the Second World War, invites conflict rather than preventing it. To exclude soldiers from the political process of planning for the resolution of possible conflict and then expect them to provide a suitable defence against attack is foolish and dangerous.

Let the trumpet call again with a certain sound, to arouse a spirit of self-confidence so that the peace and prosperity which the democracies have enjoyed for the past forty years can become universal.

# Index